SOCIALIST ARGUMENTS

SOCIALIST ARGUMENTS

edited by
David Coates and Gordon Johnston

MARTIN ROBERTSON · OXFORD

First published in 1983 by Martin Robertson & Company Ltd.,
108 Cowley Road, Oxford OX4 1JF.

British Library Cataloguing in Publication Data

Socialist arguments. — (A socialist primer; v. 1)
  1. Socialism
  I. Coates, David   II. Johnston, Gordon
  III. Series
  335   HX44

  ISBN 0-85520-650-0
  ISBN 0-85520-651-9 Pbk

Typeset in Hong Kong
Printed and bound in Great Britain by
T. J. Press Ltd., Padstow

CONTENTS

ACKNOWLEDGEMENTS

We are indebted to Her Majesty's Stationery Office for permission to reproduce our Tables 8.1 and 8.4.

NOTES ON CONTRIBUTORS

DAVID COATES (Ch. 3)
Lecturer in Politics at the University of Leeds, and the author of *The Labour Party and the Struggle for Socialism* and *Labour in Power?: A Study of the Labour Government 1974–79.*

FRANK FIELD (Ch. 8)
Labour MP for Birkenhead, director of the Child Poverty Action Group from 1969 to 1979, and founder director of the Low Pay Unit 1974–79.

BOB FINE (Ch. 5)
Lecturer in Sociology at the University of Warwick, an active member of the CSE, co-editor of *Capitalism and the Rule of Law*, and the author of articles on law, class, sociological theory and politics in Southern Africa that have appeared in journals such as *Economy and Society* and *Capital and Class.*

ANDREW GAMBLE (Ch. 1)
Lecturer in Political Theory and Institutions at the University of Sheffield, and the author of *The Conservative Nation, Britain in Decline,* and *An Introduction to Modern Social and Political Thought,* and (with Paul Walton) of *From Alienation to Surplus Value* and *Capitalism in Crisis.*

JOHN HILLARD (Ch. 2)
Lecturer in Industrial Relations at the University of Leeds, and formerly lecturer in Economics at the University of Lancaster.

BOB JESSOP (Ch. 4)
Lecturer in Government at the University of Essex, and the author

of *Social Order, Reform and Revolution; Traditionalism, Conservatism and British Political Culture* and *Theories of the Capitalist State.*

GORDON JOHNSTON (Ch. 10)
Lecturer in Politics at Leeds Polytechnic, currently researching on labourism, socialist thought and the British Labour Party.

BARRY MUNSLOW (Ch. 9)
Lecturer in the Department of Political Theory and Institutions in the University of Liverpool, on the editorial board of the *Review of African Political Economy* and *Politics*, and the author of *Frelimo and the Mozambican Revolution* and of *Southern Africa: a students' reader.*

GREG PHILO (Ch. 6)
Lecturer in Sociology at the University of Glasgow, a founder-member of the *Glasgow Media Study Group*, and the co-author both of *Trade Unions and the Media* and the three volumes prepared by the Glasgow Media Study Group, *Bad News, More Bad News* and *Really Bad News.*

JOHN WESTERGAARD (Ch. 7)
Professor of Sociological Studies at the University of Sheffield, the author of numerous publications on class structure, sociology and urban development, a member of the editorial board of *Sociology* and of the Council for Academic Freedom and Democracy, and the co-author (with Henrietta Resler) of *Class in a Capitalist Society.*

But the most beautiful of all doubts
Is when the downtrodden and despondent raise their heads
    and
Stop believing in the strength
Of their oppressors.

Bertolt Brecht
'In Praise of Doubt', *Poems 1913–1956*, Eyre Methuen 1981,
p. 334

EDITORIAL INTRODUCTION

If the political sympathies of the broad mass of working people were a simple reflection of their economic conditions, then the severe and deepening crisis of British capitalism should by now have rekindled widespread support for a democratic socialist alternative to Thatcherism. Yet so far that realignment of political sympathies has not occurred. Popular dissatisfaction with the Conservative government has not been matched by any discernible shift in popular indifference (or even hostility) to socialist ideas. Indeed if the recession has been the spur to any radical shift in general opinions and attitudes, then that shift seems to have favoured the political forces of the Right and their theoretical mentors.

This is not to say that the Left has been in retreat everywhere. The rapid growth of the peace movement stands as clear evidence of the persistence of a constituency that is open to radical ideas and initiatives. The urban riots in the summer of 1981 showed clearly too the growing sense of desperation that is widespread in the heartlands of capitalist decay, and in a whole generation of the young unemployed. And in the Labour Party, left-wing pressure has led to the adoption of an alternative economic strategy and associated social reforms of a radical kind, and has produced changes in party rules and procedures designed to sustain those radical commitments under a Labour government to come. But the amount of attention paid by the media to that internal party fight should not blind us to the shallowness of its roots in the wider society, and in particular to the absence of any parallel shift of attitudes and commitments outside the ranks of the politically active – i.e. in the broad mass of the labour movement. It is this absence of any broadly based belief in the efficacy and desirability of a socialist alternative which lends credibility to the view that the adoption of left-wing policies could actually threaten the electoral chances of the Labour Party; and it also means that, even if elected, a future Labour government would find itself without sufficient popular support for that radical confrontation with the centres of capitalist power and privilege which a genuine move to socialism must necessarily entail.

For this is the paradox at the heart of the British Left's present dilemma, the parallel absence of capitalist economic stability and mass support for a socialist alternative. Far from a crisis of capitalism shifting politics to the Left, the 1970s ended in Britain with the return to power of the most explicitly anti-socialist and reactionary Conservative government since the War. It should be said that this coincidence of capitalist crisis and Thatcherite ascendancy was not altogether surprising. The Labour government of 1974–79 did little to achieve that 'fundamental and irreversible shift in the balance of power and wealth in favour of working people and their families' which the Labour leadership had promised in Opposition, and the failure of this ostensibly 'socialist' government gave a general credibility to the equation of socialism and national decline that Margaret Thatcher's Conservatives canvassed so effectively in their return to power. The media too have been, and remain, active in the dissemination of a range of 'explanations' of the current crisis that, if only by the emphases and silences that they contain, help to discredit socialist ideas. This, of course, is only to be expected, since capitalist-induced unemployment, stagnation and inflation do more than merely waste human resources and dissipate the immense productive potential of an advanced and long-established industrial society. They also provide the material base on which men and women can come to question the moral justification and social necessity for capitalist property relationships, and so pose a threat to the privileged positions of the elites who would rule us. As a result the apologists for the present system have of necessity to be more than usually active at a time such as this, producing explanations, specifying causes and locating scapegoats that help to obscure the true nature of our situation. It is then only to be expected that socialists should face, as they currently do, a whole barrage of widely-publicized half-truths, apologetics and downright distortions whose collective impact is to present those who suffer most from the present recession as actually the originators of their own hard-pressed conditions. By so doing, of course, they also help to weaken and reduce the otherwise potentially considerable degree of popular resistance to those government-inspired measures of economic and social retrenchment which the resuscitation of capitalist profits now requires. If the 1980s are to witness a revival of a mass-based and self-confident socialist movement that is able to reverse those retrenchments and control those profits, it is precisely this barrage of official orthodoxies that has to be challenged and discredited.

The project of which this first volume is a part was prompted by the recognition of the enormous imbalance of intellectual resources that exists between those who would defend capitalism in crisis and those who would replace it by a democratic socialism. Powerful socialist arguments exist, and have long existed, against every one of the ruling orthodoxies of the day. A whole socialist rebuttal of liberal and conservative explanations of our situation (its nature, origins, laws of motion and sources of resolution) has long been available to sustain the self-confidence, the arguments and the credibility of socialist militants. But all too often those militants have been isolated, cut off from easy access to such arguments and theories, and obliged instead to operate in a world dominated by the conventional wisdoms of the ruling elites – conventional wisdoms propagated on a daily basis through the media and the education system, and conventional wisdoms which serve not simply to shape the audience that socialists must reach, but also to infect the arguments and visions of socialists themselves. If the 1980s are to see a revival of the Left on any scale in Britain, the labour movement will have to build around itself the protective wall of a sophisticated and widely-understood socialist counter-culture; and to do that it will, amongst other things, have to bridge the gap within the labour movement between its intellectuals and its activists, make more readily available its theories, and place in the hands of its militants the intellectual means by which they can grasp, build and sharpen the arguments on which the battle for the minds and support of the British working class can be won.

This project sees itself as part of that 'bridging exercise'. It attempts to bring together, in a concentrated, clear and concise form, the most impressive arguments that are available on the Left. It sees itself as a 'primer' for socialists, gathering and making easily accessible some of the most important information, arguments, theories and study guides that socialist militants might find useful in the class struggles to come. A later volume will concentrate on the general questions of capitalist analysis and socialist politics that will have to be tackled by anyone wanting to convince others of the need to move from the rejection of current orthodoxies to a full involvement in the attempt to build a new and more just social order. Our purpose in this volume is more modest, simply to collect socialist answers to the main 'explanations' of our current crisis that are

widely canvassed by our political opponents, in the hope that these
will be of use to socialists engaged in the process of winning recruits
to our cause. We hope too that they will make a suitable starting
point for a process of socialist self-education, inspiring socialists to
read widely and to refine their arguments in opposition to the more
sophisticated of the apologetics put out by the political, industrial
and cultural elites who have so far dictated the terms on which the
public discussion of the current crisis has been conducted.

We have asked our contributors to meet a number of requirements in drafting their chapters. We have asked them to lay out,
and then to answer, the most complex as well as the most vulgar of
the arguments they are attacking, on the premise that the Left must
not deceive itself about the enormity of its task, nor leave its militants exposed to outflanking by the more talented of our opponents.
We have asked them, too, to avoid the unnecessary use of that technical jargon which can so easily turn the scholarship of even a socialist tradition into a closed universe from which the uninitiated are by
definition excluded. We recognize that a new vocabulary is an important part of building a whole socialist counter-culture, but we have
asked that, where that vocabulary is needed, our contributors introduce it in ways which make the reasons for its presence obvious and
its meaning clear. We have asked, too, that our contributors present
as sophisticated and coherent a set of answers as their theme requires
and their capacities permit, and that they avoid the temptation of
balancing any simplification in their vocabulary with any crudifi-
cation of their arguments. It is our belief that the arguments of the
Left have to be many-sided and refined if they are to be convincing,
and that the intellectuals of the labour movement serve that movement badly if they underestimate either the capacities of their
audience or the complexities of the social system that they would
have that audience replace. We have asked our contributors to
ensure that they make plain the nature of the disagreements on the
Left in their particular field, so that no section of the socialist camp
need feel alienated by any gratuitous sectarianism, and so that all of
us come to recognize where unity has still to be established and
where dialogue is still required; and finally we have asked them to
add suggestions for further study to which the interested reader can
then turn.

What then are the socialist answers to the ruling orthodoxies of
the day? What should socialists say when they hear that British
industry is so uncompetitive because government intervention is too
extensive and expensive, because public corporations are too

removed from the competitive discipline of market forces, and because government policies of over-full employment have protected British workers for too long from the need to adopt new working routines and to shed 'restrictive practices' on a large scale? What are we to say when we are told that inflation erodes competitiveness and jobs because we pay ourselves too much, because our unions are too strong, and because union pressure and short-term electoral advantage combine to encourage politicians (and especially Labour politicians) to overspend on welfare and social provision? What can we say when governments claim to speak in the interests of the nation as a whole, and when they demand our loyalty against that of the 'sectional' interest of labour? How should we react when city streets are full of violent clashes between angry demonstrators and 'the poor British bobby', and when a succession of television and newspaper journalists repeatedly remind us of union militancy, welfare scroungers and outmoded working practices? What are we to say to the claims that British industry is uncompetitive because its management strata is over-taxed, that British workers are unproductive because they are cosseted by too generous a welfare state, and that jobs, housing and living standards are being jeopardized by the immigrant communities that have grown up 'so rapidly' amongst 'us'? And how are we to dispel the popular assertion that socialism is the first step on the road to Eastern European totalitarianism, that inequality and a degree of social deprivation are endemic to all societies (and not just capitalist ones), and that socialists are really no different from fascists, being just as extreme and violent, and just as opposed to the conventions of parliamentary democracy?

The chapters that follow will offer some socialist answers to this set of widely held beliefs. The first three deal directly with arguments that focus on the economy. Andrew Gamble explains the doctrine of monetarism, and offers a socialist critique of it. John Hillard examines the thesis that trade unions are to blame for the low investment and poor competitiveness of British manufacturing industry, and begins to develop a socialist explanation of the 'deindustrialization' of Britain that will be developed further in Volume 2; and David Coates surveys the range of arguments used against trade union power, and shows how socialists can and must refute these while arguing for a more openly socialist kind of trade union politics. Three chapters in the middle of the collection (by Bob Jessop, Bob Fine and Greg Philo) focus on the claims for neutrality (in the struggle between classes) made for the key institutions of the State, the police and the media, and offer socialist analyses and answers to the claim that the government must always be obeyed because its policies embody the interests of the nation as a whole, that the police constitute a force above politics, beyond the scope of public criticism and democratic control, and that the media offer a balanced, neutral and reliable treatment of issues and struggles vital to the labour movement and to allied radical causes. Finally a series of chapters examine myths periodically used to deny the necessity of the socialist task. The claim that we suffer from too much equality, and not too little, is effectively demolished by John Westergaard. The associated assertion that fraud and scrounging are now major features of a welfare system that is too extensive and generous, and too great a burden on the working poor, is subjected to a socialist counter-argument by Frank Field. Barry Munslow offers a socialist response to those who would lay the blame for our present ills on immigrant communities of whatever race and colour; and Gordon Johnston examines again the horny old refutations of socialism – as violent, Eastern European, and beyond the capacities of an inevitably defective human nature.

We hope that a strong, self-confident, explicitly argumentative and combative socialist movement will soon reappear in British politics, and that as a result the current dominance of the ideas we challenge here will long have vanished. We hope, in other words, that this collection will soon be only of historic interest, and we believe that its major task is to help to forge the kind of socialist movement that alone can make it so.

David Coates
Gordon Johnston
(Leeds)

Chapter one

MONETARISM AND THE SOCIAL MARKET ECONOMY

Andrew Gamble

During the last fifteen years there has been a sustained revival of the main doctrines of economic liberalism, and an increasingly open onslaught on the policies and institutions of social democracy. The new doctrines have been widely adopted as orthodoxy throughout the Western world and have been championed by new and vigorous right-wing political forces, especially in Britain, the USA, and Australia.

The new liberal political economy has two main strands which must be distinguished. There is the doctrine of monetarism, which is a theory of the causes of inflation, restating and developing the classical quantity theory of money, and proclaiming once more the slogan of sound money; and there is the doctrine of the free market, which is much broader in scope and attempts to identify the political conditions under which not just sound money, but the greatest possible degree of economic efficiency and individual liberty are realized. It is possible to be a monetarist without being an economic liberal, but it is more usual to find the two doctrines firmly harnessed together, especially since sound money is given such priority by economic liberals.[1] This chapter will first set out the main arguments and assumptions of these doctrines, and then criticize them. They go under various names – the new *laissez-faire*, liberal conservatism, neo-liberalism, and many more. Monetarism itself is often applied widely to indicate the whole range of ideas. The term I shall employ is *social market doctrine*, of which monetarism forms a prominent but separate part. Its major propositions will be considered in turn.

ARGUMENTS FOR MONETARISM

Inflation is always and everywhere a monetary phenomenon

This is the heart of the doctrine of monetarism which was promulgated so vigorously by Milton Friedman in the 1960s and which has since become in many places a new orthodoxy. It is a restatement of the quantity theory of money of classical economics. The underlying idea is extremely simple. In order for prices to be stable the quantity of goods and services produced in an economy and the quantity of money available to purchase them must remain in approximate balance. If anything disturbs that balance there will either be too much or too little money in the economy. In the first case balance will be restored by prices rising, in the second case prices will fall. A simple monetarist parable illustrates this. A helicopter appears over a town and unloads huge quantities of new money. The grateful townspeople reach out their hands to clutch the notes as they fall from the sky. Thinking themselves richer they attempt to spend their new wealth. But since the same quantity of goods and services is on sale as before, demand may have risen, but supply has remained the same. So shortages develop. In the short run balance can only be restored again between supply and demand if prices rise. This wipes out the increased wealth and leaves the community no better off than it was before. The price level, however, does not return to its former level.

Monetarists argue that if there is inflation, i.e. a general and sustained increase in prices, then it must be because the supply of money is increasing more rapidly than the supply of goods and services. But how can the quantity of money be increased faster than the increase in output? Firstly, because more coins and notes are being issued than is justified by the output of the economy, but secondly, and more fundamentally, because public and private borrowing are excessive. The creation of new money through credit is the basic modern mechanism of inflation, and monetarists reason that since the issuing of new notes and coins and the overall control of credit are government functions, any excessive increase in the money supply must be the responsibility of the government. So it is governments that are always to blame for inflation, and any inflation can be halted provided governments have the will and the competence to exert firm control over the money supply.

Monetarism has this stark simplicity. There is no mystery about inflation. It is always caused by an excessive increase in the supply of money, governments are responsible for the money supply, hence governments are responsible for whatever inflation exists.

But if it were really so simple why does inflation persist? Why has inflation not been ended long ago? At this point the monetarist school sharply divides. When asked, why should governments be either unable or unwilling to maintain sound money, one school holds that governments are either wicked or more probably ignorant, the victims of bad economics, as Milton Friedman explained in his Nobel Economics Lecture.[2] If they were guided by 'good' Chicago economics, instead of 'bad' Keynesian economics, then the problem would disappear. These monetarists are technicians, and on one point they outdo Keynes – they not only share his aspiration that economics might one day become like dentistry, they believe that with monetarism that day has now arrived.

The second school is less politically naive. They treat the problem of why governments fail to control the money supply as a political, not a technical, question. Governments are no longer regarded as enlightened agencies above sectional interests seeking the public good and able in principle to discriminate between 'good' and 'bad' economic advice. Instead they are composed of bureaucrats and politicians pursuing their own interests. The adoption of Keynesian policies such as the postwar commitment in Britain to full employment was not therefore the result of intellectual error, but occurred because the politicians wished to get re-elected, and the bureaucrats wanted to extend their influence and the size of their departments. So policies of high spending and high taxation and high borrowing were acceptable, and governments pursued expansionary monetary policies designed to stabilize fluctuations in output and maintain high employment with constantly rising living standards. This meant placing a higher priority on employment and growth than on stable prices. In the Keynesian view moderate inflation was the price that had to be paid if a prosperous and expanding economy was to be secured and the fluctuations of the business cycle eliminated.

For a time the new policy appeared to work. The adoption of Keynesianism was associated with unparalleled prosperity, very high levels of employment, very fast rates of economic growth, and a reduction in social and political conflicts. But monetarists argue now that it was a trick, which was only possible because governments were prepared to pump ever greater sums into the economy to maintain prosperity. The more governments attempted to maintain prosperity by boosting demand the greater were the distortions and rigidities introduced into the economy, because the incentive to hold down costs and to relate incomes to productivity was weakened. Many inefficient companies found it possible to avoid bankruptcy and many trade unions were able to postpone accepting new technologies and new working practices. Governments found that to achieve high levels of employment they had to provide ever greater injections of demand, far in excess of increases in output and productivity. This led to ever faster inflation, until eventually the profitability of many companies was undermined, the trading of higher inflation against lower unemployment broke down, and inflation and unemployment began to rise together.

Keynesianism as practised since the war is bad economics according to monetarists because it can only work by fuelling inflation and the higher inflation is allowed to go, the more damage is done to the market economy and the greater the unemployment that will be necessary to restore efficiency, growth, and high employment. Getting back to sound money is essential if the economy is to be restored to health and the present world recession ended. But social market doctrine recognizes that since governments are composed of politicians and bureaucrats pursuing their own interests, they will only halt inflation and maintain control of the money supply if it is made in their interest to do so. Social market doctrine proposes institutional reforms that can significantly reduce pressures on governments to expand the money supply, as well as introducing new constraints on the nature and content of government economic policies. As a political programme it seeks to 'unwind' social democracy, to destroy the institutional bases on which social democratic regimes have relied. There are three main prongs in this attack – on trade unions, on public spending, and on democracy, and three main accompanying propositions:

- Unemployment is voluntary
- Public expenditure is unproductive
- Democracy threatens liberty

Each proposition requires separate analysis.

Unemployment is voluntary

If inflation is a monetary phenemenon and the result of an excessive expansion of the money supply, then governments are responsible for it, and private individuals or private associations such as trade unions cannot be blamed for it. Whatever the level of pay claims these will only be inflationary if the government expands the money supply to accommodate the higher prices which they make necessary. If the money supply is not expanded, the argument runs, and workers insist on wage levels greater than their company can afford, then they may force the firm to make them redundant or to reduce its profits, but they cannot force a general inflation. In a lax monetary environment, however, companies can borrow to finance higher wages and raise prices. Where money is tightly controlled that option disappears.

But although trade unions do not cause inflation, according to social market doctrine, they can and do cause unemployment and stagnation because they interfere with the working of one of the principal sets of markets on which the smooth operation of the capitalist economy depends – the labour markets. A central argument of social market doctrine is that unemployment is voluntary. No one is forced to be unemployed. If there is a high level of unemployment its causes lie in the obstacles that must be preventing the proper workings of labour markets. Government policy should aim at removing those obstacles. Attempts to bring down the level of unemployment by raising aggregate demand will only have the effect, according to monetarists, of increasing inflation. This will alleviate unemployment temporarily but make it worse in the long run. Monetarists believe in the existence of a natural rate of unemployment which no stimulation of the economy can overcome. This rate is set firstly by the numbers of the unemployable – the disabled, the sick, the 'workshy'; secondly, by those institutions and attitudes which stop labour markets clearing (the demand for labour matching its supply) at a level which employs all those able to work. On this view thirty years of social democracy have saddled Britain with highly imperfect labour markets which mean that achieving control of the money supply and ending inflation involves keeping unemployment permanently in the low millions. The three factors which are regarded as doing most to raise the natural rate of unemployment in Britain are trade unions, social security benefits, and perhaps rather more surprisingly, council housing.

Trade unions are condemned as monopolies, as private associations which have become coercive groups, firstly because they restrict the supply of labour, so raising wages above their 'natural' level; and secondly because they obstruct changes in working practices and manning levels which would raise productivity. In the first case this means that wages are flexible upwards but generally rigid downwards, i.e. trade unions are often successful in resisting actual wage cuts and the result, it is alleged, is that fewer workers are employed because of the cost to firms of employing them. In the second case extra costs are imposed on firms, investment is curtailed, and the rate of economic growth lowered.

Social market theorists have always acknowledged that trying to cure inflation by monetary means would mean considerable unemployment. But they argue that such unemployment will only be temporary so long as labour markets are flexible, and far preferable to a continuation of inflation. Social market theorists note, however, that most labour markets are not flexible, and that adopting a strict monetary policy to control inflation may create levels of unemployment which could unleash very strong pressures for reflation and a new expansion of the money supply. They therefore argue that the government must tackle the rigidities of the labour market by destroying trade union monopoly, by cutting social security payments drastically to force more unemployed to seek employment at very low levels of pay, and by encouraging much greater geographical mobility by reducing restrictions on the ownership and disposal of council housing.

A disinflationary monetary policy raises unemployment and alters the balance of power in the factories against organized labour. This may permit productivity to be increased and wage demands to be resisted successfully. But the underlying organizational strength of trade unions may survive unimpaired, leading to renewed militancy once there was an economic upturn.[3] So social market theorists advocate measures that would permanently reduce the ability of trade unions to bargain effectively with capital. They are particularly keen to remove all the legal immunities granted trade unions, so as to make them liable to actions for damages, as well as to restrict picketing and the closed shop. The ostensible justification for such policies is that the interests of trade unionists are better served by an expanding and competitive economy than by their own unions who, acting in the mistaken belief that they are helping to raise the living standard of their members, in reality are only contributing to unemployment and stagnation.

Public expenditure is an unproductive burden on the wealth-creating sector

The first condition, therefore, for making monetarism work is to destroy the monopoly power of the trade unions, so shifting the balance of advantage at the point of production decisively in favour of capital. This is expected not only to increase profitability and investment, but also to raise employment and remove one significant source of pressure for expansion of the money supply. The second condition is a roll-back of the State. The new social market doctrine is deeply hostile to public expenditure for a number of connected reasons. Firstly, public expenditure is unproductive. It does not create wealth. Only goods and services that are traded in the market add to wealth. Since most public sector goods and services have to be financed out of taxes on private individuals, they are viewed as an expense, a deduction from the total wealth of the community. Secondly, high public expenditure destroys incentives because of the level of taxation needed to finance it. It therefore hinders and frustrates those activities which increase wealth. Thirdly, public expenditure is inefficient. It wastes resources because public sector goods and services are provided by monopolistic bureaucracies which do not face competition, so have no incentives to reduce costs. The same services could be provided far more cheaply by private firms. Fourthly, public expenditure, to the extent that it is financed by borrowing, crowds out private investment, and private spending. The State can always afford to pay higher interest rates in the competition to borrow private funds because its legal right to compel citizens to pay taxes makes it possible to raise whatever interest proves necessary. Fifthly, a high level of public expenditure creates strong pressures for Keynesian budgetary policies and expansionary monetary policies, because the government, instead of being merely involved in holding the ring, is continually involved in detailed decisions about the allocation of resources.

All this means that a major reversal of recent trends in the growth of public expenditure is necessary in order to create the conditions under which markets can function again. For only if individuals are allowed to spend almost the whole of their incomes will economic decision-making become fully decentralized and rational economic behaviour encouraged. This suggests that with very few exceptions government services should either be sold off ('privatized' is the revealing jargon term)or should be financed not out of general taxation but out of direct charges on their users. The only exceptions would be 'public goods' – those goods and services, such as clean air, which cannot be made available to one person without being made available to all. Defence and sound money are considered genuine public goods, whereas health, education, housing, and transport are considered private goods which are consumed by individuals and therefore should be paid for by those who use them.

Democracy threatens liberty

The third condition which is already implicit in the other two is that free markets are a better way of reaching decisions than is planning. Markets are decentralized and involve a multitude of independent decision-makers whose mistakes cancel out, whereas if a planning authority makes a mistake it will have devastating effects. Knowledge is imperfect and provisional, so decentralized decision-making, though apparently involving duplication of resources and effort, is actually more efficient. According to social market doctrine the only alternatives to coordinating human activities through the exchanges individuals make out of self-interest in the market is to coordinate them through the exchanges individuals make out of altruism (their regard for others' interests), or through the exchanges they are directed to make by a central bureaucracy. The second is regarded as Utopian, the third as morally and technically inferior to using markets. Planning and bureaucracy destroy efficiency and liberty.

Underlying such notions is the deeply-held belief that societies exist in a state of natural equilibrium and harmony. Markets are the principal means by which such an equilibrium can be maintained, or regained whenever some external force disturbs it. But this doctrine is not at all the same as anarchism because social market theorists recognize that the social market order is an extremely fragile construction and requires the existence of a strong State if it is to exist at all. The paradox of liberalism is that the self-interest of individuals constantly tends to subvert the general rules that regulate market exchange. So in order to prevent monopoly and preserve competition, to enforce contracts and safeguard property, and to maintain sound money, a strong interventionist public authority is required which can prevent powerful private interests from securing a privileged position. The role of the State is to guarantee the framework of general rules which the market order requires. In their ideal world bureaucracy is reduced to a minimum because the State bureaucracy is only concerned with upholding those general rules rather than with intervening in particular situations and decisions. Rule by law is regarded as preferable to rule by bureaucracy because in the former case the rules are known in advance and certain, whereas in the latter they are discretionary and therefore arbitrary.

It follows that the real safeguard of personal liberty and economic prosperity is the existence of the market order and its framework of general rules. Liberty is thought more important than democracy and the doctrine of popular sovereignty is rejected. No popular mandate can give governments the right to interfere with the market order and this is why the workings of modern democracies have received so much attention from social market theorists. In general social market doctrine favours a drastic restriction of the powers of democratic governments. Proposals have been made to remove whole areas of decision-making (particularly the control of the money supply) from the influence of democratic legislatures, and to erect new safeguards. Two-thirds majorities for certain kinds of legislation,[4] and bills of rights which would legally entrench certain 'natural' rights, such as the right to private education, private health, and inheritance, have been particularly canvassed. Democracy is only tolerable if it is so organized that economic liberty and property rights are not threatened.

ARGUMENTS AGAINST MONETARISM

Inflation

Monetarism has a simple and unrelenting logic. But all its main assumptions and propositions can be contested. No one seriously disputes that inflation is a monetary phenomenon. It is so by definition. What is controversial is that monetarists suggest there is a causal relationship between the rate of growth of money supply and increase in prices. They note that the latter are almost always associated with an increase in the money supply, but they assert that the first is the effect and the second the cause. Yet monetarists have so far failed to establish that the line of causation does run from money to prices rather than the other way round. A large body of opinion amongst economists remains unconvinced by the evidence they have produced. A major problem is how the evidence produced by monetarists should be interpreted. Monetarists say that increases in money supply affect prices but with a lag. But the lags they have proposed vary considerably – from nine months to twenty-four months. It is very difficult to make any prediction from monetarist theory about future rates of inflation that can provide a serious test of monetarist propositions.[5]

An even greater technical problem is the money supply itself. How is money to be defined and measured? Monetarists continue to dispute amongst themselves about the best definition of money. What range of financial assets and financial claims should be included? Notes and coins – certainly; current accounts in banks? – yes; deposit accounts? savings accounts?, building society accounts?; and what about the secondary banks and financial houses, and the assets and securities in international financial markets? What about Eurodollars? What about precious metals – gold, silver, platinum? What about all the near substitutes for money, all the stores of value that are used as hedges against inflation and can be employed to dodge quantitative restrictions on the supply of money? Trying to define money is to enter an ever-deepening swamp. The Radcliffe Committee in 1956 concluded that there was no satisfactory definition and that therefore the money supply could never be rigidly controlled. The Committee doubted that the money supply could be turned on and off like a tap because new forms of money would always be created to evade whatever controls were imposed, and argued that even if controls were sufficiently rigorous, there was nothing to stop the existing stock of money turning over more quickly, i.e. its velocity of circulation increasing. Monetarists have denied that this could happen, but there is growing evidence that it can, and particularly in periods of rapid inflation.

Two important conclusions follow. Firstly, even on the technical level monetarism has not established itself unequivocally. So it is not the case that monetarism offers a technique for controlling inflation in the way that dentistry offers a technique for controlling toothache. There remains a large element of faith and political judgement in monetarism, even at its most technical. Secondly, one reason why money is hard to define and why the objective of controlling the money supply may be beyond governments is because in a capitalist economy the government may be formally responsible for the currency, but it is the banking system that controls and determines the supply of money, and the government must secure their cooperation for any financial policies it wishes to pursue.

So the argument that governments are primarily responsible for inflation because they fail to control the money supply is quite inaccurate. It is the banking system that creates new money by issuing credit, and it is private enterprises that take the actual decisions to increase prices. The growth of private credit is the single most important factor in the expansion of the money supply in the last thirty years.

The secret of monetarism and the reason for its appeal is that it is a technical restatement of the case for sound money. Stable prices are good for most people (if we exclude debtors, banks, companies, and governments) because they make economic calculations much more certain. Sound money is associated with financial rectitude, the balancing of income and expenditure, and the generation of business confidence. There remains an unease about incurring debts, whether public or private, which even consumer capitalism and John Maynard Keynes have not eradicated.

But if sound money is so desirable why should it have become so difficult to attain? Why should the price level have been rising continually since the 1930s when over the whole of the nineteenth century in Britain the trend in prices was slightly down? Why has no government been able actually to halt inflation? Why has no government been prepared to phase out its budget deficit and balance its accounts?

Questions like these cannot be answered satisfactorily within the monetarist framework. Monetarists rightly say that trade unions are not the cause of inflation. But it is as mistaken to claim that governments are to blame. The problem does not arise at this level. Monetarist analysis goes wrong because it is based on such a simple-minded model of the economy. It sees the dynamic of the economy coming from individuals pursuing their own interests within markets instead of from the competitive struggle between individual enterprises to accumulate capital. The reason for inflation is not because governments are politically corrupt, but because profitability and prosperity demand it. In certain respects capitalism is a very different system from one hundred years ago. The potential fluctuations in output and employment over the trade cycle are enormous. Production in the leading sectors has become highly capital intensive, and governments have become deeply involved at many levels in maintaining the stability of the system. Managing the level of aggregate demand so as to minimize fluctuations and mitigate slumps have become very important functions of government, aimed at preserving prosperity, profitability, the legitimacy of the market order and of the State which upholds it.

Inflation as a result is now endemic in the modern capitalist economy. Since the 1940s, governments have sometimes been able to contain inflation but no government in any capitalist economy has succeeded in eliminating it. The upward movement of prices has been uninterrupted and in the 1970s the rate of increase accelerated. Monetarists assert that despite the experience of the last thirty years inflation can be halted, but their faith is insecurely founded. This is because the key to inflation lies not in government policies but in the way the economy is organized. The real cause of inflation must be sought in profitability and in the difficulties of maintaining profitability. Profits are the driving force of the capitalist economy, and the constant need which is experienced by every enterprise to increase profits and accumulate capital has contributed to the unparalleled development of the productive forces during the last one hundred years, and the exploration of every conceivable avenue for raising the productivity of labour. This has resulted in the typical structure of the modern capitalist economy, where plant is highly concentrated and control of capital tightly centralized, where labour is well organized, government functions have expanded enormously, and the interpenetration of State and capital has become indispensable to the successful functioning of the economy.

One of the most important consequences has been that since so many markets both for labour and for goods are imperfect, (i.e. companies and unions are price-makers rather than price-takers because they can influence the price at which they buy and sell), companies can within limits set their own prices. Modern companies, concerned as they are to maintain or increase their rate of profit will, when faced by any change in their costs, normally react by raising their prices. Trade unions and other groups that are disadvantaged by the rise in prices will press for proportional increases to protect their incomes. Once a spiral has begun and expectations that inflation will accelerate have become widespread, it becomes hard to break it. Monetarists believe it can be done, but the cost is heavy. Either a major slump must be precipitated by squeezing credit so hard and raising interest rates so high that output and expenditure are enormously reduced; or real competition must be restored, which would require the dismantling of the large companies, unions, and public agencies that dominate the economy. The feasibility of unscrambling the results of the last two hundred years of capital accumulation is not great. The political risks of provoking a slump that is large enough to squeeze inflation out of the economy loom rather larger. Monetarism offers no painless way of getting rid of inflation and presents a very superficial view of its causes.

Among socialists there is disagreement as to what has caused the current inflation. One approach emphasizes the underlying conflict between the three major forces in the economy – private capital, government, and the trade unions – over how the national income is to be *distributed*. The outcome is inflation because all three groups desire to spend in total more than the GNP and no mechanism exists for reconciling their competing claims. Incomes policies have at times succeeded in moderating the conflict but they have not been wholly successful because of the difficulty that arises when income from property is treated in the same manner as other incomes. Such income serves not only to finance the private consumption of the owners of property, but also is the measure of economic efficiency and the source for future investment and accumulation. Many socialists have long argued that inflation can never be controlled while capital remains in private hands, because there can never be agreement on a fair distribution of the national income, so long as society is divided between the propertied and the propertyless, and ownership of property gives an automatic and prior claim to a share in income. Inflation on this view has become endemic because governments have become committed to a vast range of expenditure in order to maintain the fabric of the economy and the legitimacy of the social order. They must accordingly tax, borrow, or print the money to finance it. At the same time many groups in the labour force are organized to fight for the best wages and conditions they can obtain. The resources each sector is able to command depend on the balance between the degree of monopoly and coercion each is able to exercise. Governments can tax, unions can strike, companies can raise prices. The interaction of all three produces an unstoppable inflation. Money supply increases passively to accommodate the price and spending decisions that flow from the conflict between them.

There is probably little disagreement on the mechanics of the inflationary spiral. But a second approach emphasizes less the problems of distribution and the problems of reconciling the claims on national income with the actual size of the national output, and more the question of *production*. For inflation can also be seen as an expression of the growing inability of enterprises to offset the tendency of the rate of profit to fall, to find ways to raise the productivity of labour fast enough to compensate for the increasing costs of maintaining and expanding their existing capital. Increases in raw material and energy costs, in wages, and in taxes, are only the triggers of the inflationary process. The problem for capital is that the cost of maintaining the stock of existing plant has become very great and the opportunities for profitable new investment have declined. One of the few things that makes this situation bearable is the permissive monetary environment tolerated by governments. So long as companies can obtain credit and can pass on higher costs in higher prices, they have a chance of surviving. If sound money were restored, an essential element of flexibility would have been removed, and recessions would be transformed into major slumps, with companies and banks of all sizes folding on every side. Much of the apparatus of intervention of the modern State has been built up to prevent this happening. The restructuring of capital to raise productivity, rationalize plant, and promote diversification into new areas and new technologies, is now carried on by means that are much less drastic than those associated with the business cycle of early capitalism. But the price is inflation. Governments have only managed to maintain a reasonable level of activity in the economy by making it easier for firms to remain profitable. The alternative in modern circumstances of attempting to adopt hard money policies is illustrated by the policies of the Thatcher government in Britain in its first two years. Although in many respects the policies fell far short of what monetarist doctrine specified, they still contributed to a slump of unprecedented severity – a fall in industrial output of 17 per cent and a doubling of unemployment. It may be *possible* to re-structure a modern capitalist economy by an old-fashioned slump, though some think it a very clumsy and inefficient method. But the real problem is that the scale of the slump that would be required, and the extent of the dislocation it would be likely to cause, make it impossible for governments to adopt if they are subject to any form of democratic accountability. Only the most authoritarian regimes would not blench.

Unemployment is voluntary

If the technical case for sound money is flawed, so too are the main arguments of social market doctrine. The proposition that all unemployment is voluntary is not heard too much on the hustings. There is a socialist as well as a monetarist common sense and such a statement sounds self-evidently absurd. It is confined to monetarist tracts and the pages of the bank reviews. But the associated idea that unions in asking for more money for their members price their members out of jobs and raise unemployment is stated openly.

The ideological basis for this notion is once again the economy of utility-maximizing rational individuals. If all economic agents are conceived as sovereign individuals, then if some of them associate to control the supply of the good they offer on the market, they will raise its price and impose extra costs on their fellow citizens. But is this the economy unions actually inhabit? Unions arose not because of an opportunity to 'corner the market', but in order to counter the unrestricted power of the employer, not just in the market-place but also and primarily in the control of the production process. The history of capital accumulation has shown how the interests of cap-ital and the interests of working people remain fundamentally opposed. In order to achieve the fastest possible rate of expansion, capital and its agents are forced to search out every possible means to prolong the working day, to increase the intensity of labour, and to raise the productivity of their workforce.

Where trade unions are weak and unable to exercise any countervailing power, then nothing prevents all the familiar horrors of capitalist labour markets and capitalist factories from asserting themselves – sweat shops; employment of children; neglect of health and safety; no controls on hours or the pace of work; subsistence wages; slums and malnutrition. But what is also true is that far from the absence of unions and other 'rigidities' in labour markets leading to full employment, what actually emerges is a permanent pool of unemployed, which rises and falls in accordance with the trade cycle. Few countries have done more than Chile to apply the precepts of Chicago economics and to unwind social democracy. But even in Chile, seven years after the coup, unemployment was still 15 per cent of the labour force.

Trade unions are one factor which makes the exploitation of labour power less favourable for capital. But too much should not be claimed for them. Wages are often high and conditions good in some trades where no unions exist, because labour power there is in short supply. Destroying the power of unions would not restore full employment. What it would do is give capital a free hand to accumulate without the restrictions which trade unions can impose. This would necessarily mean a significant worsening of the general terms of bargaining between capital and labour, and the removal of those few protections that workers have been able to achieve.

Labour markets including those in trades where unions are weak or non-existent are certainly not as flexible as social market doctrine requires. Wages do not easily adjust to changes in costs and profits. It is possible to imagine a perfectly competitive labour market in which demand and supply always balanced so that anyone who wanted a job was employed. But what would such a labour market entail? Is the price of a social market economy to be the employment of a large part of its workforce at wages that are too low to support a family? If people are faced with starvation no doubt they will accept any wage that is offered. But an economic system that can solve its unemployment problem only by employing people at subsistence or below subsistence wages has not really solved its problems at all. Capital has long been impatient with the human frailties of the workforce, one of the most awkward being that workers have come to demand a living wage as a right and often refuse to sell labour power for less.

The response of social market doctrine to high unemployment figures is to argue that almost everyone on the register should be removed. According to one pamphlet the only people who should be considered unemployed are men aged 25 to 55 who have been out of work for more than six months.[6] The unemployment statistics are renowned for their inaccuracy, but the real adjustment that is required is up, not down. For what the present figures do conceal are the large numbers of people who want employment but are not formally registered.[7] Permanent high unemployment has become a chronic structural problem for capitalist economies, and it is being exacerbated by attempts to contract the public sector.

Is public spending excessive?

The claim that public expenditure is unproductive because goods and services in the public sector are not sold in the market,[8] is a new statement of a very old idea in political economy. The original distinction was grounded in a class theory of property and exploitation. Those who lived off rents and public revenues lived off the surplus created by those in industry and agriculture. The modern notion states that all who work in the public sector or who receive money from public funds are living parasitically off those in the private sector who are creating wealth. But whereas the exactions of the landowners and the landowners' State may have been fairly clear, particularly to the new industrial bourgeoisie who contributed so much to it, there is nothing clear about labelling the modern State a burden in the same way. This is because the modern State and economy are so intertwined and interdependent that to talk of one producing wealth and the other consuming it is a great oversimplification. For what is meant by wealth? If wealth is defined as whatever satisfies human needs, then many things produced in the public sector, like education and health, would count while many in the private sector, (particularly the hidden costs of production such as advertising) would not. And what are we to make of a distinction that would make a school unproductive if it is funded from taxes, but the same school suddenly productive if it is funded from private fees? What really lies behind this revival of the distinction between productive and unproductive sectors is not an interest in determining how useful are particular services, but how productive is the labour that produces them. What counts is whether an activity produces commodities that embody and can realize surplus value. The real issue about the public sector is that in certain areas goods and services are produced and distributed in accordance with criteria other than those of profitability. This becomes a problem if they are expanded too far, because it reduces funds available for capital accumulation as well as reducing areas of social life where capital accumulation is possible. Since the tendency of capitalist production has always been for private capital to seek to invade every possible sphere of social activity, turning every good and service into a marketable commodity, the loss of any of its territory is resisted. But how did spheres from which private capital has been expelled ever arise?

There are two main ways of looking at it. From one perspective they are the result of long political struggles to increase welfare provision – struggles in which the labour movement was very prominent. They are therefore areas which represent socialist conquests, victories for the political economy of labour over the political economy of capital. Collective provision of health care, social security, and education are costs that have to be borne by capital, concessions that became necessary to preserve the legitimacy of the market order.

From another perspective the public sector has grown in order to provide services which although they are not directly productive for the private sector, are necessary in order to create conditions that allow the private sector to make profits, yet which the private sector is incapable of providing for itself. So far from being a parasite on the private sector the public sector is indispensable for ensuring the legitimacy and the profitability of the private sector it is supposed to prey on. If States did not shoulder so many of the costs of the modern industrial system – education, health, transport, and research – and provide through their expenditure vast markets for private companies, the field for private accumulation would be drastically restricted. A modern diversified industrial capitalist economy would be impossible to sustain.

Much of the current offensive against the size of the public sector is primarily an ideological offensive which assists governments not in actually reducing the total of public spending but in redistributing within that total.[9] An attempt is made to reorient public expenditure towards those programmes which either are held to provide the indispensable guarantees for a market order, such as the military machine and internal security, or appear to have a closer link to wealth creation, i.e. to providing measurable benefits for capital. What is really burdensome for capital is the expansion of those areas which are not subordinate to the requirements of accumulating capital.

But it is time that socialists went over to the attack. The arguments of social market theorists should be turned back on them. They argue that only 'public goods' should be provided by the State. The justification for cutting health and social security is that these are not true public goods because they are consumed individually – hence they should be charged to individuals. But why then are defence and law and order not in the same category? Because, say social market theorists, these are true public goods. For if one citizen is defended by spending on an army all citizens will be defended. So all must be compelled to contribute to the cost. But this assumes that there is some objective way of estimating that defence expenditure does actually provide defence rather than expensive outdoor relief, and that without it lives and property would be at risk. Who is to make that assessment on the part of the community? At the heart of social market doctrine are attitudes every bit as paternalist and collectivist as the socialist attitudes they pillory. Some things are apparently too important to be left to the individual. So social market doctrine should be challenged – either apply the same criteria to all parts of the public sector or do not apply them at all. Either propose that defence spending be paid for by private subscription to defence bonds by those who feel a need to be defended, or admit that health and education are just as much public goods as defence, and that the argument should be about national priorities and social need, about how the community should be collectively organized, and not about public and private goods.

A major reason why those who support high levels of public spending have been so much on the defensive since the world recession began is that public spending carries a stigma which private spending does not. The national accounts are set up in such a way that public spending always appears as an exaction from the private sector. It has to be financed either by the government imposing taxes on firms and individuals or borrowing from them. Most citizens accept this as one of the eternal features of nature, as immutable as the Pennines. But it only appears so because of the way in which national income is distributed. First individuals are assigned income according to the work they do and the property they own. Then a proportion of this is removed by the State through taxation. State income always appears as private income first, so taxation is always experienced by individuals as depriving them of something that is rightfully theirs. But it is not hard to imagine a different method of social accounting where all income and property belonged to the community first and where the criteria for assigning incomes to individuals were openly discussed and collectively decided. Individuals would experience such a system very differently from the present one.

One of the cornerstones of the capitalist order is that the pattern of income distribution should seem to arise spontaneously. *Individuals* earn incomes which are the reward for effort, skill, and ability. But what is concealed by the market is how the overall distribution of income is already fixed by the division of the community into propertied and propertyless, and how the existence of possibilities to earn income is determined by the organization of the economy which the State guarantees. The real issue is not whether or not income should be distributed in accordance with the attributes and performance of individuals, but whether the total income available should be distributed to individuals before or after the deduction of public funds and even more important with or without the deduction of a major share reserved for the owners of property. One of the consequences of the institutional arrangements in capitalist societies for distributing income is that modern capitalist states face periodic fiscal crises (expenditure outrunning revenue) because there is continual conflict between the government and the citizens over the size of the funds which the State can exact. In Britain local authority rates are the form of taxes over which there is most conflict, partly because the annual rates demand makes them so visible, and partly because they redistribute the most. There is least contest over the taxes which are most regressive, but also the least visible, i.e. indirect taxes like VAT.

The existing system of accounting is often defended with the claim that it preserves liberty by recognizing that it is the individual who earns and creates wealth. But this is an illusion. In modern industrial societies the ability to earn an income depends on membership of a community and on the opportunities and advantages which membership confers. Many Western capitalist states have been moving towards a kind of paralysis because of their inability to find ways of justifying and maintaining levels of public spending that are necessary for the further development of industrial society.

All the additional arguments against public expenditure are grounded in the notion that it is unproductive. The proposition, for example, that public expenditure crowds out private expenditure makes little sense when the economy is producing so far below its potential. If public borrowing were lower the recession would be still deeper. The idea that high public expenditure threatens freedom depends on the argument that it must be paid for by high taxes on individuals which destroy the incentives for individuals to work and produce. If individuals are not allowed to retain the bulk of what they earn, output and productivity will fall. But there are many causes of low productivity apart from the possible and as yet unproven disincentive of high marginal tax rates, and the tendency of this whole line of reasoning is to suggest that advanced capitalist economies would do better to dissolve into loose aggregates of fiercely independent and proudly sovereign individuals. There is a fundamental flaw in the theory which implies that it might be feasible to bestow all income on individuals, abolishing the public sphere altogether, without understanding at the same time that this would destroy the conditions for earning income.

More than most other fields, attitudes to public expenditure are riddled with ignorance and ideological distortion. The notions that the more taxes you pay the less free you are, or that when public expenditure reaches a certain proportion of the national income freedom is in danger, may be fashionable but are quite false. When Milton Friedman and Roy Jenkins both expressed the second idea in 1975 they were greeted as though they had said something profound. But the famous 60 per cent of GNP which they regarded with such alarm could as easily have been 400 per cent since so large a proportion of it consisted not of direct government expenditure, but transfer payments. Transfer payments redistribute income between generations, from those working to those who are children, who are retired, who are sick, disabled, or unemployed. These incomes are individual incomes, spent by individuals, transferred to individuals by the mechanism of the State. If the State did not do it it would be performed by private insurance companies, though less equitably and much more selectively. In neither case does the growth of transfer payments threaten freedom, or choice, or individuality. They rather obviously help sustain all three by easing the burden of major insecurities.

The argument about transfer payments can be extended. If the functions were not performed by the State they would be performed by the market. Precisely, say the social market theorists, and more efficiently, less arbitrarily, and in ways which promote choice and diversity. But this supposes that markets can always be made to function properly. Many markets, however, function imperfectly, they are constantly breaking down or being distorted. When they do work, the outcomes that emerge from them are determined by the distribution of income that already exists. Social market theorists love to analyse democracy as a political market. But the analogy can be reversed. From the standpoint of a democracy, markets are highly skewed systems of voting. Everyone has a vote, i.e. an income, but the rich have many more votes than everyone else. So large areas of the economy are devoted to supplying their needs. So long as incomes are unequal the market cannot accurately reflect individual needs and preferences. For only those needs and preferences are effective in the market which are backed by the ability to pay. So many basic needs are never met while whole areas of the economy are devoted to supplying luxuries for a very small section of the population. On a world scale the difference is even more striking. Social market doctrine, by not questioning the existing pattern of income distribution, recommends a highly unequal and artificial pattern of private consumption.

What privatization and selectivity generally mean is the destruction of services and the concentration of provision on those who can afford to pay. The result is seldom optimal. The familiar cycle, for instance, of rising bus fares and falling numbers of passengers has reached remarkable lengths in many areas, resulting in congestion in some and substantial loss of amenity in others. No one suggests that bureaucracy and planning are perfect systems. They have many faults, but they often have advantages which a policy of relying exclusively on markets necessarily abandons. The argument about crowding out should be reversed. In a capitalist economy there is much private expenditure that deserves to be crowded out by public expenditure.

Does democracy threaten liberty?

The world of liberal political economy is a very simple world. On one side are the gardens of liberty, on the other the swamps of totalitarianism. The road to serfdom passes under the arches of socialism, planning, and democracy. It is paved with every bureaucratic decision which interferes with how individuals spend their incomes. So extreme have these doctrines now become that they have spawned a new history of capitalism. It goes like this. *Laissez-faire* capitalism never existed, so the revulsion against *laissez-faire* and economic liberalism was misconceived. In the nineteenth century some first steps were taken in the establishment of a free market, but they were not ultimately successful, and *because they were not*, capitalism continued to be plagued by trade cycles, unemployment, and other disturbances. But these were not the fault of the free market. The market order when properly constituted and allowed to function properly, guarantees full employment and economic growth. (Social market theorists claim to know this because they have devised mathematical models which demonstrate it.)[10] All the ills that beset capitalism arise not from the market order itself but because of interference (sometimes by private coercive groups like unions, but most often by governments, particularly democratic governments) in the workings of the market order.

Social market doctrine has begun to recover some of the boldness of classical liberalism. Like the latter it makes universal claims. Life, liberty, and the pursuit of happiness for every individual can best be secured within a market order and a constitutional State. It is a long time since socialists have had to face the full force of such arguments. Over the last hundred years classical liberalism has been subjected to major critiques from right and left and its influence has waned. But that should not lead socialists into underestimating it now.

Socialists need to make two major points. The first is that markets are not self-adjusting, they do not naturally tend to equilibrium. To suppose that they do or can is a leap of faith. There is no empirical basis for it, and the theoretical argument for it has been subject to major challenge, because it depends on abstracting from all those elements that actually constitute markets. Marx and Keynes from very different positions recognized that a theory which was based around concepts of equilibrium, of supply creating its own demand, was seriously deficient for understanding the workings of the real economy. For in any actual economy the creation of rigidities and obstacles to the functioning of markets was not accidental or the product of malign external influences but a result of the way in which markets were in fact organized. Workers will resist if their wages are driven down to subsistence. Nation-states will seek to protect themselves from unrestricted competition. The contrast between the world of perfect competition of liberal economics, a world where all markets are composed of a multitude of economic agents, none of whom produces enough to affect the price they sell at, all of whom produce a commodity that is exactly the same and make their exchanges with perfect knowledge of all costs and prices, confront the actual economy that is dominated by huge bureaucracies – the agents of capital (the corporations), of labour (the trade unions), and of the State (the government).

The response of economic liberals is that this is a straw target. The concept of perfect competition, they say, is only an analytical device designed to elucidate how actual markets work by comparing them with the model. But this analytical device is seriously flawed. Its weakness is firstly that it is highly normative – it suggests that this is how things ought to be while purportedly explaining how things are. Secondly, it leads to the elimination of most of the actual features of markets from consideration. They are defined from the outset as non-economic and external to the market. But there is an even more damaging argument. For even if we accept the idea of perfect competition as a model and a normative standard for describing, explaining, and judging, it still fails as a defence of capitalism. Because what it must ignore is that when labour power itself is made a commodity, the classless society of independent property owners, which the model of perfect competition tacitly assumes, disappears, and in its place arises a society whose fundamental social relation is that between capital and labour. From this division of the community into property-owners and the propertyless, develops many of the distinguishing features of capitalism as a mode of production, and one of its most characteristic contradictions – between the need to subordinate everything to the accumulation of capital, and the need to find a basis for the legitimacy of the State, a basis which both expresses the universalist notions of liberalism – its proclamation of liberty, equality, and fraternity – yet its urgent wish to maintain a market order that does not challenge the division into those with property and those without.

The narrow view of democracy, which social market doctrine proclaims, (that it is simply a means to choose a government), flows from these assumptions. Socialists have always argued for a much broader vision of human potential and a belief that democracy is not only about accountability and formal legitimation, but the full development of each individual through their participation in the affairs of their associations and communities. Putting reins on democracy to safeguard property was a dominant theme of early liberalism. Locke and the Founding Fathers of the American Constitution were no strangers to it.

That it should seem radical and progressive today is because its target is the now ossified bureaucratic systems of social democracy that emerged originally to stabilize capitalist societies. The lie in economic liberalism is that it appears to offer a choice between individual liberty and bureaucracy, whereas at most it offers a choice between one kind of bureaucracy and another. It does not argue, for example, that all large companies should be disbanded, and everyone made a property-owner and self-employed. It has no quarrel with private bureaucracy, even with the giant bureaucracies of the multinational companies. All its venom is reserved for the public bureaucracies that administer the State and public enterprises. This is presented as a stand for freedom against bureaucracy, but what is really being defended is control over the economy by private capital and its agents rather than control by public authorities which are to some extent democratically accountable and open to public scrutiny. Socialism in recent years has lost some of its momentum by being so closely associated with ideas of central planning and public bureaucracy. But it still possesses its own radical critique of State power which goes much further than liberalism because it attacks the limitations on liberty and equality which arise not only from bureaucracy but also from the ownership and control of property.

CONCLUSION

The vigour of monetarist and social market doctrines is undeniable. Their great strength is that they can function on several different levels – they provide technical advice on policy, a coherent and all-embracing ideology for activists, and themes that can easily be translated into a popular common sense about economics. They owe their present importance to the problems of inflation and recession. They offer a coherent strategy for handling the recession – precipitating a controlled slump in order to raise productivity, lower wages, and restructure the economy towards long-term profitability. But monetarism has few answers if the slump turns out to be difficult to control, and if the policies encounter resistance. There is a small but growing body of opinion in the West which argues that recovery in the world economy is unlikely to come about except through much higher levels of State intervention and expenditure.[11] The different fortunes of the monetarist experiment in Britain and Chile indicate that the strategy's best chance of success requires that decisive measures be taken from the outset against the organizations of the working class, and democratic institutions suspended. But even that it seems, is no guarantee that inflation can be halted or that a broad-based industrial recovery can be initiated. Social market doctrine presents itself as a doctrine of hope and revival, but it is more likely to be remembered as a doctrine of despair and retrenchment, attempting to hold the line as best it may in the storm of the world recession, in defence of the market order and the right to be unequal.

NOTES

I should like to thank David Coates for his comments on earlier drafts of this chapter.

1. There is a growing literature on monetarism. See, for example, T. Congdon, *Monetarism*, Centre for Policy Studies 1978; H. R. Vane and J. L. Thompson, *Monetarism*, Martin Robertson 1979. For critical accounts of monetarism see especially Bryan Gould *et al.*, *Monetarism or Prosperity?*, Macmillan 1981; D. Currie, 'What's left of monetarism?' in D. Currie and R. Smith (eds), *Socialist Economic Review*, Merlin 1981
2. M. Friedman, *Inflation and Unemployment*, IEA 1977
3. D. Currie, op. cit. makes this point strongly
4. See for example, G. Tulloch, *The Vote Motive*, IEA 1976
5. See the chapters by D. Currie and Cobham in D. Currie and R. Smith, op. cit.
6. See J. B. Wood, *How Little Unemployment?*, IEA 1975
7. See *Labour Research*, Dec. 1975, pp. 246–47
8. See R. Bacon and W. Eltis, *Britain's Economic Problem: too few producers*, Macmillan 1976
9. See I. Gough, *The Political Economy of the Welfare State*, Macmillan 1979
10. See J.M. Buchanan *et al.*, *The Consequences of Mr Keynes*, IEA 1978, 85
11. One expression of this was the Brandt Report in 1980

FURTHER READING

On monetarism and the social market strategy the publications of the Institute for Economic Affairs (IEA) and the Centre for Policy Studies are important sources. The following are particularly relevant:

T. Congdon, *Monetarism*, CPS 1978
F. A. Hayek, *A Tiger by the Tail*, IEA 1972
F. A. Hayek, *Full Employment at any Price*, IEA 1975
M. Friedman, *Inflation and Unemployment*, IEA 1977
J.B. Wood, *How Little Unemployment?*, IEA 1975
G. Tulloch, *The Vote Motive*, IEA 1976
J. M. Buchanan *et al.*, *The Consequences of Mr Keynes*, IEA 1978
A. Seldon (ed.), *Is Monetarism Enough?*, IEA 1980

Socialist arguments

For an academic survey of monetarism and its doctrines see: H. R. Vane and J. L. Thompson, *Monetarism*, Martin Robertson 1979

For critical surveys of monetarism and social market doctrine see:
D. Currie, 'What's left of monetarism?' in D. Currie and R. Smith (eds), *Socialist Economic Review*, Merlin 1981;
Bryan Gould *et al.*, *Monetarism or Prosperity*, Macmillan 1981;
Andrew Gamble, 'The free economy and the strong state', *Socialist Register* 1979

Chapter two

DEINDUSTRIALIZATION:
ARE THE WORKERS TO BLAME?

John Hillard

The image is Decay —
A bowl in whose contents
Worms are breeding.
     The Book of Changes, 18

In 1980, the World in Action team visited a Thorn-EMI plant which produces the 'revolutionary' Ferguson TX television set. The line-manager revealed the open secret of British productive technique: 'If the left cheek is visible the production line is moving too fast: if the right cheek is in the air the line is slow. A nice, flat bottom is the sign that everything is going fine.' As the man exclaimed: 'the best picture of all time'. Meanwhile over at National Panasonic the Japanese manager was talking about the stereo-video wristwatch.

Blackburn Rovers (Hon. President: Mrs Thatcher) fell from First Division grace many years ago. The die-hard fans became fickle and deserted the rain-soaked terraces for the armchair comfort of Grandstand. After a long demise in the doldrums of Division III the lads eventually kicked themselves up a flight. Much to the President's displeasure, however, the 1980/81 promotion drive faltered at the last as the Blackburn board struggled in vain to discover the key to the Euro-magic of Liverpool/Hitachi.

England . . . Lord Nelson, Lord Beaverbrook, Sir Winston Churchill, Sir Anthony Eden, Clement Attlee, Henry Cooper . . . Lady Diana . . . Maggie Thatcher can you hear me Maggie Thatcher. Your boys took a hell of a beating. Your boys took a hell of a beating.[1]

Deindustrialization is an unsatisfactory term. It is more a trigger word to symbolize a vague notion of economic decadence than a precisely definable concept. Most commentators have concentrated upon the phenomenon of declining employment in manufacturing industry. In this narrow sense, deindustrialization was coined originally as a political slogan to highlight 'job-loss' – manufacturing employment in the UK, after peaking at 8.6 million in 1966, declined to 6.3 million in 1980. The 1970s witnessed a 14 per cent fall in the total number employed in manufacturing industry. But deindustrialization represents something more than diminishing industrial employment. It is a word synonymous with the English Disease, i.e. a euphemism for rapidly accelerating economic backwardness. The main theme of the following discussion centres upon the causes of the British State's *relative* economic decline but, as a preliminary, a distinction has to be drawn between those characteristics of deindustrialization which are common to the majority of market economies and those aspects of the problem unique to Britain.

Britain has not been alone in experiencing a secular fall in the level of industrial employment both in absolute terms and in proportion to the total workforce. Its widespread manifestation in market economies which, like Britain, are said to have reached a 'mature' stage of capitalist development, denotes the operation of international forces bringing about a rationalization of the labour process. As such, in and of itself, there is nothing intrinsically 'wrong' with deindustrialization. Whereas the number of jobs in British industry fell by 13 per cent between 1965 and 1977, manufacturing output actually rose by 16 per cent. This reflects the tendency of capitalist production to become more automated – a tendency which can reduce the alienation and drudgery of factory work and one which potentially frees labour to undertake socially useful tasks.

In this vein, optimistic pundits see the deindustrialization process as heralding the dawn of post-industrial society, analogous to nineteenth-century 'deruralization' which accompanied the Industrial Revolution. It is envisaged that an unfolding Service Revolution will fill the employment void created by deindustrialization, in the same way that the demands of industrialism absorbed successfully the massive reduction in agricultural employment. Such a Utopian scenario is no more than idealistic fantasy. First, to say the least, the transition from feudalism to industrial capitalism involved considerable 'adjustment' costs. Secondly, the ideologues of post-industrialism forget that the transitional shift of workers from agriculture to industry extended over many decades, which preserved the social cohesion of the British State. By contrast, the time-span for accommodating the repercussions of deindustrialization has contracted to the space of a few years.

The current depressionary phase in the Western capitalist zone is partly responsible for increased unemployment. At the best of times, it is pure chance whether a given increase in the level of investment will generate a concomitant amount of income and employment. In a depressionary context, the labour-displacing consequence of innovative investment is certain to exceed considerably its employment-generating effects in the economy as a whole. The overall decline in economic activity, however, has coincided with a revolutionary convergence of various strands of communications technology. General applications electronics makes feasible the combination of electronic and mechanical technology so as to reduce substantially the need for labour in the production process and beyond. The implications of microprocessor technology in the present circumstances render conventional remedies for unemployment inappropriate because of the scale and speed of readjustment required to handle its incorporation. Nor is it certain that the fruits of rationalization will be harvested in the mature economies of the West. Instead and on the contrary, the competitive logic of capitalist efficiency is much more likely to induce a shift by Western-based supranational capital towards newly industrializing countries, which offer the facility of utilizing the latest technology with very cheap and subservient labour.

The combined impact of slump and technological convergence is initiating a rationalization process which signifies a sudden reduction in the number of 'mature' labour units required by capital. The unleashed forces strike at the *micro*-level of the firm/industry and are reflected at the *macro* or national level as unemployment. Furthermore, there is little short-run prospect of the workers thereby displaced being re-absorbed back into the labour market. The absence of an adjustment mechanism within the Common Market to accommodate the political and social consequences of large-scale unemployment confronts senile capitalism as a whole and is not confined to Britain.

In Britain's case, however, these generally experienced exigencies of readjustment to swiftly changing economic circumstances are exacerbated by a long-term heritage of deteriorating trade competitiveness in the global market for manufactured products. Since the Second World War, Britain's share in manufactured exports has fallen from a quarter to a tenth of the world total. Between 1970 and 1977 manufacturing production increased by only 4 per cent compared to a 90 per cent increase in the volume of manufactured imports. By 1979, the share of manufactured imports in the British market stood at 26 per cent compared with 17 per cent in 1970.

Domestic production accounted only for half the new cars registered and over two-fifths of the domestically consumed durables, footwear and clothing, were manufactured outside Britain. From these indications, the general phenomenon of deindustrialization in Western capitalism is overlain in Britain by an 'internal' dimension expressed in the form of a market decline in the competitive performance of British national capital in relation to other countries.

Finally, it is important to distinguish between the historical context of Britain's industrial decline and the recent short, sharp deterioration in the fortunes of British national capital, the latter not entirely unconnected with the policy stance of the Conservative government since 1979. The Conservative Party came to power imbued with an ideological fervour which denoted a strong determination to reverse the downhill slide of industry. The programme of reindustrialization sought, in Mrs Thatcher's words, 'to direct a huge effort of National Will' to place G. B. Limited upon a commercially profitable footing. Towards this end, certain sectors of the national economy were subject to a dose of strict market discipline. The short-term impact of Thatcherism, however, far from rejuvenating Britain's industrial base, appeared instead to be metamorphosing her famed industrial wasteland into a wilderness.

During 1980 alone, 750,000 manufacturing jobs disappeared, representing a shrinkage of 10 per cent compared with the previous year's average. The annual output of manufacturing industry slumped by 15 per cent, the total standing at 17.5 per cent below the average output achieved during the 1974 three-day week. In the last quarter of 1980, gross fixed investment in plant and machinery was 16 per cent below the same period in 1979.

Whereas Thatcherism has undoubtedly worsened the problems emanating from deindustrialization, the *underlying* condition of Britain's productive base would have been perilous, Mrs Thatcher or not. Indeed, the extremism of the national government since 1979 highlights the failure of previous attempts to halt, never mind reverse, what is evidently an inevitable spiral of productive decline. It is safe to assume that Mrs Thatcher's 'bold initiative' aimed at breaking the resistance to economic advance, which has plagued the British State for over a century, will prove to be yet another false dawn. This being the case, it is probable that the objective condition of British national capital will erode further, even, in the eyes of apocalyptic commentators, to the point of disintegration. Consequently, a conscious and steady adaptation to what Samuel Brittan of the *Financial Times* glibly describes as 'severe structural change' constitutes a political target that is fast disappearing out of range.

The question is: can the institutional structure of British society withstand the political and social stresses arising from rapid economic transformation? The problem of deindustrialization has revealed a dilemma which *any* form of market solution is unable to accommodate. Since 1945, successive governments have walked a tightrope between market imperatives and pressures for representative democracy. During the boom, both sides of the equation could be satisfied, but in the twilight of the Keynesian era, the overt dictates of capital have once again become paramount. The dilemma centres on the inevitability of mass unemployment with or without encompassing the electronic revolution. Without a rapid switch to capital-oriented production, Lord Kaldor's famous spectre of 'pastoralization' will become a reality as Britain fails 'to adjust swiftly enough to the advance in industrial automation and information networks to stay afloat in a competitive world'.[2] Put bluntly, a market solution cannot combine the oil of economic efficiency with the rising tide of unemployment.

On the other hand, market logic highlights the high long-run opportunity cost of maintaining employment for non-economic reasons. The inability of British national capital to withstand global market pressures – epitomized by the fate of BL – has evoked a State response which amounts to little more than expensive cosmetic surgery. Secondly, it cannot be denied that the slush-fund approach of financial incentives has proved an ineffective trigger for promoting the regeneration of capital. In 1978–79, State support to capital in the form of subsidies, tax reliefs and grants amounted to a minimum of £7.3 billion. On the other hand, the removal of the various public props holding-up capital has deprived the latter of the margin of funds which might otherwise have been available to finance autonomous reconstruction.

Since 1979, 'rolling back the tide of socialism' and setting the market free has effected little more than an increase in the level of unemployment. By end-1981, without the temporary provision of short-term working compensation, without various government-funded temporary employment creation schemes, and without discounting over 600,000 people (mainly women) who 'disappeared' from the labour force without seeking work, the *official* figure for unemployment would have exceeded 4 million. The burden of controlling the anarchy of 'adjustment' increasingly falls on the forces of law and order. One cost of unemployment is measurable, therefore, as the social and political expenditure incurred in policing the inevitable civil strife. In other words, unemployment represents a sharp indicator of the political insolvency of an economic system. Further, there comes a critical point where the mass of unemployment jeopardizes the political stability of the system as a whole. Naturally, the mass at which the egg of consciousness cracks is a matter of intense speculation. But certainly there is evidence that the spectre of subsistence is haunting Britain:

For a person like me, redundant twice within a year, one has only to have over £2000 in disposable assets to be completely disqualified from any benefit after one year of unemployment. Who if anyone will keep the roof over my head when my resources are done? With at least 50 jobs applied for without even a single interview granted who will help, advise and encourage those of us who can see no future except the gradual decline of self-respect as small resources diminish and we sink into shabby poverty?'[3]

ARE THE UNIONS TO BLAME?

And we hear the usual comment: 'They must be mad, they must want to commit suicide.' What a ridiculous statement. These small groups do not want to commit suicide. They want to create unemployment. They want to create chaos. They want to create civil strife. Because only in this way can they bring about the structural changes that they seek.[4]

JOBLESS USEFUL AS INDUSTRIAL RESERVE, MINISTER SAYS.

Making a virtue out of the 'inevitable' unemployment caused by government policies, a junior minister described the jobless as a 'reserve' to be used to increase future production.[5]

The Moderator of the General Assembly of the Church of Scotland has condemned unemployment deliberately created as a matter of policy as being immoral and blasphemous. The Moderator's sermon was viewed as a response to the Prime Minister's Lent address in which she claimed that creating wealth must be seen as a Christian obligation. She described work not only as a necessity but a duty and indeed a virtue. She went on to urge the country to buy more British goods and to accept that there was a moral responsibility not to press for pay claims which could price people out of jobs. Finally, she wished everyone to be proud of belonging to the British nation.

As successive postwar governments have muddled through crisis after crisis down the tortuous path of industrial decline, a seemingly endless list of inconsequential scapegoats has been presented to a bemused and increasingly jaded British populace. The ultimate cause of Britain's economic ills has been placed on the doorstep of too much or too little State intervention, the activities of financial institutions, technically backward management, the pursuit of wrong government policies, *ad nauseam*. The latest culprit to occupy centre-stage as the prime progenitor of Britain's poor relative industrial performance is the organized labour movement. According to Sir Keith Joseph, 'the primary responsibility rests upon the trade unions'.[6] The case against the trade unions is worthy of critical attention not only because it is wrong, but also to demonstrate the futility of selecting *any* mono-causal explanation of the deindustrialization process. It illustrates moreover the danger of utilizing one specific area of diagnosis as the prescription for a cure-all.

Sir Keith Joseph's hard-line attitude towards the organized labour movement expresses a 'pop' version of extreme economic theory which presupposes that market forces *in themselves* can bring about the adjustments necessary for the restoration of industrial health. In the ideal world of self-regulating 'pure' competition, the theoretical assumption of 'complete price/wage flexibility' ensures the long-run correction of market 'disequilibrium'. But, like all systems of artificial abstraction, the ideal world of neo-classical economics is an illusion – never has such an economy existed. Neo-classical economics, ostensibly a striking testament to the virtues of individual freedom, ignores an economic reality where the vast majority of individuals is precluded by material deprivation from undertaking all but the most meagre of economic choices. In a society characterized by a wealth distribution skewed positively in favour of a small minority such an idealization of individual freedom serves only to legitimize the perpetuation of massive inequality.

The ideological significance of the dull grey worm of neo-classical economics lies in its function of providing the justification, however immoral, for eliminating 'imperfections' within the market which stand in the way of capital's unfettered ability to pursue the goal of profit. In terms of the logic of capital, the sole criterion of economic success is profit. The key to profitability is the quality of investment and the utilization of that investment expressed as (labour) productivity. After allowing for inflation in the cost of replacing assets, after paying interest and tax, after compensating for the contribution of labour, what remains is profit – the 'seedcorn' to finance future investment. Historically, the gross rate of return on British national capital has consistently lagged behind her major competitors. What, then, according to the perspective of capital has 'caused' the strong underlying decline in profitability since the early 1960s and its concomitant low investment?

Low productivity is the central issue as it underlines all the others; it is the issue of our national future . . . Low productivity and irregular production have resulted in low investment and low investment has contributed further to low productivity. The market is the only force powerful enough to have any chance of curing the British disease.[7]

Here, in elemental form, is the chain of causation of the deindustrialization process as seen by the proponents of the free market. Low productivity leads to low profitability which inhibits investment and a vicious circle of decline is set in motion. The starting point, it should be emphasized, is low productivity. Deindustrialization is diagnosed, therefore, as arising primarily from what is called a supply-side imperfection, namely the freedom of workers to organize collectively.

Trade unions insist upon overmanning and restrictive labour practices, thus reducing the output and the profit from new investment and indeed, in many cases, aborting new investment altogether because it does not seem worthwhile. [Only] profits are the source of investment, expansion, research and development and increased job security.[8]

Such a viewpoint demands the creation of a free market in labour as the only remedy capable of restoring industrial competitiveness.

Productivity is an elusive, almost mystical concept. Most simply, it can be viewed as a measure of the *economic* efficiency with which various inputs are translated into output. Unfortunately, there exists no satisfactory method of isolating and quantifying the relative contributions of the different inputs. In bastardized versions of neo-classical economic theory, as espoused by Sir Keith Joseph and his like, productivity is discussed almost exclusively in terms of the contribution of labour, with much loose talk about worker laziness, restrictive practices, overmanning and irresponsible wage bargaining. It is assumed that trade unions serve to restrict output and thereby 'rob' employers of their rightful profits. Such a presumption slides over several features of the relationship between labour and productivity which, once recognized, destroy entirely the case for Sir Keith Joseph's political programme.

First, it is important to put the record straight. The decline in profitability of British industry cannot be ascribed to the growth of real average labour earnings exceeding that of labour productivity. From 1963 to 1975, the annual average growth rate in manufacturing output per person (3.2%) outstripped the growth of the real product wage (2.9%). In the decade up to 1974 British output per person employed grew at an annual rate favourably comparable to the Western average.[9] Nor does the carefully organized regime of superstition concerning the alleged strike-proneness of British industry stand up to scrutiny. An international comparison of the number of days lost per 1000 employees conducted by the Department of Employment revealed that between 1965 and 1974 Britain lagged considerably behind Canada, the US and Italy in the league table of industrial disputes. In terms of hard facts as opposed to beer-joint innuendo, 'very little weight if any should be put on the argument that productivity growth in the UK has been retarded by increasing inefficiency . . . in the form of overmanning and underproduction'.[10]

Secondly, in the real world, the contribution of direct labour productivity comprises but one of a variety of elements that determine the overall competitiveness of industry. The deterioration in the competitive efficiency of British-based manufacturing industry up to the mid-1970s reflected its *general* performance relative to other countries. In areas such as product design, quality control, marketing and after-sales service, British companies were markedly inferior to their major competitive rivals. Moreover, it is generally agreed that the pound was overvalued in the 1960s, thereby artificially inflating export prices while simultaneously encouraging import penetration.

Thirdly, although the annual growth of labour productivity faltered badly in the second half of the 1970s, it is extremely misleading to lay responsibility at the door of the trade unions. Not only has the world energy crisis reduced economic growth as a whole, but also, especially since 1976, the British authorities have chosen to pursue internal policies directed towards economic and financial retrenchment. By 1981, as a result of demand deflation more than anything else, British industrial capacity was being under-utilized to the extent of at least 25 to 33 per cent. To be sure, it is more than improbable that *underlying* productivity can be improved in surroundings of declining economic activity and large-scale unemployment.

In fact, productivity is mainly dependent upon the level, rate and quality of investment, and therefore it is equally permissible to argue that low productivity is a *consequence* of low investment and not the other way round. No less an authority than the Bank of England *Quarterly Bulletin* has noted that 'even before the recession, gross investment was falling below trend, and net investment probably more so; this is likely to have reduced the underlying rate of productivity'.[11] It is not surprising that German and Japanese workers are more 'productive' when it is realized that, on average, they have three to four times the capital equipment at their disposal than a British worker. Between 1960 and 1975, net investment in British manufacturing industry was a quarter less than France, a third less than West Germany and half that of Japan. The average life of British plant and machinery is thirty-five years – double that of France, Germany and Japan.

The proponents of the free traders' mentality turn a blind eye to the cumulative impact of a sustained failure to invest within British industry. It is conveniently forgotten, for example, that the 1950s witnessed high levels of British profitability in relation to her main competitors. Here was a golden opportunity to renovate British capital but the profit windfall was not transformed into an advanced industrial framework. There was, and still remains, no automatic guarantee within capitalism that surplus value will be translated into productive investment.

The growth of British productive potential was stunted at a time when her competitive rivals were engaged in reconstructing their productive facilities. This lost opportunity dealt a fatal blow to the long-run competitive capability of British national capital.[12] A temporary respite was gained from the vestige of captive imperial markets and from the easy pickings of the armaments drive. Yet the post-war inflationary boom masked and perpetuated an historical imbalance between Britain's productive capabilities and her position in the world market. Internally, welfare capitalism diverted too great a proportion of national capital into consumption rather than into productive investment. Once released, worker aspirations flooded the circuit of national capital with pent-up demand repressed through two world wars and an intervening slump. Over-consumption expressed itself as inflation which, in turn, eroded the rate of surplus exploitation. By 1980, British consumption amounted to 80 per cent of GDP compared to 75 per cent in West Germany and 70 per cent in Japan. This is what Lord Lever has christened 'the historic distortion in our credit system'.[13]

Lord Lever contends that Britain is presently reaping an industrial whirlwind because of her consistent failure to renovate her productive capacity. In his view, the lowest rate of private industrial investment in any OECD country has caused low output and productivity, low profits, a demoralized workforce with the second lowest take-home pay in the EEC and aggravated inflation. His analysis provides convincing evidence of a unique structural flaw within the British economy which has persistently inhibited productive investment, especially in those industries experiencing the most rapid growth in world trade during the postwar period. Yet, having pin-pointed investment as the crucial variable, Lord Lever falls into the same trap as his neo-classical adversaries by confusing one proximate expression of the structural distortion with its foundational cause. His diagnosis concentrates upon the unwillingness of the financial institutions to extend long-term credit to industry and their impo-sition of low gearing ratios (the ratio of lending to equity capital).

Given the structure of economic relations in Britain, however, the private savings institutions (banks, pension funds, insurance com-panies and building societies) are compelled to pay careful heed to market imperatives. Their attitude is painfully rational – if market signals indicate that British industry is inefficient, uncompetitive, technically incompetent, managerially bloated and organizationally rigid, then it deserves to go to the wall. The historically abysmal replacement rate of return on British national capital explains the reluctance of the savings institutions to become involved in long-term industrial lending.

The British savings system constitutes a perfect framework for a perfect economic system – and British industry is far from perfect. The private savings institutions possess neither the political incli-nation nor the economic muscle to force reconstruction upon unprofitable industry. This puts paid to the Lever solution of utilizing the savings institutions as the mechanism of industrial resurgence. It takes a vivid imagination to envisage the Governor of the Bank of England leading a team of commercial bank kamikaze pilots to save Britain's industrial hinterland from absolute derelic-tion. In sum, the perceived problems of economic indolence, polit-ical fragmentation and social injustice can be measured as 'an investment gap of £100,000 millions [and one which] is getting wider each year'.[14] What still requires explanation, therefore, is the long-term neglect of productive capital.

Returning to the main theme, whereas trade union activity com-prises an important element in the complicated chain reaction which expresses itself as deindustralization, the primary responsibility does *not* rest upon the freedom of workers to associate within collective organizations. In the final analysis, the ideological and material onslaught against trade unions is best understood as representing an unresolved *political* issue centred upon the way in which work is organized. The ability of trade unions to obtain 'concessions' from capital – health and safety at work, protection from unfair dismissal and so forth – inhibits the 'optimum' extraction of surplus value from a given amount of investment than would be the case if trade unions did not exist. In effect, organized labour challenges the market reality of hierarchial control over workers in production which treats labour as a disposable commodity. Put differently, trade unions, by representing the interests of labour as a corporate class, constitute a hindrance to the institutional mechanism whereby surplus value is extracted in a market economy.

Historically, trade unions emerged organically as a collective response to the excesses of early industrial capitalism when labour, including women and children, was exploited almost without limit in the relentless pursuit of accumulation. There existed a power imbalance within society which favoured a minority possessing class against the majority who were forced to rely upon the individuality of their labour power to subsist. From their inception, trade unions were forced to struggle within an established order where the rules of the political game were strictly formulated. In practice, the activities of trade unions were treated as legitimate only when they behaved within the substantive rules. In this way, trade unions not only posed a potential and actual threat to the unhindered ability of capital to pursue the goal of profit, but were themselves infected by the cultural mores of the British establishment.

It comes as no surprise, therefore, that as institutions *within* capitalism, trade unions reflect many of the reactionary characteristics of capital for which they are rightly condemned. As collective organizations devoted to the raising of wages and the improvement of working conditions British trade unions, far from representing the socialist vanguard, have consistently sought instead (and in vain) to promote the prosperity of national capital. What power trade unions do possess is transformed as it passes through the filters of Labourism into negative, conservative 'moderation'. Nothing more vividly demonstrated the reality of contemporary trade union power than the sight of the TUC leadership begging Mrs Thatcher to enter into a dialogue only to be summarily dismissed and told to come back nearer Christmas 1984. If organized labour were as powerful as popular mythology suggests then burgeoning unemployment would surely have elicited a stronger response than a pale imitation of the Jarrow march.

Notwithstanding, the very existence of an independent trade union movement represents and reflects an irreconcilable tension between capitalism (property) and democracy (persons). What Sir Keith Joseph regards as restrictive practices (the equivalent of greenfly afflicting the rose garden of capital) can be viewed equally as bargaining rights. As intrinsically defensive organizations, trade unions have struggled to protect workers from the worst excesses of a production system wholly geared to the accumulation of capital. Yet the pursuit of democratic control over production by a participatory association of individuals is incompatible with capitalism, which depends upon absolute managerial control over the labour process for its optimum reproduction and expansion. Those countries free from institutional 'imperfections' – usually as a result of the physical repression of organized labour – enjoy considerably higher levels of labour productivity than Britain. But the claim that British trade unions are to blame for low productivity on these grounds indicates a sense of morality far removed from the civilized virtues usually promulgated by all but the most extreme right-wing apologists for private capitalism.

As Keynes, Orwell and others proved convincingly in the 1930s and 1940s, the destruction of market 'blockages' in itself cannot guarantee the achievement of civilized economic goals such as work for all and distributive justice. The 'free' market in the inter-war period was epitomized by slump, mass unemployment and right-wing extremism. It was partly for these reasons that the British State effected a compromise between capitalism and representative democracy at the end of overt hostilities in 1945. The privately coordinated market system was 'politicized' to the extent that the State undertook minimal redistributive responsibilities. Most important, an all-party agreement to promote and maintain 'a high and stable level of employment' reflected the necessity of avoiding a return to the economic conditions of the pre-war period which would have posed a very real threat to the political stability of capitalism. In the event, the political commitment to full employment has proved an unattainable long-term goal. The mixed economy turned out to be an untenable transitional form.

The material basis for the mixed economy finally disintegrated in 1976 when the Labour government, under the external diktat of the IMF, jettisoned the social-democratic obligations which underwrote the postwar settlement. The historic compromise was held together for another three years by the patriotism of the organized labour movement and its willingness to rest content within the conventional pale of uncritical allegiance to the Constitution. Meanwhile, behind the facade of the Social Contract, the Labour government accepted the dogma of monetarism, de-capped the pound in 1977 and spent a billion pounds' worth of social expenditure cuts upon modernizing the 'independent' nuclear deterrent.

On accession, Mrs Thatcher terminated the Social Contract and overnight the trade unions came to be regarded as the 'organized muscle of militant labour', a twentieth-century equivalent of the feudal barony acting outside the authority of the Crown. What is more, the workers were alleged to be standing in the way of the resurrection of virile free enterprise. In the name of the Crown, Thatcherism sought to resolve the contradiction between capitalism and democracy by the subjugation of the equal liberties of the majority to the will of the minority who own and/or control the processes of production and distribution. It quickly dawned, however, that the demise of welfare capitalism did not imply that a reversion to a free market and the pursuit of the competitive ideal would reveal the economic Phoenix.

On the contrary, a free market reconstruction of Britain's industrial base *as it is now* cannot be achieved otherwise than by a massive reduction in the real standard of living for the majority and through what amounts to a reversion to nineteenth-century sweat shop conditions within the workplace. The utilization of irrational conservative therapy to reconstruct the economy is motivated, above all, by a desire to reproduce the existing form of economic relations within British society. The subversion of democratic control over macroeconomic phenomena through the passive acceptance of large-scale unemployment constitutes the high price to be paid in pursuing this blind mission.

THE NATURE OF THE BRITISH STATE

A constantly weakening industrial base, a dominant financial sector oriented towards foreign investment rather than the restructuring of British industries, a non-technocratic state quite unable to bring about the 'revolution from above' needed to redress this balance; everything conspired to cause an inexorable spiral of decline.[15]

All that one can say in general is that the structural disequilibrium may be so deepseated, and the economic and political environment may be such, that in spite of the benefits of North Sea oil, it may not be possible to bring about the required modifications in the production system without fundamental institutional changes.[16]

Britain's economic malaise stems largely from its productivity problem, whose origins lie deep in the social system.[17]

A great deal of intellectual effort has been expended on the search for an explanation of Britain's enduring economic predicament. A truly comprehensive analysis would start and finish with a British version of Gibbon's *Decline and Fall of the Roman Empire*. In essence, the structural impediment militating against productive transformation has arisen because of *the historical nature of the British State*. This somewhat bland statement encapsulates the problem, yet its inner significance is difficult to apprehend because the underlying form of the British State is hidden by antiquity, thereby making it inaccessible and, as it were, unquestionable. What exists as a hidden form becomes manifest in the interaction of societal elements, but the temptation to isolate one (or a combination) of these elements as the ultimate cause of productive decay discounts the catalyst without which the overall chain reaction would not occur.

As the first nation to embark upon industrialization, Britain enjoyed an early supremacy in production and world trade which permitted a 'peaceful' adaptation of her ancient institutional structure. Whilst her potential rivals were subject to the throes of bourgeois revolution, Britain reaped the benefits of internal stability and consolidated her position in the expanding world economy. Uniquely, the British bourgeoisie failed to achieve State power, its pre-eminence being held in check by an alliance of the landed aristocracy and banking capital. The rise of banking capital reflected the external orientation of the British State. Banking capital acted as a deposit box for storing and recycling the excess spoils of imperial accumulation. From the outset, banking capital responded passively to the requirements of productive capital. There never evolved a formal two-way link between the banking institutions and the company sector of manufacturing.

By contrast, later arrivals on the industrial scene consciously utilized banking capital as an effective instrument to achieve industrial 'take-off' or resorted to State-directed economic development as the means of 'catching-up'. In Britain, the fruits of imperial plunder provided the material basis for the economic autonomy and political dominance of banking capital at the expense of productive potential. The lack of integration between banking capital and productive capital hampered the flow of surplus value into productive accumulation so that 'institutions successfully created to ensure the stability necessary to early industrialization were distinctly less appropriate for the problems of sustaining subsequent development'.[18]

Worse still, when the world monopoly position of British productive capital was undermined by imperialist competition in the late nineteenth century, banking capital found itself locked into the international economy in its role as a financial centre. As Nairn comments[19]:

Less and less able to compete with the new workshops of the world, the ruling elite compensated by extended control of the world's money market . . . Successful enterprise moved away from industry and, far from dislodging the elite or state, formed a new alliance with them on the foundation of City-centred imperialism . . . Long after the centre of industrial gravity had moved to North America and Continental Europe, they kept their pre-eminence in the area of capital investment and exchange.

The externalized growth of the City of London, founded originally upon the material strength of British production became a Frankenstein detached from the development of productive forces. Correspondingly, the money imperatives of finance overtook the real needs of production as the predominant influence within the national economy.

The political and ideological hegemony of externally-oriented banking capital promoted a reliance upon external indicators to guide the rudder of national economic management. Despite the changes brought about by the First World War – particularly the shift in the balance of economic power towards the US – inter-war governments retained the belief that a stable currency was the price to be paid for a stable economy. The return to the gold standard at its prewar parity in 1925 represented a strategic victory for the interests of banking capital. The Treasury, acting as the City's broker within government, argued successfully in favour of deflation to force the productive economy into line with external factors. A strong pound was brandished as an international virility symbol but the national economy was subject to the deprivations of an over-valued exchange rate, severe credit contraction and cuts in public subsidies. The ransom for propping-up the City of London's inflated and meaningless prestige was extracted from 'Elsewhere' in the form of productive stagnation and large-scale unemployment.

Despite the ostensible acceptance of Keynes' reformist solution, which implied that the external value of sterling should conform to its internal value as set by national policy and not the other way round, the sacrifice of the national economy to the demands of the City continued after the Second World War. Governments of all persuasions strove to restore the City as an offshore island for coordinating Western imperialism. In Cold War surroundings, the creation of conditions favourable to 'the re-establishment of sterling as a general international currency and of London as an open financial market place'[20] involved the maintenance of an overseas diplomatic and military presence which was way beyond the nation's productive capacity. The ultimate imperative compelled the preservation of

Britain's rank within Western imperialism although the creeping contraction of the British Empire suggested a diminution of the resources available to underwrite such an illusion of grandeur. Accordingly, the innately conservative framework of ancient institutions was ill-equipped to reconcile Britain's internationalist stance with the political compromise afforded to the labour movement in Command Paper 6527 of 1944.

The veiled objective to maintain the external strength of sterling imposed a strait-jacket upon the conduct of demand management. The preservation of a fixed exchange rate from 1949 to 1967 and the operation of sterling as a second-reserve currency required periodic doses of deflation to be imposed on the national economy to assuage the confidence of the Sterling Area. Under the changed conditions of welfare capitalism, however, the British mixed economy had entered 'a situation where reductions in marginal demand began to check the efficiency of supply by more than they held down demand itself'.[21] Under these circumstances. Keynesian deflation, usually in the form of primary credit restriction, succeeded far more in discouraging investment than in moderating consumption, thereby worsening the national disequilibrium. Conversely, measures designed to promote accumulation through reductions in rates of taxation instead encouraged a faster growth in consumption compared to the development of productive facilities. The national economy became afflicted with inflationary bottlenecks, balance of payments deficits and the imposition of periodic stop phases to guarantee external stability. Consequently, 'the continuous round of stop-go cycles deeply depressed business expectations, limited efforts to expand output and to raise productivity, and made existing investment less productive than it should have been'.[22]

In the midst of visible productive decay, governments, caught inside an electoral web spun by the full employment commitment, were forced to react to the poor performance of British national capital. Increasingly, the State became a ward for the unwanted, which, not surprisingly, further deprived productive capital. Incidentally, the laughable 'crowding-out' hypothesis is pure disinformation. The opiated idea that deindustrialization sprang from the public robbery of private endeavour fails to realize the *responsive* growth of public employment in relation to a disappointing real growth rate. If anything, private profligacy crowded out public enterprise.

Whatever, the continued external policy orientation worked against the accumulative needs of productive capital. The defence of the City's privileged position as a haven for footloose capital took precedence over any concerted strategy designed to promote productive accumulation. As Fausten concludes[23]:

The meaning of British balance of payments policies during the two post-war decades was to maintain sterling parity as a symbol of her former position in international monetary relations, and the heavy weight assigned to the interest rate mechanism at the expense of the real sector of the economy was a reflection of the traditional sentiment of, or was actively intended to reaffirm, the superiority of finance over industry.

Within the State, the unchallenged supremacy of the Bank/Treasury Axis in the decision-making process has ensured that 'among those making economic policies, the rentiers' or bankers' mentality, with its emphasis on restriction and stagnation, still holds sway'.[24] The Treasury insisted upon short-term forecasting and displayed an effete reluctance to apply anything other than arm's length control measures. However, 'the dead-heads with brilliant minds' opposed successfully the introduction of productive planning, thereby sabotaging any political initiative aimed at encouraging productive transformation. Balogh summarized the dilemma[25]:

The Treasury's preponderance among departments inexorably involves the danger of the Government being swayed by the Treasury's own departmental cares, and prejudices the interests of industry for the benefit of finance and the City.

Although the 1970s witnessed a public relations shift in emphasis – flexible exchange rates, the establishment of an industry section in the Treasury, a tortured retreat from sterling's reserve currency role – the perpetual conflict between the Treasury's 'orthodox financial accountancy' and 'social accountancy' remains unresolved. In any case, the City has in the meantime carved a new niche for itself as an international financial entrepôt specializing in the Euro-dollar market, 'while its political position is buttressed by the intervention of the International Monetary Fund in the determination of economic policy'.[26] Or as Keynes predicted in 1944[27]:

I feel great anxiety that, unless we move with no uncertain steps along the other path, the Bank will contrive to lead us, in new disguises, along much the same path as that which ended in 1931.

As well as the limitations placed on the productive economy by the historic severance of City-based international banking capital, the legacy of imperialism left behind an important section of British capital with substantial overseas operations. The activities of British multinational capital have remained largely independent of the national economy and, despite the inevitable erosion of the 'home' base, the interests of 'big' capital have coincided with the external inclination of economic policy. By 1973, the value of foreign production by British companies was double that of their exports from Britain. In the same year, the overseas production value of German and Japanese companies amounted to just over a third of their respective domestic outputs.

Whereas overseas investment may be regarded as rational from the viewpoint of individual shareholders, it contributes little to the generation of national income and employment. Bearing in mind the precarious profitability position of British national capital, the bonfire of controls to create greater individual freedom militated further against productive efficiency by encouraging the export of capital. It is hardly coincidental that an over-valued exchange rate between 1979 and mid-1981 (combined with the relaxation of currency controls) gave a considerable discount for British companies investing in foreign markets and in the US. Nor is it astonishing to discover that, in 1980, overseas production by the top fifty privately owned manufacturing companies had risen to well over three times the value of their exports.[28] Hence, 'the very *strength* of the cosmopolitan activities of British capital has helped to undermine further its strictly domestic economy. The overseas strength of British big *capital* has compounded the debility of British *capitalism*.'[29]

To summarize, the preponderance of banking capital and multinational capital has dictated the underlying logic of national economic policy. The systematic bias in favour of external prerogatives has so circumscribed the political sphere as to make it appear wholly natural and unavoidable. Once it is realized, however, that the economic function of the British State in relation to national production is severely curtailed because 'the dominant fraction of capital earns most of its income sharing in surplus value created elsewhere in the world',[30] the shape of the economic problem takes on an entirely different form. Such an awareness extends the scope of debate beyond the narrow limits of discussing what are, in reality, innocuous and strategically irrelevant issues. Set against the unquestioned legitimacy of subjugating the level of internal activity to the whims of external confidence, the reactive, contingent and subordinate behaviour of the organized labour movement can be placed in its proper perspective. Cognizance of the essential nature of capitalist power in relation to the British State also illuminates the striking divergence between the rhetoric of Thatcherism and its actions.

In all, whereas welfare capitalism left intact the underlying form of economic relations and its captive political and ideological apparatus, the increased mutual interdependence between capital and the State failed to engender an effective corporate-bureaucratic alliance capable of promoting a productive renaissance. The re-emergence of global capitalist crisis has revealed that Britain's productive base, judged by Western standards of competitive performance, is verging on the abyss. Yet the existing institutional structure is patently unable to accomplish the changes necessary to transform productive capital. The private enterprise horse bolted long ago to greener pastures around the globe. Britain is left with an old industrial nag dying on its feet. Then again, the failure of social democracy to transcend the productive barrier denotes that the root of the problem is explicitly *political*: 'a slow, cumulative collapse determined not by the failure of 'British capitalism' alone, but by the specific underlying structures of an archaic state and the civil class system it protects'.[31]

NOTES

1. Norwegian football commentator reacting to his country's historic victory over England in the preliminary round of the World Cup, Sept. 1981
2. P. Large, 'A shortage in the software department', *The Guardian*, 12 Apr. 1978
3. The *Sunday Times*, 15 Jan. 1981
4. Sir James Goldsmith, *The Times*, 21 Jan. 1981
5. *The Times*, 27 Jan. 1981
6. Sir Keith Joseph, *Profits are the source of investment*, HMSO 1981 (contribution to the *Sunday Times* seminar: Banking on Britain, 25 Feb. 1981)
7. 'The sparks are falling on the gunpowder', (leader article) *The Times*, 13 Nov. 1979
8. Sir Keith Joseph, op. cit.
9. R. Bacon and W. Eltis, *Britain's Economic Problems: Too Few Producers* (2nd edn), Macmillan 1978, pp. 9–10
10. G. B. Stafford, *The End of Economic Growth?*, Martin Robertson 1981, pp. 74, 104
11. Quoted in T. D. Sheriff, *The Slowdown of Productivity Growth*, National Institute of Economic and Social Research, Discussion Paper No. 30, p. 11. Sheriff adds: 'The reason for believing that the level of investment will affect the growth of productivity is

that technical progress is hypothesised to be embodied in new capital stock – the greater the volume of investment, the greater the rate of technical progress and the higher the level of productivity. The greater and younger the capital stock, the higher will be the output per head.' ibid., p. 12

12. For an insider's view of the impact of neo-liberalism upon the Conservative government in the 1950s see E. Boyle, 'The economist in government'. in J. K. Bowers (ed.), *Inflation, Development and Integration*, University of Leeds Press 1979
13. Lord Lever, speech delivered to the *Sunday Times* seminar: Banking on Britain, 25 Feb. 1981
14. F. E. Jones, 'British manufacturing industry, the missing £1000,000 million', *National Westminster Bank Review*, Apr. 1978, 16
15. T. Nairn, 'The twilight of the British State', *New Left Review*, 101–2, Feb–Apr. 1977, 5
16. A. Singh, 'U. K. industry and the world economy: a case of deindustrialisation?', *Cambridge Journal of Economics*, *1*. (2) June 1977, 134
17. R. E. Caves and L. B. Krause (eds), *Britain's Economic Performance*, Brookings 1980, p. 19
18. W. P. Kennedy, 'Institutional response to economic growth: capital markets in Britain to 1914', in L. Hannah (ed.), *Management Strategy and Business Development: An Historical and Comparative Study*, MacMillan 1976, p. 159
19. T. Nairn, op. cit., 12, 15
20. S. Strange, *Sterling and British Policy*, Oxford UP 1971, p. 64
21. N. Macrae, *Sunshades in October*, Allen and Unwin 1963, p. 27
22. S. Blank, 'Britain: the politics of foreign policy, the domestic economy and the problem of pluralistic stagnation', *International Organisation*, *31* (4) 1977, 691
23. D. K. Fausten, *The Consistency of British Balance of Payments Policies*, Macmillan 1975, p. 154
24. S. Pollard, *The Gold Standard and Employment Policies Between the Wars*, Methuen 1970, p. 44
25. Lord Balogh, 'The Bank of England – some defects in organisation and functioning – First Report from the Select Committee on Nationalized Industries', *The Bank of England*, HC 258 1969
26. F. Longstreth, 'The City, industry and the State', in C. Crouch (ed.), *State and Economy in Contemporary Capitalism*, Croom Helm 1979, p. 161
27. Letter dated Feb. 1944

28. 'British manufacturing multinationals', *Labour Research* Sept. 1981, 190–2
29. R. Rowthorn, 'Imperialism in the seventies – unity or rivalry?', *New Left Review* Sept. – Oct. 1971, 46–7 (emphasis in original)
30. R. Minns, 'A comment on finance capital and the crisis in Britain', *Capital and Class, 11* 1981, 108
31. T. Nairn, op. cit., 10

FURTHER READING

J. Bellini, *Rule Britannia*, Jonathan Cape 1981
A. Gamble, *Britain in Decline*, Macmillan 1981
T. Nairn, *The Break Up of Britain* (2nd edn), New Left Books 1981

Chapter three

THE QUESTION OF TRADE UNION POWER

David Coates

Amongst the most insidious arguments faced by the labour movement in the present recession are those which single out the trade unions for particular condemnation and blame. Right-wing politicians, prominent industrialists, university professors and leading figures in the media have combined in recent years in a very effective campaign against trade union industrial and political power, seeking to persuade the public at large that the poor performance of British capitalism is best explained by the dominant position that unions have supposedly come to occupy in the distribution of power in contemporary British society. Opinion polls stand witness to the impact of that propaganda. In September 1978, to take one typical example, a MORI poll for the *Daily Express* found that 82 per cent of its sample thought that the trade unions had too much power, and that 80 per cent agreed with the statement that 'most trade unions are controlled by a few militants and extremists'.[1] Perhaps even more disturbingly, that same poll found those two views held by as many as 73 per cent and 57 per cent of the union members in the sample, and did so at the very end of a period in which, ironically, union compliance with a Labour government's incomes policy, far from achieving that most basic of union goals, rising wages, had in fact done the reverse, and had reduced real living standards by 8 per cent over the three years in which the policy had held.[2]

The precise nature of the criticisms levelled against the unions change over time. There are fashions in 'union bashing' which come and go, varying with the particular issue in contention between the classes, varying with the general level of militancy and political assertiveness coming from the unions themselves, and varying too with the particular strategy for union incorporation and working-class control then dominant in government circles. But over time a very standard range of arguments tends to appear with disturbing regularity.

Socialist arguments

The first set tends to concentrate on the internal state of the unions and the representativeness and quality of their leaders. Union leaders are often criticized for their low intellect and loose grasp of economic reality[3]; or for being unrepresentative in their militancy of the general views of their own rank and file.[4] Moderate union leaders are rarely so criticized – unrepresentativeness apparently only matters when it means trouble – but union leaders threatening industrial action will often be condemned, either for failing to educate their membership in the wider national interests that their militancy is supposed to threaten (and so, by implication, for being too representative of an irresponsibly led rank and file) or, more commonly, for being unnecessarily responsive to the extreme views of the relatively small numbers of union members who participate regularly in union branch activity. Apathy at branch level, and the failure of the democratic process in union government, are then singled out as explanations of why 'extremists' are able to infiltrate key levels of the union structure, and why shop stewards in particular are able to offer leadership that is unrepresentatively militant and even at times politically motivated.[5] Indeed, on one famous occasion, this strategy of argument was applied to part of the national executive of the Seamen's Union, which was then described by the prime minister of the day as nothing more than 'a tightly-knit group of politically motivated men' because of their refusal to call off industrial action.[6] Though politicians are rarely so paranoid in public now, the media do little to dispel the impression that militants are unrepresentative of the silent majority in the union movement; and this is coupled, at times, with the claim that unions have a propensity not simply to misrepresent that silent majority but actually to tyrannize it, and so to constitute a threat to the very individual workers that they claim to exist to defend. Unions are supposed to do this either by forcing reluctant workers to join their ranks or lose their jobs (in closed-shop arrangements) or by compelling terrified individuals to obey strike calls to which they are opposed (by mass picketing, and by refusing to work after a strike with individuals who have insisted on working through it).

A second set of criticisms tends to concentrate less on internal union politics than on the nature of the goals to which those politics are addressed. Unions are often criticized for being greedy, excessively materialistic and solely concerned with the narrow sectional interests of their own members. When these criticisms are levelled, they are often accompanied by the claim that this means that the unions refuse to subordinate their preoccupations to the wider interests of the community as a whole[7] and instead, through their single-minded protection of their own members' interests, actually threaten directly the living standards of the weaker sections of society (unorganized workers, the old, the poor and the sick, even the self-employed and those on fixed incomes). Indeed, this criticism is occasionally couched in the language of the Left, as when Paul Johnson in 1975 dismissed trade union defence of 'free collective bargaining' as having more in common with capitalism and gangsterism than with socialism, and castigated the unions as a 'positive and growing obstacle to the accomplishment of socialist goals'.[8]

But the real focus of so much criticism of the unions turns on their supposedly excessive industrial power. Unions are supposed to be a major (or indeed on some accounts *the* major or the *only*) cause of high prices and low profits. They play this role, so the accusation runs, partly because of their capacity to win high wages through the exploitation of their monopoly power in the labour market, and partly through their defence of overmanning and a whole set of other restrictive practices. They play it too through their willingness to use industrial tactics deemed to be 'illegitimate' and 'unfair' by their critics (the blacking of goods, the taking of sympathy strikes, the use of flying and mass pickets). They supposedly undermine industrial competitiveness too by the sheer cost, impact on output, and alienation of customers, that arise from strike action *per se* and they are, in the popular mythology of the Right, the main barrier to the modernization of British industry through technological change. Their crime here is often two-fold: they are supposedly Luddites, blindly opposing the destruction of jobs by new technology; and they are a disincentive to investment, with the visibility of their industrial power deterring both domestic and foreign investors from placing their money in the new manufacturing plant and equipment that is vital to industrial regeneration. And for all these reasons, the excessive industrial power of the unions is then often presented as a major cause of the economy's poor competitiveness, low productivity and lack of economic growth.

Finally, trade unions are criticized for their excessive political power. They are said to have a privileged legal position, free from the constraints which apply to other organizations and individuals, which they are prepared to defend even (as in 1971) at the cost of confrontation with the government, and which constitutes the base of their excessive industrial leverage. They are said to have a particularly tight hold on decision-making within the Labour Party, able to shape the policy of a Labour government because of the

Party's dependence on union finance, and because of the unions' voting strength at party conference and on the national executive committee. And the commitment of successive governments to full employment, and the increasing interconnectedness of industrial processes, is said to have so strengthened trade union power that the unions can now regularly veto government policy, and destroy the electoral credibility of governments so vetoed, by 'holding the country to ransom'. It is this political power which, to some commentators, threatens parliamentary democracy[9]; and, to others, combines with the industrial power of the unions to explain why inflation, unemployment and industrial stagnation are so persistent a set of features of British life in the last quarter of the twentieth century.[10]

GENERAL COMMENTS

What then are the socialist answers to all that? Let me begin with a number of remarks that apply generally to unions and their critics.

The first is that it is not without its significance that so many of these views are expressed most loudly by people who have a vested interest in the reduction of union power. They come from managers whose industrial control is threatened by union assertiveness. They come from owners of capital, whose privileged position in society and hold on material possessions does not require a union to protect it. They come from financiers involved in the export of capital, and from bankers whose rates of return would benefit from the creation of a supine labour force. And they come from a whole set of academics and journalists who identify with these elites, and from politicians who need to appease them. It may be that what they say is correct – we will have to see if that is so in a moment – and it is illegitimate to dismiss an argument simply because of its source. But I think that we have a right to be sceptical of arguments against unions that are canvassed by people whose general political and social views are so hostile to left-wing causes, and whose social position, and industrial and political practices, are so distant from, and unsympathetic to, the interests of the less privileged majority, for whom unionism is a vital safeguard and defence.

The focus of all this criticism is also worth dwelling on for a moment. It is true that not all unions are being singled out for condemnation. There seems to be a general recognition, except on the extreme Right, that the size, bargaining strength and industrial militancy of unions vary, and that many unions do not have the capacity to hold the country to ransom. The focus of the criticism tends to be on the big unions, on the unions recruiting in the manufacturing sector of British industry, and on unions recruiting in the public sector bureaucracies and public utilities. It does not generally extend to the unions of workers in agriculture, in shops and small offices, or even in small manufacturing and processing plants. Indeed the significance of the Grunwick dispute lies precisely here, in that even a mass picket supported by miners could not give those workers enough power to force the recognition of their union by their employer, let alone compel him to negotiate better wages and conditions of service with union representatives. And yet at the same time the criticism of union power does not extend to the organizations and restrictive practices of professionals – to consultants, doctors, accountants, and lawyers – even though they enjoy a degree of control over entry to their jobs, working conditions and pay that even the print unions must envy. What is a 'restrictive practice' in the hands of a printer becomes 'professional self-government' in the hands of a lawyer; and because this is so, I think we have a right to say that there is a distinct class bias in so much of this criticism.

Moreover, the critics of union power gain the penetration that they do as much by what they fail to say as by what they emphasize. For by concentrating on the activity of unions, they fail to situate union power in the wider context of the social processes and institutions to which that power is a reaction. Three features of that context are worth stressing here: the imbalance in the labour contract; the capitalist nature of the work process; and the concentration of social and economic power in the hands of a capitalist class.

To take the imbalance in the labour contract first: it cannot be stressed too much that union activity is an attempt to redress an unevenness of power between the individual worker and his or her employer.[11] When a worker sells his labour power to a firm, his whole life-situation depends on the wages he can earn, such that to lose that wage is to endure considerable material and social deprivation. Yet the employer has no such stake in the contract with this worker. For him one worker is just an extra unit of cost, an element at the margin of his calculations, to be held or dispensed with at the whim of the market. And because the wage contract is central to the worker but marginal to the employer, the balance of sanctions between the two is heavily stacked against the former unless the union intervenes on his behalf. Moreover, in that wage contract, the worker sells not just his labour power but his freedom, in that he agrees to subordinate himself for the length of the working day to the authority structure of the firm, to its managerial and supervisory directives. At the very least this means that the issues likely to adversely affect workers in the workplace (low wages, poor conditions, too fast a pace of work and so on) have a 'perishable' quality. They will just automatically work themselves out to the employers' liking unless the union or the workgroup act quickly to stop them. Trade unionism therefore has an essential part to play in redressing this imbalance of power, protecting the individual worker (through the strength of collective action) against the force of managerial sanctions, against the otherwise automatic and dictatorial drift of managerial decision-making, and against the excessively exploitative wage contract to which the isolated worker is exposed. So trade union power, to the degree that it exists, draws on a membership who are systematically disadvantaged as individuals in the face of the concentration of industrial power in the hands of capital. Labour, that is, has to 'catch up' with capital before any equalization of power between them can be achieved, and the activities of the unions should be seen, measured and judged in that light.

Moreover, it is not just that individual workers are powerless in the face of managerial sanctions. That after all would be a feature of any class-based system of industrial production, whether capitalist or not. What has also to be said is that unions in Britain are trying to 'catch up' and improve their power position in a society which is capitalist, and in which as a result their members, as workers, are subject to particularly onerous market processes. The whole thrust of capitalist production is geared to the making of profits through the expropriation of the surplus value of labour power, and in industrial terms this means that individual workers are perpetually subject to two pressures. They are persistently subject to managerial attempts to increase that rate of expropriation, to alter, that is, the 'effort – wage' bargain in favour of effort, by intensifying the pace of work and by increasing its length. And in this process workers are treated not as people but as commodities, as things, as units of cost, as resources of production that are of no more intrinsic value to the employer than is the machinery and raw material he has also purchased. In addition, because of the force of capitalist competition and the perennial pressure on profits that is a feature of that competition, individual workers can expect their own work practices, and even their jobs themselves, to be periodically threatened by the introduction of new machinery, and to experience this threat in a context in which the suffering that will result to them in this 'rationalization process' will not directly enter the calculations of management at all. Union power then becomes essential to redress this balance too: to defend existing 'wage – effort' bargains against the remorseless pressure to intensify the work process, and to protect jobs and working practices against the systematic tendency to rationalize them both away. So often in the media we are left with the impression that industrial experience would be peaceful and harmonious if only unions would stop their agitation; but as long as that industry is subject to the dull market imperatives of a capitalist system workers will continue to experience the work process as one of alienation, inequality, exploitation and generalized insecurity, regardless of the presence and activity of unions as such; and we have a right to say back to the media that if they are genuinely concerned with these features of industrial life, it is to capitalism and not to the unions that they should address their criticisms.

There is a third sense too in which union power, to the degree to which it exists, is still attempting to catch up, and that is in the general area of social and political power. Those who criticize the unions for attempting to move resources in favour of working people and their families tend to be silent on the morality of the highly unequal distribution of resources that still remains. And yet the distribution of wealth in Britain is highly uneven, the distribution of income only slightly less so, access to senior positions in industry, finance and administration remains highly skewed in favour of the children of the privileged, and patterns of consumption in this society are still heavily structured by class.[12] If you ask who is paid most in this society, whose working conditions are easiest and most in their control, who has easiest access to the bureaucracies and centres of power, whose life-styles are most affluent, whose health is better and who lives longest, the answers are always the same. The higher up the class structure you go, the better you do on all of these, and trade unionism has still to make a significant impact on this.

It is as well not to be misled by the appearance of things. The visibility of the activity of trade unions is no guide to their power. Unions still operate in a world in which a relatively small class of men own and control the key industrial, financial and administrative institutions to which union members sell their labour. They operate in a world, moreover, in which the vast majority of the decisions which they as unions wish to influence are taken privately by the agents of those owners. And unions have to operate within a culture (a set of popularly held ideas that is assiduously propagated by the media) that is distinctly unsympathetic to their activity. This culture is prone to assume that the use of militant tactics by unions is self-evidently illegitimate unless the unions can prove otherwise. It is prone to grant to governments the right to specify the 'national interest' even when their policies are blatantly partisan; and it is prone too to accept as quite proper the use of sanctions *against* unions (and indeed against governments sympathetic to the union cause) by managers, industrial owners, multinational corporations, foreign governments and international financial agencies, all of whom are quite capable of presenting the pursuit of their own selfish interests in a way which suggests that they are really only acting in the interests of the community as a whole.[13] And the result of that 'cultural camouflage', and the concentration of industrial and financial ownership that it seeks to hide is that, unless unions act, a capitalist class quietly continues to rule; and just because these people cannot always be seen, don't stand on picket lines and don't pass resolutions in open conference, it does not mean that they are not there. This is a point to which we shall need to return in the concluding section of this argument.

UNION GOVERNMENT AND GOALS

The criticisms of the quality and character of union government are the easiest to dismiss. Though the democratic process in union government may work less than perfectly, the unions remain the only major set of private institutions making their decisions in that way, and subjecting their leaders to the control of elections, elected executive committees, annual conferences, democratically arrived at rule books and even, in some cases, final appeal courts. So even at its worst, union government is still more democratic than is decision-making in industry, the City, the civil service and the media. And when it does break down, undermined by leaders determined to have their own way, those leaders are not necessarily always on the left politically, or excessively militant in their industrial policy. On the contrary, rigged elections, fixed agendas and the disregard of union procedures can more easily be used to frustrate militancy than to force it. No union leader can afford, persistently and regularly, to disregard his members if his own spokesman role before employers and politicians is to maintain its credibility, and this pressure is particularly acute on a leader keen to fight militantly for his members' interests. For a militant union has to mobilize its members, and this need for the voluntary support of an entire membership at times of crisis is a powerful democratic control on left-wing leadership, and is so even in unions in which, in quieter times, involvement in decision-making devolves on to the shoulders of only a few. Moreover unions vary in their internal structures and traditions, and the 'popular bossdom' and oligarchic control of a union like the GMWU has to be set against the active factions, decentralized power structure, sophisticated electoral systems and traditions of rank and file involvement in union decision-making that characterize more democratic unions like the miners and the engineers. And though at times of strike calls, critics of unionism prefer individual balloting to the more normal union procedure of a show of hands in a mass meeting, socialists have the right to argue back that the mass meeting affords at least some protection from the anti-strike propaganda of the employer and the media, and gives a sense of their collective power to workers who would otherwise be isolated and alone. Some unions do, in any case, take individual ballots, and they are often amongst the most militant (the miners in 1972 and 1974, the railwaymen in 1971); and anyway the concern of those outside the unions who would generalize this procedure is not, as far as I can tell, for greater union democracy, but for fewer strikes and a more supine labour movement.

Nor is there much evidence to support the thesis that union leaders are unrepresentatively militant. Studies of shop stewards have shown that they are elected (and subject to regular re-election) by very high percentages of their 'constituents' – 70 to 80 per cent turnouts are not uncommon; that they tend to be no more politically radical or industrially militant than their members (and that where they are, they are supported in spite of their political views); that their workload is overwhelmingly concerned with the detailed protection of individual workers and working practices against perennial managerial threats; and that when they do call for militant tactics to be used, it is not uncommon (as at BL recently) for their militant calls to be overthrown by rank and file decisions, even at mass meetings. What could be more representative and democratic than that? And those critics of national union leaders who bewail the militancy of an Arthur Scargill or a Mike McGahey have a very inconsistent attitude to the relationship between leadership and democracy. For they are the same people who persistently call for union leaders to 'put their house in order', discipline their militants and subordinate their policies to wider national concerns, and to do so in spite of union policy to the contrary. The vast majority of union leaders have succumbed to some degree to these pressures with such regularity down the years that one can often argue that union democracy is under threat – but threatened from outside and not from within, destroyed by the forces of conservatism and moderation and not by those of militancy and political radicalism.

Indeed it is at this point that it is worth mentioning the way in which many trade union leaders, far from being disproportionately radical and militant in their activity, are much more likely to be unrepresentatively moderate in their views and their industrial policies. Trade union leaders come under very heavy pressure from the media, from senior businessmen, and from civil servants and politicians to restrict union demands, and to subordinate union policy to the wider dictates of a 'national interest' that is seen as coterminous with enlarged industrial profits and strengthened managerial control. Union leaders are also often reluctant to jeopardize the financial and legal integrity of the union organization by too vigorous a support of strike action or by too prolonged a confrontation with the policies of government. Many shop stewards have latterly shown similar propensities to conservative leadership, encouraged in this by the special status accorded to them by sophisticated personnel managers, and ever-conscious of the vulnerability of their workmates to redundancies caused by the movement of capital away from areas of labour militancy in a time of general recession. Far from being industrial wreckers, these men should be more properly seen as under great pressure to act as 'the managers of discontent', 'lieutenants of capital in the intensified exploitation of the workers', and in need of mass support and socialist principles if they are to retain the resilience to pursue industrial policies that do actually erode the power of capital or block the reactionary policies of governments.[14]

The closed shop is a more difficult area for socialists. Union members can be justifiably resentful of individuals who willingly pocket pay rises won by union action but who refuse to join the union or who actively erode its power by crossing its picket lines. And they have a right too to see a streak of hypocrisy in those who condemn the unions' power to throw the occasional worker out of his job because he or she refuses to take a union card, but who are silent on capitalism's daily capacity to throw hundreds of individuals out of employment for no 'crime' at all. Liberal critics of trade unionism are quite happy to argue for compulsory taxation, for example, on the grounds that people should not be allowed to 'free-ride' (to benefit, that is, from the collective provision of goods and services, such as defence, without paying for them); and yet it is just this argument, on the closed shop, that they choose to ignore in defence of individual freedom. But an individual freedom to live off the backs of others is a freedom which is not worth having, and the right to negotiate and maintain a closed shop is an important way of protecting the organizational strength of unions which is perpetually under threat from so many other forces. But socialists have to recognize too that the closed shop is potentially a double-edged weapon. If it produces a coerced membership, it can become a threat to strong trade unionism, by encouraging the union leadership to exaggerate its actual degree of voluntary support. If it is applied too rigidly, it can provide a field-day for trade union critics quick to seize on the hardship of the workers made redundant by its terms, and so undermine support for unionism in the community as a whole. And in the wrong hands, the existence of a closed shop agreement can actually jeopardize the position of union militants. For it should not be forgotten that it is often employers and right-wing union leaders who use closed shop arrangements to consolidate a conservative union presence in industrial relations, not least by allowing union leaders to use the employment sanction to discipline their own militants; and it is against such misuses of the power that the closed shop brings, rather than against the principle of the closed shop itself, that socialists in the unions should direct their fire.

It must be conceded too that the goals which unions pursue are, in the main, closely tied to the individual wages and working conditions of union members. But why this should be a criticism is far from clear. Those issues are of vital concern to the living standards of workers and their families. It is capitalism, not they, who deny them property rights, and so leave them totally dependent on their money wage for survival; and within capitalism, no other institution exists to protect those wages from the managerial concern to cut costs. At times, of course, that union preoccupation manifests itself in fights between unions, and the conflict of worker against worker; and this is both understandable (it always bears a direct relationship to the wage structure and employment practices of capitalism over a long period) and undesirable from a socialist standpoint.[15] Capitalism has long set worker against worker (by trade, industry, region, skill, even race, religion and sex) and it is hardly surprising that this manifests itself in the kinds of demands that individual unions sometimes put forward, and which particular craft unions have come to have a vested interest in defending and promoting. It must be said that to the extent that unions help to set worker against worker, or to restrict their horizons to immediate questions of pay and conditions of employment, then union activity weakens, rather than strengthens, the attempt to forge a socialist majority in the labour movement. In that sense it is both legitimate and necessary for socialists to condemn sectionalism, racism and sexism whenever these manifest themselves in certain union goals and practices. What is not legitimate, however, is for right-wing critics of trade unionism like Paul Johnson to argue that, because these occasional features of union activity are anti-socialist, it is necessary to weaken unionism as a whole in the pursuit of the socialist goal. On the contrary, strong unionism of a democratic, collectivist and egalitarian kind is vital to the entire socialist project.

For it has to be recognized that the unions have always played a vital part in the wider struggle for social and political reform. No other organized section of the community has a record which can match that of the unions here. It was trade unionists who made up the bulk of the activists in the fight for the extension of the franchise. It was the unions who pressed for old age pensions, unemployment benefits and industrial insurance. And it has been union pressure (and not that of industry, the City or the Conservative Party) that has consolidated a welfare state, which affords at least some protection from market forces to the poor, the sick, the young and the old. If those groups are still (as they are) insufficiently protected, that is not because unions have been too strong but because they have been too weak, and have failed to defend and extend welfare provision with sufficient vigour. And their failure here has not been caused by their greed and their sectionalism, but by their willingness to subordinate both their industrial demands and their calls for social spending to the parsimonious dictates of a so-called 'national interest' whose content has been specified by the very class of men who now castigate unions for their selfishness. It is the pedlars of capitalism who, at the present time, are all for cutting welfare provision, and letting the poor suffer, in order to facilitate the making of profits and the accumulation of capital; and if the unions have not pressed as hard as they should in the poor's defence, it is because they too have been contaminated to a degree by the arguments of those who put profits before people, and class privilege before social justice.

THE INDUSTRIAL POWER OF TRADE UNIONS

What then of the industrial power of trade unions in Britain? The first thing to say is that it is grossly exaggerated. Unions still operate in an industrial system in which the vast majority of key decisions are made unilaterally by management, without consultation (let alone negotiation) with the workers directly affected by them.

Unions do not have a say in the location of factories, the levels of investment, the size of the labour force, the sales policy or design of the product to be sold; and when a Labour government after 1974 tried half-heartedly to give them such a say (through the introduction of planning agreements and the extension of industrial democracy) Labour ministers met a quite hysterical but highly successful campaign of resistance from an outraged managerial class.[16]

If trade unions have power, it is on a very narrow range of issues: wages, working conditions, levels of manning, speed of work . . . . And even here that power is more negative than positive, a power to block unacceptable managerial initiatives rather than to dictate wholly new sets of working practices. It is a shared power too, a capacity to negotiate and to bargain, not (as with management's power elsewhere in industrial decision-making) to decide unilaterally. And it is a power that only certain trade unionists enjoy, and only at certain times. It is just some unions who have a particular bargaining strength, because of the strategic importance of their industry (either to the economy as a whole, or to a complex and interlocking set of production processes), or because of the high level of demand for the commodity they produce, or because of its immediate perishability (as with newsprint). Most unions are not so fortunate. Yet some are – the miners are an obvious case – and their power was matched, at least on this narrow range of issues, by work groups and shop stewards in 'sections of engineering, and a few other manufacturing industries'[17] in the years of the long boom (between 1948 and 1973). Management in those industries in those years often had to negotiate levels of manning, the pace and organization of work, overtime and company bonuses with stewards. But workers in the public sector, and in transport and distribution, lacked that leverage, and yet even they were prepared (in 1969 and in the winter of 1978–79) to engage in major national strikes in the pursuit of wage settlements that were handled in engineering by localized bargaining by stewards.

So we can go this far with the conventional wisdom of the day. The miners do have industrial muscle, shop stewards were powerful in a restricted section of the engineering industry in the 1960s, and national strikes against government policy have been a feature of the 1970s. But we have to point to other things too. For all the claims about trade union monopoly power, wages in Britain are amongst the lowest in Western Europe; and if monopoly power is a problem in British industry, it is a problem of monopolies not in the labour market but in the structure of industrial ownership itself. For the unions here face a higher degree of industrial concentration, of monopoly power, in the ownership structure of British industry than do unions in any other major industrial power.[18] It is these vast industrial monopolies which are the source of inflation, exploiting their market position to restrict output and artificially inflate prices; and it is their (and not the unions') multinational scale of operations and intimate connections with the large banking networks that draw capital away from the UK, and erode the bargaining power of British workers and their representatives.

The economy which those multinational companies are helping to 'deindustrialize' does suffer from internationally low levels of industrial productivity. Yet this is not because the unions have set their face against new machinery. On the contrary, they have called persistently for new investment, and have cooperated regularly in schemes for greater productivity. But British capital has gone abroad in search of easier pickings, and the defensive strength of trade unionism does play its part here. Pickings are easier abroad because labour movements are weak, and because British workers have insisted that their interests be recompensed to some small degree, through a more controlled and negotiated introduction of new technology, by the buying-out of old working practices, and through high government spending on the social services. When they are criticized for that, socialists have the right to ask their critics what is their attitude to the sweat shops of Asia and Brazil, and to the unprotected working conditions and low wages of the Western European 'guest workers' – for that, in truth, is the alternative they are implicitly canvassing. And if it is not, socialists must point out that the export of capital is self-fulfilling, creating overmanning by restricting the scale of machinery available for each worker to use, and consolidating resistance to change by enhancing the generalized insecurity to which the labour force of any under-capitalized competitive economy must necessarily become subject. Socialists have the right to say, that is, that the protection of jobs here will be best served, not by a reduction in trade union power, but by an international campaign to strengthen trade unionism on a world scale, and by the removal of decisions on the distribution and character of investment from the hands of a tiny, privileged, self-seeking and unrepresentative capitalist class.

Nor, it should be said, is the British economy particularly strike prone by international standards.[19] Strikes in Britain tend to be concentrated in a few industries: in coal-mining, the car industry, in engineering and in shipbuilding. The costs of those strikes are invariably exaggerated by the media, partly by ignoring the costs to workers of tolerating the old conditions, partly by ignoring the way in which output can quickly be made up after the strike, by ignoring the money saved by the employer in wages during the strike, and by failing to point out that, in a recession, a break in production can often be a boon to a hard-pressed sales director.[20] In any case far fewer days are normally 'lost' through industrial action than arise from the illnesses and accidents caused by the pressures of the work process or from the enforced idleness of the unemployed. Nor should strikes be taken as an index of absolute power, as they always are. Even workers going on strike lack the range and potency of sanctions enjoyed by capital (stretching as these do from the capacity to discipline individual workers, through their easy access to government, to their capacity to move their money abroad); and it is intriguing to see how, in such a context, militant tactics by workers come to be defined by politicians and the media as 'unfair' just as soon as they start to have an impact on those powers of capital. The use of flying pickets was condemned, you may remember, because just for a short time they gave striking miners the kind of leverage on government policy that capital exercises on a daily basis without condemnation at all. But even so, workers go on strike not because they have power but because they lack it, and are driven with great reluctance and at considerable financial cost to themselves to withdraw their labour in sheer frustration. This was certainly the case in the strikes of the low paid in the public sector at the end of the 1960s and 1970s, when they were driven to strike successfully against incomes policy (the point the media stress) because of their systematic loss of pay and position in the years in which the policy held (the point the media tend not to stress); and they remain just as vulnerable after the strike as before, as the firemen and others have been discovering since 1979, as further government retrenchments erode the gains of their militancy slowly over time, and now, as I write, threaten their very employment itself.

For the industrial power of the unions is now being seriously eroded by government-induced unemployment and the intensification of international competition brought on by the world recession. The bargaining power of labour always weakens in a capitalist crisis. The working practices and shop-floor strength of work groups in British engineering industry are being rapidly eroded by new managerial initiatives. What else, after all, is the 'BL saga' and that of Chrysler UK all about? Wage settlements in the private (and now increasingly in the public) sector are being driven down well below the inflation level. And unemployment has soared to 3 million officially by late 1981, and in truth to nearer 4 million.[21] The unions have found no answer to this crisis and its unemployment, and the struggles of workers everywhere are sporadic, defensive and modest in their aims. All these features of contemporary industrial life make a mockery of the anti-union case, and stand as a clear indication not of the power of labour but of the moral, social and economic bankruptcy of capitalism.

THE QUESTION OF POLITICAL INFLUENCE

When the unions turned to the State in the nineteenth century, they did so in the first instance to win the legal right to exist, and then to strike. It took a century of political agitation to win those rights in the 1906 Trades Disputes Act, and without the rights enshrined there (immunity from prosecution for actions taken in the furtherance of a trades dispute) it would be impossible for unions to pursue their conventional business without exposure to crippling financial penalties. Those rights have been threatened many times, either frontally (as in the 1971 Industrial Relations Act) or incrementally (as with the Conservatives' proposals in 1980 and 1981). The fact that they are unusual in English law shows how entrenched are the rights of individual property and corporate capital in that legal system; and the mutterings of judges against trade union legal 'immunity', and their narrow and unsympathetic interpretation of the labour law passed between 1974 and 1979, tells us more about the social background and political views of the judiciary than it does about the excessive legal position of union bargainers. The unions' legal position is in no sense one of 'privilege'. 'Indeed it indicates the extent to which the values of capital-holders dominate that such a word should be used for labour and yet not used to describe the enormous protection, such as limited liability, which capital gets.'[22] Even after the Labour government's favourable legislative changes of the mid-1970s, it remains the case that unions have no way of obliging a reluctant employer to negotiate in good faith, workers still do not have the right to strike without losing their jobs, judges are still capable of denying legal immunity to unions using industrial power on issues more political in nature (such as a boycott of South Africa), and pickets are still subject to police harassment and tight legal constraints. As Robert Taylor has said, the legal changes between 1974 and 1979, which are themselves now under attack, 'have done little more than provide trade unionists in Britain with rights enjoyed by others in the western world over the past decade. Moreover by innumerable decisions in courts and industrial tribunals they have been circumscribed, in some parts rendered quite ineffective'.[23] No wonder trade unionists have increasingly looked to their collective strength, and not to their legal rights, as the only way effectively to defend and advance the interests of union members.

When we turn from the unions' legal position to the more general question of their political power, we can say this. There is no doubt that the unions enjoy a very special place in the decision-making process within the Labour Party, with union votes dominating party conference, with union nominees holding eighteen of the twenty-seven elected places on the party's NEC, and with the party heavily dependent on the unions for finance and sponsorship.[24] There are very close connections of ideology, programme and friendship between leading union figures and Labour parliamentarians, and these have been given institutional expression since 1971 in the existence of the Liaison Committee, on which leading TUC members, NEC figures and parliamentary representatives meet to formulate Labour Party policy. And it cannot be denied that, after 1970 at least, Labour parliamentarians did respond to the unions' political demands in a quite unprecedented way. The Labour government entered office in 1974 with an agenda of policies largely derived from union preoccupations: new labour laws, the renegotiation of the terms of entry to the EEC, economic expansion, new public ownership, State control of the big monopolies through planning agreements, greater social spending, the extension of industrial democracy, and a redistribution of wealth downwards. Since the Labour government did its best to implement that programme in its first eighteen months in office it is not altogether surprising that many of the recent critics of union power draw heavily on that period for their evidence.

But again appearances are misleading in a number of crucial senses. The year 1975 marked a high point of union influence, as rare as it was brief; and there are a number of reasons for that. One is that the unions have never exploited their constitutional position inside the Labour Party to the full, and show no sign of doing so even now. This is partly because unions are economic bargainers, to which political infighting is of secondary importance, and to which hard-pressed union leaders can only devote a limited amount of their time. It is also because the unions are rarely if ever united on political questions, and so do not speak with one voice. It is also because union leaders fear that too deep an involvement in Labour Party politics could cost them members, divide the TUC, and alienate Labour voters from a party 'in the grip' of union domination. But it is also because leading union figures do actively subscribe to the ruling views about the supremacy of parliament and the autonomy of MPs, and are very wary of any action that smacks of dictation. Certainly all the recent studies suggest that the unions have been very restrained and moderate in their internal dealings with the Labour Party.[25]

More important even than that, it must be stressed that the leverage which the unions enjoy over Labour Party policy-making in Opposition diminishes rapidly when the party moves into power. Stronger political forces, in the civil service, in the City, in industry and abroad, then come directly into play. Union leaders can argue, lobby, issue their own budget proposals, agitate for them, even organize marches and strikes, but they lack the sanctions of the pressure groups of capital. Certainly between 1974 and 1979 the radical parts of the Labour government's programme were blocked by opposition from these groups, in spite of sustained union pressure. Industrial democracy was blocked by a CBI campaign. Planning agreements were aborted by the refusal of multinational companies to negotiate them; and incomes policies, cuts in government spending and rising unemployment were forced on a Labour government by currency speculation and the IMF. All that the unions could salvage was their new body of labour law (to be attacked after 1979 by the Conservatives), and the capacity to veto a fourth year of voluntary incomes restraint. That veto power on that one issue continues to give the unions some political leverage, but that is hardly a power to dictate general economic policy, for all their special relationship with the Labour Party.

One final point on the relationship between the unions and the Labour Party is also important, namely the vulnerability of union leaders and members to appeals for solidarity and support from Labour politicians. The close involvement of unions in Labour Party decision-making may well give the unions considerable leverage when the party is in Opposition, but the flow of influence is much the other way round with Labour in power. As Labour politicians succumb to conservative pressure, union leaders in particular are slow to offer unambiguous opposition: partly from reasons of personal loyalty and friendship; partly because of their own involvement in the detail of the retreat; and partly because they know that to fight Labour in power is to let the dreaded Tories in. It is hard to imagine a Conservative government getting away with the three years of almost totally unchallenged pay restraint that Labour achieved between 1975 and 1978, and this is a pattern we are all too likely to see again.

Nor should we assume that the more regular appearance of union leaders in the corridors of power necessarily tells us anything about the rising influence and political ambitions of unions as such. There is no doubt that the unions have won the right to be consulted, and that this opens channels of influence to them. There is no doubt either that a Labour government is more likely to use those channels regularly than is the Thatcher type of Conservative government. But the ambitions and preoccupations of the unions have remained remarkably constant over the years: to advance and protect the wages, jobs and working conditions of their members. That this takes them into politics now reflects, not changes in them, but the much greater role played by governments in these matters. The State now directly employs 40 per cent of all trade unionists, and makes policy (on incomes and so on) that directly affects the rest; and as a result trade unions have now to deal with the State to settle questions which, between the wars, would have taken them no further than the offices of the managing directors of the key private firms.

This involvement of union leaders in the higher circles of power is not without its dangers to the members they represent. There is the ever-present risk that union leaders so involved will be coopted as agents of the policies they are supposed to oppose, and obliged to act as 'managers of discontent', unpaid assistants in the implementation of government policy. We saw this happening to men like Jack Jones and Hugh Scanlon in the period of incomes policy after 1975, and will no doubt see it again. As Richard Hyman has observed, 'it is a commonplace of industrial relations that unions can readily be transformed, at least partially, into an agency of control over their members to the advantage of external interests'.[26] And even when that does not occur, it is quite illegitimate to look at a body like the N E D C, see the equal number of union and business representatives there, and conclude from that that in some crucial sense the power of business and labour is now equal. Capital rules through its ownership of the means of production, and its power lies far from the corridors of Westminster. All the trade unions have is their collective strength, and that can so easily be dissipated and eroded by the 'responsibilities' of participation. As Leo Panitch put it recently[27]:

Socialist arguments

Trade union power is based on the effectiveness of its collective organisation. But the power of capital is based on control of the means of production, and this control is not transferred to the interest associations of business by individual firms. This means that these associations' incorporation via state structures is less significant for capital than is the incorporation of trade unions for labour, precisely because these associations play a less critical role for their class as agencies of struggle, of representation and of social control than do trade unions for their class.

This is an important point, for both union leaders and business spokesmen have a vested interest in pointing to union involvement in government committees as an index of union power. For both ignore the political leverage that capital enjoys because it owns the means of production, and can quietly take its decisions privately, far from the glare of publicity that surrounds the committees of the State.

THE CHARACTER OF UNION POWER

So do the trade unions have too much power? The answer to that question seems to be 'No', no matter how 'power' is to be understood and measured. If power is to be equated with *participation* in decision-making (in collective bargaining, and in the committees of the State)then union power has increased significantly this century and shows little sign of abating. But that equation is itself false. There is no parity between the parties to a collective agreement in a context in which management is still able arbitrarily to restrict the issues negotiated to matters immediately relevant to the wage contract; and the involvement of unionists in parity of representation with business spokesmen in government circles, as we have just seen, still leaves capital in control of the means of production and union leaders dangerously exposed to incorporation into a government ethos and set of policies dominated by the concerns of business and finance. If, on the other hand, power is to be measured by *effects*, by the capacity of a union to achieve its goals (either positively, by achieving high wages and so on, or negatively, by blocking unacceptable initiatives by management and government) then again union power is limited. The range of issues on which unions can hope to have influence is very narrow, and union leverage drops rapidly (both in collective bargaining and in negotiations with the State) as soon as questions of wages and working conditions are left behind. And even in that narrow range, the positive power to win high wages and secure employment is being eroded by the world recession, the declining competitiveness of British capitalism, and the antagonism of the Conservative government. The power to block is weakened too by the debilitating effect of unemployment on industrial militancy; but for some unions, as we have seen, the power to prevent voluntary incomes restraint and even industrial relations legislative change still remains. But union power should not be measured by the criteria of 'participation' and 'effects'. It should be measured by the *unions' place in the whole structure of social, economic, cultural and political relationships in the society*; and when that is done, it is easier to see the true state of trade unionism in Britain in the 1980s.

Since this is a difficult point to explain briefly, let me proceed by analogy and diagram. Critics of trade union power can be said to implicitly liken power relationships to a football match, with the ball (say government policy) being pushed from the Left by the unions and from the Right by the pressure groups of capital (see Fig. 1). The argument then is that the pressure from the Left has grown, and has become disproportionate, moving the ball from X to Y. But the point to grasp is that the football match is not being played on level ground, but on the side of a hill (see Fig. 2), with the unions pushing upwards, against the gradient; and what we have to note is both the movement of the ball X to Y and the gradient of the hill (g). The strength of the second diagram is that it suggests that unless unions act, forces at work in the society will erode the interests of union members, and that it is possible for unions to move the ball slightly up the hill (as arguably they did in 1974–75) without fundamentally altering the inequalities of power that surround them. It is in this sense that union activity has been described as 'the labour of Sisyphus'.[28]

The question then becomes, what are the forces pushing that ball downhill? I think that there are least four. The first (a) is the sheer inequality of class power and privilege in a capitalist society. Unions have to fight (even strike) for pay awards far smaller than those which accrue automatically to senior management and professionals.

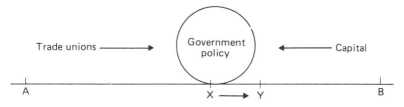

Fig. 1

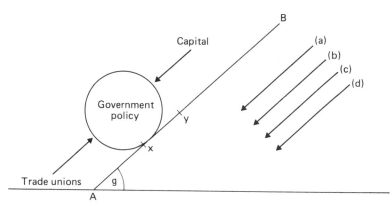

Fig. 2

The second (*b*) is the general framework of law and the disposition of the State burcaucracy, both of whom give (and will continue to give) primacy and legitimacy to the interests of capital unless, and to the degree that, trade unions can assert their counter-interests successfully. The third (*c*) is the sheer weight of the dominant ideologies of the day and the associated conventions of parliamentary democracy, both of which systematically erode trade union power. And the fourth (*d*) is the impact of market forces on trade unionism in the midst of a capitalist recession.

Let me expand slightly on (*c*) and on (*d*). Socialists should not underestimate the power of the media, in shaping public attitudes to trade unionism and in undermining the self-confidence of union members themselves. As was argued earlier, when unions strike they are invariably condemned for taking such action, with almost no regard to the relative merits of the issues involved. But when capital strikes (by not investing) or the IMF speaks, there is no parallel condemnation. On the contrary, these are legitimized by the media as the 'realities' to which trade unionists should subordinate themselves. Least of all should the unions strike against the State. This is to threaten the conventions of parliamentary democracy. And yet capital uses its industrial power to bend government policy to its will regularly, and meets no equivalent condemnation.

This all weakens union resolve, and that resolve is weakened further in a recession by the power of market forces and the associated employment and pricing policies of capitalist firms. The rate of capital accumulation sets the real limit to union bargaining strength even in a period of capitalist expansion. In the long boom, after 1948, rapid capital accumulation quickened the growth rate of productivity, and altered the balance of class forces in favour of labour, and so created easier conditions for trade union negotiators. And what the unions gained in the boom they stand fair to lose in the recession. For the uneven militancy of unions in Britain now is no accident. It reflects the genuine dilemma faced by workers and their representatives in a context in which they too need a healthy economy to guarantee their jobs and living standards, but in which the capitalist nature of the recession means that those jobs and living standards have to be cut in the pursuit of those profits that might eventually bring that health. In such a context, market and class forces persistently erode trade union gains. High wages are eroded by high prices. Job security is undermined by intensified competition. Non-inflationary social spending is restricted by the failure of productivity to grow in the manufacturing base of the economy. And trade unions find, whether they like it or not, that their militancy can discourage private investment, and hence undermine the long-term basis of successful trade unionism, namely a rapidly growing and fully employed economy. In such a context trade unions do not have power. They have a choice – Hobson's choice – and there is no way they can win.

Trade unions and their members are victims of a capitalist crisis, not its cause[29]; and as that crisis intensifies, even the meagre gains made in the boom years will (and have already) come under increasing attack. Unemployment is being used as a weapon for eroding the control of work groups over aspects of the work process. Inflation is being used as an excuse for cutting the social wage; and the dwindling competitiveness of British capitalism is being used as a smokescreen under which to attack the legal rights of trade unions and their members. In other words, the ball is being pushed downhill and the gradient steepened against trade unionism by market forces and government policy.

Trade unionism as such offers no way out of this dilemma.[30] Unions are at once both part of and an antagonism to capitalism. Their very existence constitutes, and gives expression to, a perennial challenge by workers to the dominance of capital, and a perpetual threat to the capacity of the ruling class to make profits and enjoy privileges. But unions are also very much capitalism's product. They arose as capitalism exploited and concentrated its working class. Their organization and goals mirror the structure and wage practices of capitalist industry.[31] Their officials must, of necessity, bargain on a daily basis as though capitalism and its irrationalities were immovable; and their practices help to incorporate a whole working class into a subordinate position within capitalism, pursuing only a modest role and a limited set of goals. This is not to say that the preoccupation of unions with winning 'short-term gains within capitalism [then] negates their role as agencies in class struggle'. It is rather to argue that this preoccupation 'does account for the relatively low ordering in their operative priorities usually given to public ownership and controls over capital, let alone to the project of bringing the working class to power in the sense that the bourgeoisie is in power in capitalist society.[32] And it is to make clear too that the job of socialists is to help to defend these institutions as the bedrock of a self-confident proletariat, and as a first line of defence against capitalist attacks on workers' jobs and living standards, but that socialists need to argue in addition for a political party and a political strategy that can go beyond unionism, to the replacement of capitalism itself. As Marx said[33]:

trade unions work well as centres of resistance against the encroachments of capital. They fail partially from an injudicious use of their power. They fail generally from limiting themselves to a guerilla war against the effects of the existing system, instead of using their organised forces as a lever for the final emancipation of the working class, that is to say, the ultimate abolition of the wages system.

NOTES

I would like to thank David Beetham, Andrew Gamble, David Held, John Hillard, Gordon Johnston, Robert Looker, Dick Taylor, Sue Thomson and my father for their comments on an earlier draft of this chapter.

1. R. Taylor, *The Fifth Estate*, Pan Books 1980, p. 14
2. L. Panitch, 'The limits on corporatism', *New Left Review*, No. 125, 38
3. See, for example, P. Johnson, 'A brotherhood of national misery', *New Statesman*, 16 May 1975, 652–6
4. See, for example, Sir Keith Joseph, 'Solving the union problem is the key to Britain's recovery', Centre for Policy Studies 1979, pp. 3–4
5. For a discussion of subversives, see P. Ferris, *The New Militants*, Penguin 1972, Ch. 6
6. Sir Harold Wilson, in the seamen's dispute of 1966, quoted by P. Foot, 'The seamen's struggle', in R. Blackburn and A. Cock-

burn (eds), *The Incompatibles: trade union militancy and the consensus*, Penguin 1967, p. 190

7. See, for example, Mrs Thatcher, quoted in R. Taylor, op. cit., p. 116; or G. Dorfman, *Government versus Trade Unionism in British Politics since 1968*, Macmillan 1979, p. 132

8. P. Johnson, op. cit., p. 652

9. See, for example, S. E. Finer, 'The political power of organised labour', in R. Rose (ed), *Studies in British Politics*, Macmillan 1976, p. 356

10. See, for example, *Inflation and the Unions*, IEA 1972, pp. viii, 6

11. This has been put extremely well by V. L. Allen: '. . . an employee on his own is at a marked disadvantage in labour market transactions. In all labour markets there are many employees and few employers so that employers are in a position where they can select employees according to their own criteria, dispense with them if need be, discriminate between one employee and another, displace employees by machines, contract out of labour market transactions altogether. The employee cannot avoid the market superiority of the employer for he is forced on to the labour market because only by selling his labour can he subsist. He is in an inherently unstable position which is reflected in the determination of his wages, conditions of work and hours of work. In other words, because of the operation of the market situation it is the employer who argues, negotiates, acts, from a basis of power.' *Militant Trade Unionism*, Merlin 1966, p. 12

12. On this, see J. Westergaard and H. Resler, *Class in a Capitalist Society*, Heinemann 1975; and the chapter by John Westergaard in this volume, pp. 146–168

13. For evidence of the way that the media distort union activity, see P. Beharrell and G. Philo, *Trade Unions and the Media*, Macmillan 1977; and the later studies by the entire Glasgow Media Study Group, published by Macmillan as *Bad News* and *More Bad News*. For the impact of this on the consciousness of workers, see R. Hyman, 'Industrial conflict and the political economy', in R. Miliband and J. Saville (eds) *The Socialist Register 1973*, Merlin 1973; and for a discussion of the general character and content of this anti-union culture, see V. L. Allen, op. cit., Ch. 1, and D. Coates, *Labour in Power? A study of the Labour Government 1974–1979*, Longman 1980, pp. 208–10

14. These quotations are from C. Wright Mills and Trotsky; and the whole question of union leadership is discussed at length in

T. Lane, *The Union Makes Us Strong*, Arrow Books 1974, and in D. Coates, op. cit., Ch. 5

15. On this, see R. Hyman, *Industrial Relations: a Marxist introduction*, Macmillan 1975, pp. 177–8
16. On this, see D. Coates, op. cit., pp. 131–42
17. R. Hyman, 'British trade unionism in the 70s', *Studies in Political Economy*, 1 (1), 1979, p. 104
18. The top one hundred companies were probably responsible for two-thirds of manufacturing output in 1980, a higher degree of market domination than applied even in the USA.
19. For the figures on this, see R. Hyman, *Strikes*, Fontana 1972, pp. 31–3
20. On this, see H. A. Turner, *Is Britain Really Strike Prone?*, Cambridge UP 1969
21. On the missing million unemployed, see *New Statesman*, 27 Mar. 1981, 4–5
22. V. L. Allen, op. cit., p. 168
23. R. Taylor, op. cit., p. 289
24. Ibid., pp. 99–111 for details
25. See in particular L. Minkin, 'The Labour Party has not been hijacked', *New Society* 6 Oct. 1977, 6–8; and L. Panitch, 'Socialists and the Labour Party: a reappraisal', in R. Miliband and J. Saville (eds) *The Socialist Register 1979*, Merlin 1979, pp. 51–74
26. R. Hyman, *Industrial Relations*, op. cit., p. 68
27. L. Panitch, *New Left Review*, No. 125, op. cit., 26–7
28. 'Trade unions cannot suppress the law of wages. Under the most favourable circumstances the best they can do is to impose on capitalist exploitation the 'normal' limit of the moment. They have not however the power to suppress exploitation itself, even gradually . . . once industrial development has attained its highest possible point and capitalism has entered its descending phase on the world market, the trade union struggle will become doubly difficult. In the first place the objective conjuncture of the market will be less favourable to the sellers of labour power, because the demand for labour power will increase at a slower rate and labour supply more rapidly than is the case at present. In the second place, the capitalists themselves, in order to make up for losses suffered on the world market will make even greater efforts than at present to reduce the part of the total product going to the workers in the form of wages . . . Trade union action is reduced of necessity to the simple defence of

already realised gains and even that is becoming more and more difficult . . . Trade unions can neither determine the dimensions of production nor the technical progress of production . . . The objective conditions of capitalist society transform . . . the economic functions of the trade unions into a sort of labour of Sisyphus which is nevertheless indispensable.' (Rosa Luxemburg, *Reform or Revolution* (1900), reprinted in Mary Alice-Waters, *Rosa Luxemburg Speaks* (Pathfinder Press, New York, 1970) pp. 50 and 71)

29. As Robert Taylor op. cit., p. 16 has observed, 'in most vital respects the unions are what they have always been – defensive, voluntary pressure groups, under sporadic attack from the class bias and common law traditions of the British legal system and the blandishments of governments, at the mercy of the ebb and flow of uncontrollable, impersonal market forces.'

30. For a classic statement of this, see P. Anderson, 'The limits and possibilities of trade union action', reprinted in T. Clarke and L. Clements (eds) *Trade Unions Under Capitalism*, Fontana 1977, pp. 333–50

31. As Alan Fox puts it, '. . . trade unions strive to effect marginal improvements in the lot of their members, and to defend them against arbitrary management action. They do not – and here we come to the crucial point of what issues are *not* at stake in management/worker relations – attack management on such basic principles of the social and industrial framework as private property, the hierarchical nature of the organisation, the extreme division of labour, and the massive inequalities of financial reward, status, control and autonomy at work. Neither do they try to secure a foothold on the majority of decisions made within the organisation on such issues as management objectives, markets, capital investment and rate of expansion. Very rarely do they seriously challenge such principles as the treatment of labour as a commodity to be hired or discarded at management's convenience.' (quoted in Clarke and Clements, op. cit., p. 142)

32. L. Panitch, *New Left Review*, No. 125, op. cit., 43

33. K. Marx, *Wages, Prices and Profits*, in Marx and Engels, *Selected Works*, Lawrence and Wishart 1968, p. 229

FURTHER READING

R. Taylor, *The Fifth Estate: Britain's Unions in the Modern World*,

Pan Books 1980

T. Clarke and L. Clements (eds) *Trade Unions Under Capitalism*, Fontana 1977

T. Lane, *The Union Makes Us Strong*, Arrow 1974

R. Hyman, *Strikes*, Fontana 1972

R. Hyman, *Industrial Relations: a Marxist introduction*, Macmillan 1975

K. Coates and T. Topham, *Trade Unions in Britain*, Spokesman 1980

Chapter four

THE DEMOCRATIC STATE AND
THE NATIONAL INTEREST

Bob Jessop

. . . the most comprehensive contradiction in the Constitution consists in the fact that it gives political power to the classes whose slavery it is intended to perpetuate: proletariat, peasants and petty bourgeoisie. And it deprives the bourgeoisie, the class whose old social power it sanctions, of the political guarantees of this power. It imposes on the political rule of the bourgeoisie democratic conditions which constantly help its enemies towards victory and endanger the very basis of bourgeois society. It demands from the one that it should not proceed from political emancipation to social emancipation and from the other that it should not regress from social restoration to political restoration.[1]

Socialists and their opponents will probably adopt very different attitudes to this alleged contradiction in democratic constitutions. For socialists it is clearly paradoxical that an economic system based on the exploitation of the labouring mass by the capitalist minority should be combined with a political system which apparently gives sovereign powers to the numerical majority and their elected spokesmen. Does this mean that democratic forms of rule are merely a sham and that all capitalist states – whether democratic in form or not – function to maintain the 'dictatorship of the bourgeoisie'? Or does it mean that the economically exploited and politically oppressed majority have yet to recognize the need for social as well as political emancipation and that a democratic road to socialism must therefore await the development of such a revolutionary consciousness? Or does it mean, as liberals and conservatives might well argue, that the paradox is false? Perhaps the very fact that an allegedly exploiting class is prepared to concede political power to the people as a whole indicates that capitalist societies are not really exploitative and oppressive. Perhaps they combine the sovereignty of the consumer in the market-place with the sovereignty of the citizen in the political system so that freedom and equality can be found in both the private and the public life of the community. Is it not true that the modern State is the first to allow the entire adult population to share in the exercise of political power rather than restricting this right to a minority? Might it not be the case that capitalism is a precondition of political freedom and that any attempt by socialists to abolish the free enterprise system could also lead to the abolition of democratic government? Perhaps the road to serfdom does indeed lie in the direction of creeping socialism and perhaps freedom has survived because the people have so far resisted the siren call to cast their votes for socialist revolution.

In the following pages we shall consider how a socialist might respond to such arguments. We begin with a slightly more detailed account of the case that liberals and conservatives (whatever their actual party allegiance) might present in defence of the claim that the modern, democratic State is the vehicle through which the national interest and popular government are reconciled. This requires us to look at four strands of argument: that the modern State is uniquely democratic in form, that the modern State is also uniquely responsive to popular demands and interests, that the modern State operates to maintain the public interest at home and abroad, and that the problems and limitations of the modern State can be solved through gradual reforms and a greater sense of realism. We then present four lines of counter-attack which are addressed directly at these arguments to reveal their limitations and show how a socialist analysis can provide a much better account of the capitalist State. Finally we shall offer some brief remarks on the most suitable approach to a democratic, socialist transformation of the modern State.

THE NON-SOCIALIST DEFENCE OF THE DEMOCRATIC STATE

The democratic form of the modern State

Liberals and conservatives would be quick to stress that the leading capitalist societies are almost all characterized by a constitutional and democratic form of government. They have a constitutional system based on the rule of law and the law itself stems from a legislature and/or executive that is accountable to the will of the people as expressed through elections and other forms of political participation. There is no legal monopoly of power in the hands of the economically dominant class and the democratic rights of the citizen are guaranteed to all members of society. Moreover, however powerful such bodies as the British Cabinet or the US Presidency may have become, their powers still derive from the authority of the people and their occupants must face re-election at regular intervals on the basis of past performance. In the short term they are also subject to control by the elected representatives of the people in legislative assemblies and must win the cooperation of affected interests when formulating and implementing policies. In addition every citizen has the right of peaceful protest against government actions and enjoys the protection of the judicial system in the exercise of his/her liberties. In these and other ways the system of government in the advanced capitalist societies ensures that the State is an impartial instrument of popular (or, at least, popularly accountable) rule.

The bases of State power

Liberals and conservatives would also take pleasure in telling us that politics in these societies is not organized along class lines in the way that socialists often suggest. They would surely point out that political action is not structured in terms of a polarized class struggle involving two monolithic, cohesive, mutually antagonistic class forces. Not only is there no civil war between two hostile, armed camps locked in class struggle but it is also clear that elections cannot be seen as the peaceful expression of such a struggle. Instead of an open war (whether violent or peaceful) between bourgeoisie and proletariat, it would be argued, there are innumerable political forces organized along various lines and promoting diverse interests. Some of these may well be economic in character but others are equally assuredly non-economic. Indeed liberals and conservatives would be keen to point out that the cleavages around which modern party systems are organized are just as likely to be religious, linguistic, regional, ecological, agrarian-industrial, or nationalist as they are to be rooted in the alleged opposition between capital and labour. It is just as common to find workers and employers on the same side of a political conflict as on opposed sides and there are many key issues where this supposedly fundamental antagonism is quite irrelevant. Attempts to polarize politics around such an alleged antagonism have always failed and will continue to do so because they do not correspond to the real world. Liberals and conservatives attach great significance to the fact that no party committed to the total overthrow of capitalism (whether communist or socialist in identity) has ever received an electoral mandate from a clear majority. They would argue that such divisive, extremist politics cannot succeed in a democratic system and it is only those socialist parties committed to a national, moderate programme that have won office. From this they would conclude that there is a basic consensus in modern societies on the need to sustain economic and political freedom and that the electorate will only support parties – whether of the Right, Left, or Centre – which share this basic outlook.

In opposition to the thesis that politics is (or should be) rooted in a fundamental, dichotomous, irreconcilable antagonism between labour and capital, liberals and conservatives advance the claim that politics is essentially diverse, pluralistic, negotiable in nature and therefore cuts across social classes as well as other social groupings. In a complex, highly differentiated society, they would argue, power is necessarily dispersed among many groups, institutions, and organizations. In such a society there can be no single elite or dominant group – whether based on some exclusive economic prerogatives or on a monopoly of political control. Instead there will be many powerful groups, each with restricted areas of influence and each based on different power resources. Moreover, whilst inequalities may perhaps exist in the distribution of certain power resources, these are not cumulative but cancel each other out. Thus workers have the strike weapon and the vote to counter any abuse of the managerial prerogatives and financial muscle of the capitalist; and, if workers and employers act in collusion to exploit a temporary monopoly position, they can be countered through consumer boycotts and government action. The political system is just as open to checks and balances of this kind as the economic system. In addition to party conflicts and pressure group struggles based on the most varied and heterogeneous issues, significant roles are played by civil servants, the electorate, international organizations, and so forth. Likewise, in so far as the economic and political systems are institutionally and organizationally distinct, their activities must be coordinated where necessary through a complex and pluralistic system of bargaining among the representatives of various economic and political interests. Add to this the complications introduced through extra-economic issues such as language, gender, race, religion, disarmament, and sport, and it soon becomes apparent why liberals and conservatives will deny that politics can be reduced to a simple opposition between bourgeoisie and proletariat. There is no singular pyramid of economic and political power with capital at its apex and workers at its base. Instead there is a dispersal of powerful individuals and groups throughout society and, in so far as this heterogeneous system of checks and balances is subject to any unified control, it is a control established through the political system and accountable to the people through the ballot box.

The purpose and role of government

In this context liberals and conservatives would also argue that the State is not an instrument of class rule but serves instead to maintain the public interest in domestic affairs and to promote the national interest in international matters. These twin interests are not at all identical with those of any given section of society and it is frequently necessary for the State to act against the interests of capitalists as well as those of workers. The State must 'hold the ring', mediate among competing interests, and represent the public and national interest in opposition to sectional interests. This holds not only for the alleged conflict between capital and labour (which is really, according to liberals and conservatives, a whole series of conflicts with cross-cutting constituencies) but also for regional, linguistic, sexual, racial, urban, cultural, and all other conflicts. A wide range of policies can be cited to show that the State does not act to favour the interests of capital to the exclusion of the workers (or vice versa): instead the State acts in the public interest against all sectional interests. If it systematically advanced the interests of one particular section of society at the expense of the rest, it would lose support at elections either directly or through popular reaction to the resulting social unrest. On some occasions the State will appear to favour a given sectional interest because this happens to coincide with the public or national interest; on other occasions this interest will be disadvantaged and a different sectional interest will seem privileged for the same reason. Liberals and conservatives will therefore insist that specific instances of short-term disadvantage cannot be cited in a one-sided manner as evidence for a systematic, long-term bias in the activities of the State. For a democratic State is ultimately accountable to the people as a whole and not to any sectional interest.

Problems with the State

If all this sounds too good to be true, liberals and conservatives would certainly agree that the State is not really perfect. But they would also argue that its failings cannot be attributed to the rule of capital as if capitalism itself were the source of all political evil.

Instead the problems of the State are seen as flowing from inadequacies in the system of democratic accountability and/or the pressures arising from unrealistic popular expectations. Sometimes the State does seem too partial to certain sectional interests even in the long term because the latter have managed to entrench themselves in particular positions of influence. But this can apply as much to the influence of trade unions or other supposedly exploited groups as it does to particular financial and managerial interests. Liberals and conservatives argue that where this happens it is the whole society that suffers and the solution lies in extending the scope of democratic accountability. For, if the State is captured by particular interests and/or if different ministries or branches promote sectional demands at the expense of the public or national interest, the State will lose its ability to manage economic and social affairs in a relatively unified manner and to secure the conditions necessary for economic stability and social cohesion. This can be seen in the way that the penchant for clientilism and patronage in Italian politics has weakened the State's ability to act in the overall interests of capital (let alone labour) in economic and social matters. Similarly the dominance of metropolitan interests in the political process at Whitehall and Westminster has aggravated the economic and social decay of less well represented areas and prompted the response of Scottish and Welsh nationalism as well as the political disenchantment of declining English regions. The problems of sectionalism are often aggravated by excessive expectations among the electorate about the capacities of government in a complex world. This can lead to an over-extended State and overloaded government. The solution proposed by liberals and conservatives to such problems involves limiting the scope of government and educating the electorate in the facts of life. They would certainly argue that problems of overload cannot be solved through further extending the role of the State. The greater the degree of State intervention, the greater the dangers of bureaucratic despotism or simple mismanagement. In short, according to liberals and conservatives, even if there are problems with the State in capitalist societies, they are not rooted in capitalism or class relations. They have political roots requiring political action – greater popular accountability to combat sectionalism, greater popular understanding of the limits of good government to counter the dangers of overload and the anti-democratic backlash of frustrated expectations. Thus liberals and conservatives would conclude that any attempt to resolve problems of insufficient political freedom through abolishing economic freedom and imposing State control over everything is a recipe for serfdom rather than the Utopia of socialist democracy.

A SOCIALIST CRITIQUE OF CAPITALIST DEMOCRACY

The form of the State

How would a socialist respond to such arguments? Let us begin with the claim that the modern State is uniquely democratic and can only survive in association with the free market. It is certainly true that the State in capitalist societies has a distinctive form that sets it apart from pre-capitalist states. There is no legal monopoly of political power in the hands of the economically dominant class and, at least in the last half century or so, opportunities for political participation have been extended to the people as a whole in most advanced capitalist societies. But this does not necessarily mean that the modern State is impartial in its effects on class relations: perhaps it only means that the manner in which it secures the political rule of capital over other classes is different from the ways in which States in pre-capitalist societies secured the political domination of their exploiting class or classes. To investigate this possibility we should examine the actual historical development of bourgeois democracies and consider their role in securing some of the conditions necessary for capitalism.

We should first concede that the arguments surveyed above do gain at least some support from the history of democratic government. It is certainly true that freely elected representative government based upon universal adult suffrage nowhere preceded capitalism and that all major advanced capitalist societies do currently have such a political system. Even so it should be emphasized that democratic forms generally had to wait until the present century before they were fully established and that capitalism managed for generations with authoritarian government, a restricted, property-based franchise, and severely limited political rights and liberties. During the transition from feudalism the State could not be democratic since it needed to use force to establish the conditions in which a free market economy based on wage-slavery could be made to work (e.g. through the dispossession of peasants from their land and the creation of a reserve of industrial labour). Even during the supposed hey-day of competitive, *laissez-faire* capitalism all that was necessary in political terms was a constitutional State that could secure the monetary, legal, and administrative framework for the operation of free market forces. This does not mean that the government had to be democratic in form nor even that the State's relations to its subjects in political (as opposed to private, economic) terms had to be regulated through the rule of law. Indeed it would have been dangerous to extend full citizenship rights to the working class as long as profits hinged on the extension of the working day and the intensification of labour (as opposed to technological and other means of improving productivity from which both worker and capitalist could gain increased earnings) and as long as there was only limited room for material concessions to win working-class support in the electoral process. In short, although capitalist societies may have democratic forms of government, there is no economic necessity for this and democratic government can sometimes threaten the survival of capitalism.

Nonetheless it could be argued that capitalism makes it possible for democratic government to develop for at least two reasons. Firstly, in economic terms, capitalist exploitation during production occurs only after a formally free and equal exchange has occurred between workers and employers in the labour market. This implies that the employers have no immediate need to monopolize political power to force the working class to labour for them – provided only that workers accept the legitimacy and/or inevitability of free market forces. This represents a major contrast between capitalist and pre-capitalist class-based societies and is a significant factor in differentiating their respective forms of State. Secondly, in political terms, capitalism needs some form of *Rechtsstaat* (constitutional State based on the rule of law) standing outside and above the clash of competing economic interests and able to secure the various conditions in which market forces can operate. This means that, even though the State in capitalist societies need not be directly involved in economic exploitation and can assume the form of an impartial, constitutional State, it is still indirectly implicated in the process of exploitation in so far as it maintains the conditions in which market forces can secure the economic domination of capital. At the same time the existence of such a constitutional system of government does prepare the ground for the extension of formal freedom and equality to the public sphere through the struggle for citizenship rights and democratic accountability.

The development of democratic government in this context was certainly far from a slow, peaceful, continuous process without ruptures or reversals. It emerged unevenly and haltingly at different rates in different countries in response to a wide range of pressures and in many respects it is still incomplete. In some cases more or less peaceful mobilization by internal political forces was sufficient to bring about the piecemeal extension of formal democratic government; in other cases it was imposed at the command of foreign powers in the aftermath of military defeat.[2] But the real question at issue is not the historical, contingent association between capitalism and democratic forms of rule (which socialists would not want to deny): it is the extent to which these forms of rule have any real democratic content and do not simply serve as a cloak for the economic and political domination of capital.

In practice democratic rights are often eroded by a number of very serious obstacles resulting from deliberate political action and/or the unintended effects of particular institutional arrangements. Among the former we could mention deliberate attempts to rig the outcome of the electoral process through gerrymandering constituency boundaries, adopting voting systems that favour established parties over new ones, providing State support to some parties rather than others, proscribing radical parties, using the powers of economic management to create short-term economic conditions favourable to parties in office, the use of news management techniques to influence public opinion, the resort to various 'dirty tricks' to discredit and disorganize opposing parties (as revealed, for example, in the 'Watergate' episodes), and so forth. Moreover, even where such deliberate barriers to formal democracy are minimized in the electoral process, similar barriers may be erected to prevent elected representatives controlling the exercise of State power. This is most evident in the insulation of key parts of the governmental system from effective control through legislative assemblies and/or popular consultative bodies with real teeth. Here we could mention the forces concerned with law and order (police, secret services, military) and the departments concerned with essential economic functions (central bank, exchequer, economic management, energy, nationalized industries, etc.) as well as other ministries and/or quasi-non-government organizations (or 'quangos') concerned with a host of crucial social issues (education, broadcasting, race relations, sexual equality, the press, health care, etc.). In addition we should note the self-denying ordinance of governments in relation to major areas of economic conduct in the private sector (such as investment decisions, pricing policies, foreign trade, and, in many cases, wage negotiations); and in relation to other 'private' activities where appropriate values and institutions and/or self restraint and mutual aid are insufficiently developed to prevent individual or collective self-indulgence from producing excessive social costs (e.g. the balance between private and public transport, the patriarchal bias of the mass media, racial discrimination, and alcoholism). In short, not only must we ask questions about the breadth of the electorate, the equality of votes, the real freedom of electoral choice, and so forth, we must also examine how far elected assemblies actually control the political executive and administration and consider what powers lie beyond the scope of legitimate government intervention and democratic accountability.

But committed socialists should not stop here. Formal democracy is also subject to significant structural constraints which hinder its effective operation as a vehicle of popular control. Such constraints can be loosely divided into three main groups. Firstly, there are real obstacles to effective political participation owing to the unequal distribution of individual resources (e.g. education, money, leisure, political contacts) and the uneven incidence of opportunities for collective action (e.g. the relative social isolation of housewives, the long-term unemployed, the chronically sick, rural communities, small businessmen, etc.). Secondly, there are various factors that serve to limit the political agenda and define certain issues as lying beyond the scope of government action. In this context the role of the mass media and the major political parties is especially important and entails major problems for socialists and others outside the mainstream in placing 'private' and/or taken for granted issues on the political agenda. In recent years this has been apparent in the controversial and hard-fought battles to politicize questions of women's liberation, industrial democracy, sporting contacts, gay rights, private medicine, intermediate technology, the use of the 'sus' law in policing ethnic communities, and so forth. Thirdly, it is essential to recognize the crucial structural constraints involved in the institutional separation between the economic and the political in capitalist societies. This separation is a double-edged sword in the development of democratic politics. For, whilst the dominance of exchange relations and market forces in economic organization means that the State need not be directly controlled by capital to ensure its continuing economic domination over wage labour, the general exclusion of the State from private economic activities means that it is continually forced to react to economic events rather than control them and must ensure the continuing smooth operation of market forces as a precondition of its own survival. In this way capital retains significant *indirect* control over the State through the latter's dependence on the continued health of the economy.

This third set of constraints is particularly important in imparting a capitalist character to the democratic form of State. For most of the other factors cited so far involve at most systematic deviations from real democratic control without ensuring that it is capital itself that takes the place of the people in controlling the political system. This criticism can also be levelled against the socialist argument that economic and political elites are drawn largely from the same social and educational backgrounds and that political leaders often have vested interests in capitalist activities through shareholdings, directorships, etc. But this argument at most helps to explain the channels through which policies favourable to capital might be developed and cannot show that politicians will pursue the general interests of capital rather than their own personal economic interests in particular enterprises or sectors. Indeed it could even be the case that politicians and public officials without close personal, financial, or organizational links to particular capitalist interests would be better placed to promote the global, hegemonic interests of capital. Nor should we neglect the role of formal democratic politics (even if this falls short of real popular control) in constraining the more obviously self-oriented activities of political leaders from any social background. It is for these reasons above all that we must pay particular attention to the implications of the separation between economics and politics for the capitalist State.

This separation entails a specific relation between the capitalist State and the capitalist economy. Firstly, political power is debarred from organizing production according to its own criteria – property is private and the basic core of productive activities remains outside any effective political control. Secondly, in so far as the State depends on tax revenues or other forms of surplus extraction for its resources, its capacities are indirectly determined through the rate and volume of private productivity and profitability. In particular this means that the 'governing groups' in charge of the political system (politicians and officials) have a vested interest in securing capital accumulation as a precondition of their own survival as people who live off (and not just for) politics. Fourthly, in so far as the State is democratic in form, however, these 'governing groups' cannot retain power unless they win sufficient votes at the ballot box. This means that they must try to reconcile the requirements of capital accumulation and the demands of the electorate. This involves a specific form of politics through which the needs of capital can be presented as the interests of all the people and it requires a certain degree of self-restraint on the part of particular capitalist interests as well as a flow of concessions to maintain the support of other interests. There is a delicate balance between the needs of accumulation and the needs of popular support and any imbalance will show itself in economic crises and/or social unrest. In this context there can be no guarantees that capital will eventually win out but the structural constraints considered above certainly work to its advantage in influencing the balance of political forces.

The effects of this separation are reinforced through the growing internationalization of the capitalist economic system. For this means that many important factors determining domestic economic performance lie outside the control of the individual nation-state and must be taken as basic parameters of economic intervention and social welfare policies. This is reflected above all in the need for governments to maintain international and domestic confidence in the business environment and the prospects for profitable investment. In the period of the gold and gold-dollar exchange standards and fixed exchange rates this constraint was especially strongly linked with changes in the balance of payments and was policed through the dominant world financial powers (initially Britain, then the USA) and/or through international capitalist bodies such as the IMF and World Bank. With the growing internationalization of production through the multinational corporation this constraint is further reinforced in two distinct directions. The growing international mobility of capital increases pressures on the State to maintain conditions favourable to investment or face the consequences of capital flight; and it also enables the multinationals to avoid many political constraints and controls at the expense of immobile, home-based capital and wage-labour. This is not to suggest that home-based capital and labour are powerless in the face of government but merely to record the differential enjoyed by international capital. For this puts the burden of adjustment in the face of economic crises on the least mobile and most vulnerable sectors.

So far we have considered only the form of the State in capitalist societies and the constraints under which it operates. Even here we may have conceded too much to the liberals and conservatives by restricting our arguments to more or less democratic political systems and by ignoring those fascist, military, and other authoritarian regimes which resort to open war against the organizations and representatives of the working class and other subordinate groups in order to maintain the economic and political domination of capital. In addition we have ignored the extent to which formally democratic States circumscribe the rule of law and infringe their own legality for 'reasons of State' related to the narrow self-interest of politicians, officials, and State clients and/or to the broader pursuit of the interests of capital (e.g. the role of official secrecy as a cloak for government mistakes and delinquencies, illegal telephone tapping and mail interception, the use of torture and assassination, government connivance in the breaking of Rhodesian oil sanctions, and so on). But even working under this admittedly self-imposed restriction we have already developed some powerful replies to the liberal and conservative claim that the modern democratic State is an impartial and neutral instrument of popular rule. In particular we have argued that democratic government is largely formal in nature and that there are serious gaps and deficits in the social and economic conditions necessary for an effective exercise of democratic rights; that the scope of formal democratic control is severely limited so that crucial areas of State activity itself as well as the productive core of the capitalist economy lie beyond effective popular control; and that the separation between the economic and political under capitalism puts severe constraints on the State's ability to act against the interests of capital. But our critics might well reply that the imperfection and distortions in the system of formal democracy could be eliminated if sufficient pressure was applied and that any State is bound to be constrained by the economic environment in which it is located. They might also argue that there is still a sufficient degree of democracy for the people to change the economic environment itself if they really wanted. In response to these claims socialists should not only repeat the above-mentioned criticisms in greater detail but should also move beyond questions of form and external constraints to consider the basic dynamics of the political process itself. This must be our next task.

The bases of State power

Capitalism has quite specific effects on political life. For it defines all economic agents as formally free and equal in the market-place regardless of their class position and further fragments and isolates them through the effects of competition within as well as across classes. The same sort of individualism and fragmentation is also found in social and political life and all sorts of relations are treated as sites for the pursuit of competitive advantage. Capitalism also denies a formal monopoly of political power to the economically dominant class and provides the basis for the development of formal democratic government and the rule of law. Together these features form the foundation for a quite distinctive form of politics: the politics of *hegemony*. Hegemony involves political, intellectual, and moral leadership rather than the forcible imposition of the interests of the dominant class on dominated classes. Such leadership is exercised through the development of a national-popular project which specifies a set of policies or goals as being 'in the national interest' – policies or goals which actually serve the long-term interests of capital at the same time as they advance certain short-term, narrow economic and social interests and demands of subordinate groups. Hegemonic leadership requires systematic consideration of the demands and interests of various individuals and social groups, compromise on secondary issues to maintain support and alliances, and the continuing mobilization of support behind the national-popular project. It should also be emphasized that hegemony involves leadership and not merely the mechanical reproduction of mass demands and in this sense it requires a dual strategy. Firstly it requires an approach that progressively polarizes political forces around the hegemonic project through an educative process as well as straightforward material concessions. But it also requires an approach that progressively neutralizes or eliminates counter-hegemonic forces as well as using force against any openly violent oppositional groups. This educative process involves developing and maintaining a collective will, a 'national–popular' outlook, a common world view and shared definitions of common sense, which are adequate to the needs of social and economic reproduction. Many different institutions, organizations, and agencies are involved in the struggle for hegemony; and hegemony in turn involves (indeed, requires) the pluralization of social forces rather than their polarization around a basic class cleavage. In this sense the socialist would not dispute the basic description of bourgeois democratic politics as pluralist in nature and, indeed, would argue that such a pluralization is a basic precondition for the effective operation of such democratic politics. But, in contrast to liberals and conservatives who are happy to accept this pluralism at face value, the socialist will attempt to explain its historical roots in the development of the capitalist system as well as its functions in securing political class domination.

Liberals and conservatives correctly identify the wide range of issues and social cleavages that form the basis of political action and are also right to note that political parties frequently have non-class bases of electoral support. But they do not consider how this obvious pluralism is related to the long-term political interests of capital. For democratic politics is not just a question of securing an electoral majority in the context of 'one man–one vote–one value' but also raises the question of formulating policies that will prove realistic in terms of the overall balance of forces and structural constraints confronting a party or coalition in office. It must be emphasized here that power is not parcelled out in equivalent lots to each and every citizen along with the vote but depends instead on the differential strategic location of particular individuals and social forces in an ever-changing national and international economic, political, and ideological conjuncture. Thus the politics of electoral mobilization must be practised within the limits imposed by the overall balance of forces and structural constraints. For politicians and parties that go beyond these limits will either be electorally unpopular (because their policies and programmes will seem sectional, extreme, or unrealistic) and/or will be obliged to undertake U-turns and embrace the current orthodoxies should they secure election. This applies to all parties that choose to stand outside the prevailing consensus or notion of 'common sense' as it exists and changes from time to time. Thus, whilst there are certainly political parties with regional, religious, national, ethnic, linguistic, and other bases of electoral support, they must either temper their representative role in the light of the above-mentioned constraints or accept a marginal role in the formulation of government policies and the long-term exercise of political power.

In this context it is important to note again that the democratic process depends on a flow of material concessions which come ultimately from the accumulation process. This has two significant implications – governments cannot afford to disrupt the accumulation process in the economy in the long-term without losing the resources to win political support and, secondly, as the nature of the accumulation process changes, there must be a succession of hegemonic projects seeking to adapt national-popular objectives to changing reproduction requirements. This can be seen in the transition from *liberal social imperialism* in the era of late nineteenth-century imperialism to the *Keynesian–welfare state project* associated with problems of demand management and social reproduction in the immediate postwar period and, most recently, to attempts to implement *corporatist* and/or *monetarist strategies* to promote industrial restructuring and supply-side economics and to cut the allegedly parasitic burden of welfare payments and bureaucracy. Where the prevailing ideas of 'common sense' become inadequate to the needs of capital, crises of hegemony occur and there is a struggle to redefine or replace the world view which establishes the framework for political struggles among moderate forces. This consensus typically encompasses all major parties (either wholly or through one of their party wings) and it thereby defines the 'centre' ground of politics. This can be seen in the era of 'Butskellism' in the 1950s in Britain (a contemporary concept coined to highlight the convergence between the 'One Nation' policies of Tories such as Rab Butler and the social democratic reformism of the Gaitskellites in the Labour Party) and in the continuing flirtation of social democrats and 'right–progressive' Conservatives with corporatist economic and social engineering in the 1960s and 1970s. With the emerging crisis of the Keynesian–welfare state project, however, the two parties have diverged in their efforts to establish a new hegemonic project. The Thatcherite experiment is proving increasingly unrealistic and is already subject to significant U-turns and even greater pressure to return to the middle ground. It remains to be seen whether Labour's 'alternative economic strategy' is any more viable.

The problems involved in the pluralist character of democratic politics in capitalist societies can be illustrated from the history of social democratic parties. Radical workers' parties, as Adam Przeworski notes, face three strategic choices when engaged in political struggles on the terrain of democratic capitalist societies. Each must choose

(1) whether to seek the advancement of socialism through the political institutions of the capitalist society or to confront the bourgeoisie directly, without any mediation; (2) whether to seek the agent of socialist transformation exclusively in the working class or to rely on multi- and even supra-class support; and (3) whether to seek improvements, reforms, within the confines of capitalism or to dedicate all its efforts and energies to its complete transformation.[3]

Historically social democrats have chosen to participate, to seek supra-class alliances, and to struggle for reforms. Yet this creates a series of double-bind or 'Catch-22' situations for such parties.

Firstly, participation in democratic politics makes it increasingly difficult to pursue insurrectionary strategies or tactics or even to combine economic and political action to put pressure on a duly elected government. At the same time it leads to the embourgeoisement and bureaucratization of the social democratic party and the withering away of mass participation and internal democratic decision-making. In the second place social democratic parties found themselves trapped in an inexorable electoral logic: the proletariat proper remained a numerical minority in a political system which defined majority rule as the key to political power. The social democrats were forced to choose either to maintain their class purity as a vehicle of working-class representation or to aim for political power through seeking electoral support beyond the working class and thus developing into a 'people's party' or *Volkspartei*. Yet the very act of broadening their appeal to the masses, the 'people', 'consumers', 'taxpayers', or simply 'citizens' necessarily weakens the general salience of class as a determinant of the political behaviour of individuals and thereby undermines the initial class basis of support for the social democrats. The party must now appeal to workers in terms of interests and concerns they share with other individuals in other classes and not in terms of issues specific to the *sui generis* collective position of the proletariat in contradistinction to other classes. Yet this in turn opens the path to other parties to appeal to workers as individuals, consumers, taxpayers, masses, people, etc., and thereby reinforces the classless image of bourgeois democratic politics. And, in the third place, once committed to a broad-based populist politics and abandoning an alternative economic strategy premised on the abolition of capitalism, the social democrats are obliged to develop feasible programmes that combine wide electoral appeal with capitalist rationality. They must accept the logic of private capital and the separation of the economic and the political – with all that this entails for the management of capitalist economies. The very capacity of social democrats to mitigate the social effects of market forces and to regulate the capitalist economic system depends paradoxically on their ability to protect the profits of private capital in an increasingly international economy. In short the combined logics of parliamentarism and market forces dictate that social democrats commit themselves to maintaining bourgeois hegemony.[4]

Thus there is no need for socialists to deny the claim that politics in capitalist societies is pluralist in character. This has quite specific roots in capitalist social relations and provides the basis of the distinctive form of capitalist politics. But this conclusion does not mean that socialists are therefore opposed to pluralism. Rather we are committed to developing a counter-hegemonic project which will progressively polarize the majority of these pluralist forces around support for socialist democracy and progressively neutralize support for capitalist hegemonic projects. It is not pluralism as such that is to blame for the failure of social democracy to abolish capitalism but the failure to develop a long-term socialist strategy adapted to political struggle in societies radically different from Tsarist Russia. In this context it is essential for socialists to take full note of the different problems confronting revolutionaries in 1917 and those facing socialists in the West today.

The role of the State

It cannot be denied that the State acts against particular capitalist interests as well as against the interests of particular groups of workers or, indeed, other sectional interests. But this is not really surprising and does not prove the impartiality of the State. For the interests of capital in general are by no means identical with those of particular capitalists. One cannot simply add up all the diverse and conflicting claims of particular capitalist interests, satisfy them all equally (even supposing that they might not be contradictory), and thus secure the interests of capital as a whole. In this sense the mobilization of capitalist support behind an appropriate hegemonic project can be seen to be just as important as the mobilization of support from subordinate classes and groups. For an effective hegemonic project defines the political and ideological framework within which conflicts between particular interests and the so-called 'general interest' are fought out and it thereby legitimates the sacrifices of short-term interests needed to secure the long-term interests of capital. It cannot be stressed too often that the role of the State is not to promote the narrow, economic interests of particular capitals but to secure the social conditions in which market forces can operate to maximize capital accumulation in the long-term. This is not to deny that the modern State goes well beyond the provision of the monetary, legal, and administrative framework for capital accumulation and is now directly involved in all manner of economic activities. For, in so far as market forces fail (or are expected to fail) to secure the technical, economic, and social conditions necessary for profitable investment and acceptable levels of employment, the State is subjected to various pressures to compensate for these failures either through subsidies to the private sector and/or through nationalization and related forms of direct State involvement in economic production and social welfare. Here it should be emphasized that the State intervenes not so much in response to actual or anticipated market failures as to their repercussions in the political arena. In this context the structural biases built into the capitalist State make it more open to pressures for the restoration of conditions favourable to capital than to pressures for a transition to socialism. This structural asymmetry is reinforced to the extent that such pro-capitalist measures can be linked to the national–popular goals defined in the prevailing 'hegemonic project'. In other words, the State is a political force concerned with the collective interests of capital rather than an economic agent devoted to short-term profit and its role (even in the case of State intervention in directly economic matters) is one of *political* management rather than the narrow-minded, short-sighted pursuit of mere economic interest. It is this fact that lends so much credence to the liberal and conservative claim that the State represents the 'public interest' or 'national interest'.

Two difficulties occur in socialist arguments here. We cannot give any cast-iron 'guarantees' that the State will invariably pursue the long-term interests of capital. For the very separation of the economic and political and their organization according to quite different rules and procedures means that *it is always problematic for capital how far political action will promote rather than undermine accumulation*. State intervention depends upon political struggles and economic constraints whose overall effects are contingent. Although there is a certain bias built into the structure of the governmental system and there are important economic constraints on political action, the final outcome of State intervention depends on the complex interplay between institutional forms and the changing balance of forces mobilized in support for and resistance to the actions of the State. There is a certain openness in the form of the capitalist State which is only resolved through actual political struggles. Moreover the long-term interests of capital cannot be treated as harmonious and non-contradictory (e.g. there is a frequently remarked contradiction between the requirements of accumulation and those of legitimation) and, since different courses of accumulation are possible (e.g. under the dominance of banking capital in Britain or industrial capital in Japan), they are not necessarily unambiguous. In many cases the long-term interests of capital appear only *post hoc* through the emergence of economic, political, or ideological crises to which the State must then respond as quickly and appropriately as possible. Indeed, given the importance of crises as a basic steering mechanism of State intervention and the frequently 'trial-and-error' nature of attempts to strike the right balance in promoting the long-run interests of capital, it is particularly important for socialists to avoid simple-minded conspiracy theories and recognize the complexities of political action.

Secondly, given this inherent *indeterminacy* or openness, it would be wrong for socialists to insist that the modern State is *essentially* bourgeois. This would defuse the case for political struggle within the present form of State and imply that democratic rights and liberties have no value (an error notorious in the analyses of the Comintern during the rise of fascism). We cannot assume that the State in capitalist societies will always act in the interests of capital and we must therefore attempt to shift the balance of forces within the State itself as well as outside it in order to produce policies favourable to the advancement of our own hegemonic project. Otherwise we run the risk of oppositionalism – the defence of immediate, short-term, particularistic interests and an emphasis on resistance at the cost of a general, long-run, socialist strategy. We shall return to this issue in our closing remarks.

Problems with the State

Socialists recognize that not all problems and contradictions are reducible to class exploitation. They are committed to the abolition of capitalism through the extension of democratic control over the economic system and see this as inseparably tied to the extension of democracy in the political region and civil society more generally. The struggle for democracy is not identical with the struggle against capitalism and, if socialists are to win hegemony, they must link the struggle for socialism with the struggle to extend democracy in other spheres. Here we have a particular duty to extend democracy against its enemies on the Left as well as the Right. This is not the place to consider the awful spectre of Stalinism which continues to haunt democratic socialists; but we must note that democracy is also under attack in the so-called 'Free World'. In addition to the appalling record of the advanced capitalist powers in the field of human rights in the less developed capitalist societies and their support for military dictatorships and political repression abroad[5], we must also draw attention to the increasing atrophy of parliamentary institutions and civil liberties in the advanced capitalist states themselves together with a growing ideological antipathy to democracy. In this respect socialists ought to confront the liberals and conservatives head on and ask them to justify the gradual destruction of the democratic system they seek to defend.

The changes that can currently be observed have been well portrayed by Nicos Poulantzas in his recent work on *State, Power, Socialism*. Thus he notes the rise of 'authoritarian statism' in the advanced capitalist societies and describes its main features as follows: firstly, a transfer of power from the legislature to the executive and the concentration of power within the latter; secondly, an accelerated fusion between the three branches of the State – legislature, executive, and judiciary – accompanied by a decline in the rule of law; thirdly, the decline of political parties as the principle vehicles of political representation and the leading forces in the organization of hegemony; fourthly, the growth of a complex of networks cross-cutting the formal organization of the State and exercising a decisive share in its activities without proper accountability and publicity (e.g. the role of the Cabinet Office network in Britain); fifthly, the continued expansion of the forces of 'law and order' and their increasing involvement in pre-emptive policing and surveillance rather than the punishment of clearly defined crimes.[6] Such changes occur in response to the dramatic growth and increasing centrality of State intervention in the economy itself (as opposed to more traditional political functions such as maintaining law and order and defending the territorial integrity of the nation-state). But they are also reinforced through the growing difficulties capital finds in securing its hegemony through the operation of the parliamentary system and political parties. For not only does the capitalist solution to economic crisis require serious hardship and sacrifice for the bulk of the population but these are also times of growing politicization of popular, non-class forces.

These difficulties are reflected on the ideological level in increasing concern among liberals and conservatives with the functioning (or malfunctioning) of democratic government. There is concern about overloaded government (to be resolved through government withdrawal from key areas of economic, social, and intellectual activity) and about the threats to capital accumulation posed by radical left-wing parties (to be resolved through restricting the powers of elected assemblies and transferring crucial functions to independent and/or technocratic bodies that can be insulated from popular control). This growing concern is almost certainly linked to the rise of the interventionist State in place of the liberal constitutional State. For, whereas the minimal State or 'nightwatchman' State could secure the general external conditions for capital accumulation merely through maintaining the monetary, legal, and administrative framework for competitive capitalism and thereby free the capitalist class to concentrate on industrial management and opportunities for profit in the market, State intervention is now so important for the expansion of capitalism that politics has become too serious a business to be left to politicians and the vagaries of public opinion. Thus the indirect, external constraints on democratic politics are reinforced through direct involvement in policy-making and implementation for a new breed of industrial statesmen and/or the deliberate insulation of vital economic ministries and boards from parliamentary (let alone effective popular) control. But this has its own dangers for capital in so far as economic management cannot be separated from political management. This is evident in the problems of growing particularism and short-sighted clientilism in State intervention at the expense of the long-term general interests of capital as well as in the growing diversion of working-class and popular protest into extra-parliamentary channels. In turn this is likely to lead to a 'two nations' politics at the expense of the 'one nation' approach supported by liberals and conservatives. In short, if we consider the current developments in the form and functions of the modern State, there is a growing divergence between democratic ideals and actual practice.

CONCLUDING REMARKS

An adequate view of the State is crucial for socialists engaged in the struggle to transform social relations. There are important elements of truth in the liberal and conservative view of the democratic form of the modern State and the pluralistic nature of bourgeois politics and it would be foolish to reject this view out of hand. Instead we must try to develop an alternative account that integrates any elements of truth at the same time as it avoids the overall limitations of this perspective. Thus socialists must explain why the democratic form of government is possible under capitalism (without being necessary to and/or entailed in capitalism) and must also show why such democratic government is limited in form and in practice by the existence of capitalism. In particular we should emphasize that the formal freedoms and rights essential for an effective system of popular control are insufficiently developed and are further weakened by the lack of social and economic conditions which would enable the majority of citizens to make good use of these freedoms and rights. We should emphasize that the actual scope of democratic control is extremely limited (with crucial areas of economic, political, and social life escaping even formal accountability) and that even this limited scope is currently under attack. We should emphasize how the freedom of manoeuvre available to the State is constrained by the separation between the economic and political regions and the ultimate dependence of the State on the continued profitability of the capitalist economy. At the same time we should note that the process of economic management is also a political process and that the pluralistic nature of bourgeois societies means that capital cannot simply impose its interests on other classes or groups in a forcible manner. Instead we find a distinctive form of politics: the politics of hegemony. It is on this terrain that socialists themselves must engage in political action without getting trapped in the contradictions encountered hitherto by social democracy. This requires a three-fold political strategy oriented to the long-term conquest of political, intellectual, and moral leadership. Socialists must 1. work within the existing system to reveal its limitations while winning such short-term concessions as may be possible, 2. develop an alternative hegemonic project that links short-term sectional interests to the pursuit of a democratic, socialist system and justifies necessary short-term sacrifices in terms of the strategic goal, and 3. seek to transform the separation between the economic and the political through the introduction of a coordinated system of industrial self-government and democratic economic planning and to reorganize the State itself through the extension of democratic accountability. This three-fold strategy requires socialists to work at a distance from the State, within the State, and against the State. For only in this way can we secure the conditions in which a democratic transition to socialism will prove possible. The existence of democratic forms and pluralism are important elements here and we must insist that their full potential can only be realized in a democratic, socialist society.

NOTES

1. K. Marx, 'The class struggles in France: 1848 to 1850', in *Surveys from Exile*, Penguin 1973
2. On this, see G. Therborn, 'The rule of capital and the rise of democracy', *New Left Review*, May–June 1977, *passim*
3. A. Przeworski, 'Social democracy as a historical phenomenon', *New Left Review*, July–Aug. 1980, 27–8
4. On this, see Przeworski, op. cit., *passim*
5. On this see N. Chomsky and E. S. Ehrman, *The Washington Connection and Fascism*, Spokesman 1979, *passim*
6. N. Poulantzas, *State, Power, Socialism*, New Left Books 1978, pp. 217–31

FURTHER READING

N. Chomsky and E. S. Ehrman, *The Washington Connection and Fascism*, Spokesman 1979

Socialist arguments

D. Coates, *Labour in Power?*, Longman 1980

C. Cockburn, *The Local State*, Pluto 1977

A. Gamble, *Britain in Decline*, Macmillan 1981

B. Jessop, *Theories of the Capitalist State*, Martin Robertson 1982

C. B. MacPherson, *The Life and Times of Liberal Democracy*, Oxford UP 1977

K. Marx, 'The class struggles in France 1848 to 1850', in K. Marx *Surveys From Exile*, Penguin 1973

R. Miliband, *Marxism and Politics*, Oxford UP 1977

N. Poulantzas, *State, Power, Socialism*, New Left Books 1978

A. Przeworski, 'Social democracy as a historical phenomenon', *New Left Review*, 122, July–Aug. 1980, 27–58

G. Therborn, 'The rule of capital and the rise of democracy', *New Left Review* 103, May–June 1977, 3–41

Chapter five

LAW, ORDER AND THE POLICE

Bob Fine

INTRODUCTION

'Law and order' has become a major political issue under the Conservative administration. Thousands of black and white youths have taken to the streets and have directed their anger first and foremost at the police; democrats have taken-up the fight against augmented police powers and diminished police accountability to public bodies; civil libertarians have drawn attention to the erosion of the capacity of the law to serve as an agency of discipline over the police and have fought to restore the law's capacities in this regard; left-wingers have called for the expulsion of the police from those areas where they have appeared as 'an army of occupation' and for their replacement by community self-defence organizations.

In the normal run of events it is conservatism that knows how to make capital out of the 'law and order' question. The ordinary citizen's respect for the law, desire for order, fear of crime and dependence on the police are sentiments that Conservatives are well practiced in stimulating and exploiting. Socialists, despite our long and fine tradition of analysis and critique of bourgeois law and order, have tended to flounder around the issue. The right wing of the socialist movement have been anxious to demonstrate that they are no less committed to law and order than the next Conservative; civil libertarians have waged a rather lonely battle to protect the rights of free-born Englishmen and women; and the extreme Left have been equally isolated in their denunciation of law and order as a mere mask for the despotism of class or State rule. Many socialists have sought merely to bypass the issue by deflecting attention onto wider social, economic and political problems, like bad housing, unemployment or Thatcherism.

The political atmosphere is changing. Law and order is now becoming an arena of struggle for socialists around which we are gaining substantial popular support. Theoretically there has arisen a new interest in socialist critiques of law in general and law and order in modern Britain in particular.[1] Practically, we find a renewed interest in developing defensive strategies against the intensification of repression and in developing offensive strategies for the institution of popular forms of justice. The most pressing question for socialists is in what direction to steer this struggle and how can we best channel the current unrest in order to provide a real alternative to conservative law and order orthodoxy. In this chapter I wish only to sketch out the parameters of the debate: to consider first what has actually taken place in the law and order arena in recent years by focusing on the shifting relation between the police and society, and then the variety of socialist responses – strategic and theoretical – to these developments.

We shall see that the relation between the police and society is not static: neither are the police simply a democratic force representing the people as a whole, nor are they simply the instrument of class or State oppression. Rather the character of the police has changed with the extension of its powers and the erosion of avenues of democratic accountability. We witness as a result a gradually increasing alienation of the police from society. Among socialists debate has centred around the significance of this alienation: whether it marks a deviation from a fundamentally democratic system (that needs to be restored through reform) or whether it serves as a clear sign of the oppressiveness of all the forces of law and order (that need to be overthrown). Is it the task of socialists to curb police powers, restore avenues of accountability to public bodies, democratize the police and so improve relations between the police and the community? Or to exploit the increasing alienation of the police from society to tear away the veils of illusion that the police are a democratic force, to intensify and channel direct resistance against the police, to lay the groundwork for alternative forms of popular justice and so to exacerbate relations between the police and the community? In other words, is it the role of socialists to attenuate the contradictions in the exercise of police power or to intensify them? Most socialists and socialist groupings do not take simply to either one of these options. But we do find at one pole a 'reformism' that is *exclusively* committed to reform and, at the other, an 'ultra-leftism' that is *exclusively* committed to denunciation. The major problem facing socialists is to learn how to combine forms of struggle, to overcome the limits either of reform of the police or of direct action against the police. At a time when it is a practical necessity for socialists to find ways of uniting the spirit of revolt of those resisting the police on the streets with the struggle of the labour movement to bring the police under some kind of democratic control, the linkage of resistance and reform in the arena of law and order is particularly urgent.

POLICE POWERS

The conventional view of the police – and the view the police themselves project – is familiar: the police appear as the 'thin, blue line between anarchy and order', the 'long arm' of the law, the force that defends the interests of society as a whole and serves the community, that protects the rights of the individual to liberty, private property and life against assault by others, that prevents, detects, catches and deters criminals. The litany is well rehearsed. It is one of the key images of bourgeois consciousness: of a police that mediates impartially between the competing forces of civil society, that maintains order – keeping a necessary balance between helping old ladies to cross roads (*Dixon of Dock Green*) and swooping down mercilessly on hardened thugs (*The Sweeney*). So strong is the force of this ideal on the conservative mind that for many it appears heretical even to question whether it is realized in practice; to such a consciousness criticism itself appears as a sign of illegitimate disrespect for authority. Those, however, who wish to retain their critical faculties and who wish to understand the police as they are and not as they should be in the sacred texts – must examine the shadow that falls between the image and the act.

What has come to the fore in the wake of the recent urban unrest is a new and more offensive police presence to handle the problem of 'public order'. We have witnessed the arming of the police with protective shields and helmets, tear gas and high-speed landrovers. The Home Secretary, William Whitelaw declared that henceforth armoured cars, plastic bullets and water hoses will be available to the police. The government has turned once again – as during the prison officers' strike – to the use of army camps for detention of convicts, and to the use of army training for the police. It has threatened to legislate a new Riot Act to increase police powers and has put its full support behind the most offensive of police operations. The aggressive tactics of special units like the Special Patrol Group (SPG) or the Police Support Units (PSU) have become especially notorious.

While the current spate of riots has brought sharply to public view a new militarized aspect of policing, what we now see is in fact the tip of an iceberg of changes which have been taking place for a couple of decades.

The size and cost of the police force has grown sharply (numbers have increased even during the current public expenditure cuts). Special units designed for paramilitary control of riots, picketing, demonstrations and terrorism as well as for offensive anti-crime operations have been formed. The first SPG was established in London in 1965 and now they have spread to at least twenty-four out of the fifty-two forces in the country. Police Support Units – in 1974 envisaged as a wartime 'civil defence' expedient but now serving a similar function to the SPGs and the like – have become widespread. The Special Branch, designed to counter 'terrorism' and 'subversion', has grown from 300 officers based at Scotland Yard at the beginning of the 1970s to over 1,600 officers in most forces in the country by the end of the 1970s. More than 12,000 officers have been trained in the use of firearms and many forces have special firearms units. There has been a notable shift in police strategy from 'community' patrolling to what Sir Robert Mark called 'fire-brigade' policing, i.e. 'reactive' policing using 'the car, the radio and computer' to enter communities only when crime or disorder is seen to arise. We have witnessed the centralization and concentration of police with their restructuring into a smaller number of operational areas and with it the development of a computerized control system, including the use of the Police National Computer in Hendon. Police representatives – whether chief constables, the Police Federation or the Association of Chief Police Officers – have developed an active political role in lobbying government and spreading their very conservative views on a wide range of social issues, from jury trials and trade union law as well as directly policing matters.[2]

These internal changes have been coupled with the extension of police powers in law: e.g. the Prevention of Terrorism Act among other things gives the police the power to arrest and detain anyone suspected of involvement in 'the use of violence for political ends'[3]; the Scottish Criminal Justice Bill increased the political power of detention in normal cases[4]; the police have been granted judicial and political sanction to vet juries in political trials as was revealed in the ABC trial[5]; and the Royal Commission on Criminal Procedure has recently recommended an extension of police powers to arrest, to enter premises without a search warrant, to detain suspects, to refuse access of detainees to a lawyer, to fingerprint suspects and to use improperly obtained confessions in court.[6]

Many of these changes in the character of the police were introduced with little or no public debate in Parliament or elsewhere. For instance, there was no discussion in Parliament about the introduction of SPGs, PSUs or of the arming of the police. The Prevention of Terrorism Act, introduced in 1974 by the then Home Secretary, Roy Jenkins, was passed as a 'temporary' measure, the 'draconian' powers of which would automatically lapse unless emergency conditions justified renewal; it was approved by Parliament without division, came into force the next day and has been renewed ever since without discussion. Behind our backs and documented only thanks to the hawk-eyed efforts of a few socialists and democrats, the police have been transformed into a far more powerful force than one could have imagined twenty years ago.

POLICE ACCOUNTABILITY

The police in theory are presented as serving the community and enforcing the law. If this ideal is to be anything more than hollow rhetoric, then there must exist mechanisms whereby the community and the law can impose their respective will on the police. Such mechanisms do exist and always have done so – but always in ways which strictly limited the amount of democratic scrutiny and control possible. The socialist historian, John Foster, records how, at the beginnings of the modern police force during the period of Chartist revolt, the struggle by Chartists to secure control of the local watch committees was thwarted by transferring power over the police to more inaccessible and invisible bodies.[7] This history illustrates the fact that in capitalist society the police are a class force which must be kept remote and alien from the will of the mass of the people. However, this does not mean that it has not been possible to exercise some degree of public scrutiny and influence over the police; the fact that this has existed in Britain is one mark of the fact that Britain is a social democracy and differentiates the British police from those police states where there are no democratic forms of influence.

What has taken place in recent years is an historical erosion of popular influence over the police, or to put the matter the other way round, of police accountability to public bodies. This drift is a matter of great significance; for while it is true that the police are not and never have been a popular force under direct democratic control, still the extent to which inhibitions on the power of the police are imposed by open and public bodies is a crucial determinant of the character of the police and a crucial index of the strength and struggles of the working class. The Conservative ideal that the police 'serve the community' has always been a myth in that control over the police has systematically been retained in hands other than those of the mass of the people.

Socialists argue that the lack of democratic control indicates that the police are a class force, serving not the people as a whole but the interests of the bourgeoisie. But this alternative conception does not mean that the police are *merely* the instrument of the dominant class or that the character of the police is fixed by their class function. Rather the nature of the police depends on the relations *between* the classes, on the outcome of class struggles and on the *influence* which the working class and their allies manage to wield. Thus those who argue that the police are simply a democratic force ignore the actual insulation of the police from democratic control. Those who argue that the police are simply a class instrument ignore the different forms of police that emerge out of class struggle. This was the kind of mistake made at their cost by the German Communist Party when they dogmatically asserted that there are no 'class distinctions' between democratic policing and a system of reprisals, of brutal force and police terror, since both are instruments of the bourgeoisie. Trotsky's response to them pinpoints the deficiencies of this approach[8]:

The ruling class . . . does not exist in a vacuum. It stands in definite relations to other classes. In a developed capitalist society, during a democratic regime the bourgeoisie leans for support primarily on the working classes which are held in check by the reformists. In a fascist regime . . . capital leans on the petty bourgeoisie which destroys the organisation of the proletariat. Is there a difference in the class content of these two regimes? If the question is posed only as regards the ruling class, then there is no difference. If one takes into account the position and inter-relations of *all* classes, from the angle of the proletariat, then the difference appears to be enormous.

We are not talking about democracy versus fascism here; but we nonetheless need to pay the closest attention to the signs of a gradual drift to a more authoritarian form of State, for which a less accountable police is one prop, and the shift in class relations that this drift expresses.

There has been a recent renewed interest among socialists in police accountability, which has led to the production of numerous writings on the question. This material has been very useful in illustrating the historical decline of police accountability, although some critics measure 'lack of police accountability' against a timeless and unstated ideal of what accountability should be, and thereby neglect its real historical development.

Accountability has declined in two respects: first in terms of political control over the police by open and democratically elected bodies, and second in terms of legal control over the police through the enforcement of citizen's rights in the courts. On the first form of control, what has happened is a move away from some accountability to elected representatives of local government to, on the one hand, the granting of local powers to chief constables, and, on the other hand, centralized control by the Home Office, shielded from any public intervention beyond the turnover of Home Secretaries and the occasional question in Parliament. This was the nub of recommendations of the 1962 Royal Commission into Police Powers and then the effect of the 1964 Police Act[9]: to concentrate power in the Home Office centrally and chief constables locally, and to diminish democratic control through the shift from watch committees to police authorities. The powers of these police authorities were heavily circumscribed; for instance, they are not permitted even to advise on what the chief constable deems to be an 'operational' decision, they may require the chief constable to make a report 'when required' but he can refuse to disclose any information which he deems in the public interest ought not to be disclosed, they have little power over appointments and dismissals, etc. One-third of its members are Justices of the Peace appointed and not elected and hold an important balance of power between the elected representatives. Further, there has undoubtedly been a lack of political will on the part of the local government representatives on the police authorities to move against the chief constable and to use even the faint powers they do possess. Most observers agree that police authorities have become little more than a rubber stamp for the chief constable and the Home Office, though it is interesting that when public discontent with the police is strong, police authorities can provide an effective forum for mobilizing and channelling public opinion (as recently has been the case in the Merseyside Police Committee under Margaret Simey). In London even the slight degree of accountability enforced in the counties through police authorities does not exist, the 'Met' being responsible directly and uniquely to the Home Office.

Further, there is an alarming tendency for the police to put themselves, and for conservative politicians to put the police, above any kind of public control. It seems characteristic that when Ted Knight, the leader of Lambeth Council or Councillor Lansley, the chairman of the Lambeth Community Affairs Committee asked the police to withdraw during the recent Brixton riots in order to defuse the conflict and restore order, they were both told to mind their business and we heard from a police spokesman that 'the only people who control the streets of London are the Met'. We have recently heard more than one chief constable publicly declare that they did not care what the public thought or said. And far from disciplining them, the Home Secretary, William Whitelaw, pronounced it unthinkable that any reasonable politician would deny the requests of a chief constable. The official rhetoric is that the police 'serve the community'; in actual fact there is a diminishing control that the 'community' can impose on the police.

In respect of the law too, police accountability has been eroded. The scrutiny by the courts of the exercise of police power is a crucial plank of the 'rule of law', whereby State power is not unbridled but exercised within legal limits. In a variety of ways the courts act as a restraint on the exercise of police power: through civil suits and criminal prosecutions against individual malpractices; through the Judges' Rules on police treatment of detainees; through legal restrictions on police rights to stop people, enter their premises, search them, detain them, interrogate them and so forth; and through the requirement that the police have to take suspects before a court and to secure their conviction, sometimes before a jury. The police are thereby presented as servants of the law; the 'independence' of the judiciary serves in part as independence from the police and therefore as an inhibition over police power. Such judicial overview has always had an only limited efficacy. This is partly because the law itself is an imperfect means of inhibition (it is effective only after the event, it rests only on individual cases, it is reliant on the police as its 'arm' etc.)[10] and partly because of the inbuilt tendency on the part of judges to side with the police in cases of dispute.

Nevertheless those legal constraints that do exist are crucial forms of inhibition on police power. Consider, for example, the judicially enforced 'right of silence' for suspects.[11] Ever since the abolition of trial by ordeal it has been a basic principle of the rule of law that the guilt of an accused person must be proved by evidence brought by the prosecution; the right of the accused to choose to remain silent is the essential bulwark against the possible extraction of confessions and self-incriminating statements by force of pressure. The importance of strict enforcement of the right to silence as a curb on police powers over suspects was fully appreciated, for instance, by the 1929 Royal Commission which sought to impose stringent conditions on interrogation[12]:

We are now dealing with persons in custody and such persons are from the nature of things at a disadvantage because of their position. As one witness expressed it to us 'the whole of the influences around them appear to be hostile' and we think that a right of asking questions in these circumstances is in itself a source of danger . . . The simple and peaceful process of questioning breeds a readiness to resort to bullying and to physical force and torture.

The right to silence means that failure or refusal of a suspect to answer questions concerning an alleged criminal offence cannot be evidence against him or her at a subsequent trial. This right may be judicially enforced by the use of the 'exclusionary rule' in the courts: if the prosecution cannot prove that suspects' admissions were obtained without any threat or inducement from a person in authority concerned with the interrogation, they can be ruled inadmissable and there is no judicial discretion to allow them in at trial. This is the formal means by which the law imposes restraint on police power. In actual practice it is well documented that police regularly use all kinds of physical and psychological pressure, or as Commissioner McNee put it, methods 'bordering on trickery and stealth' in their investigations and frequently violate this right. Further, the courts have been extremely reluctant to exclude 'relevant' evidence in practice. However, even if the 'right of silence' and the exclusionary rule are not very effective inhibitions on police power and perhaps increasingly ineffective in recent years[13], yet they do represent *some* restrictions.

Recently there have been moves coming from the courts and from political quarters – pushed hard by the police themselves – to do away with these curbs on police power. For instance, the 1972 Criminal Law Revision Committee advocated their erosion of the right to silence in utilitarian terms of police efficiency and the search for evidence of guilt, and was unable to find any good reason why such a curb was ever brought into being[14]:

Since the object of a criminal trial should be to find out if the accused is guilty, it follows that ideally all evidence should be admissable which is relevant in the sense that it tends to render probable the existence or non-existence of any fact on which the question of guilt depends . . . We have aimed at reducing the gap between the amount of evidence which should be given and the amount which is in fact given. This is done chiefly by provisions designed to discourage the accused from refraining from giving evidence if a prima facie case has been made out against him . . . and by abolishing certain privileges of refusing to answer certain questions. We justify these reforms which we recommend for this purpose not only because of the changed conditions to which we have referred but mainly on the ground that there is no clear reason why the restrictions should have ever existed.

These recommendations were not accepted, but other signs pointed in the same direction. When the House of Lords considered whether a judge had discretion to exclude evidence of a crime obtained by an *agent provocateur*, Lord Diplock ruled decisively that it was no part of the courts' brief to impose discipline on the police[15]:

It is no part of a judge's functions to exercise disciplinary powers over the police or prosecution as respects the way in which evidence to be used at the trial is obtained by them. If it was obtained illegally there will be a remedy in civil law; if it was obtained legally but in breach of the rules of conduct for the police, this is a matter for the appropriate disciplinary authority to deal with.

The same Lord Diplock is also famous (infamous) for setting up the emergency courts in Northern Ireland (bereft of juries) in which confessions extracted at special interrogation centres serve as sufficient ground for conviction and in which, in the few cases that were contended, it is the defendant's task to prove that confessions were illegally extracted. Such judicial 'trust' in the police is reflected in the writings and rulings of Lord Denning when he declares that it is 'the duty of every responsible citizen to support the police' and when he belittles the right of silence[16]:

If a man makes a statement to the police and it is given in evidence in the Court, as often as not he will turn round and say it was extracted by threats, or was made up or that he was framed.

Increasingly the right to silence has been made to appear either as an anachronism or as a mere technical ploy on the part of 'known criminals'.

The recommendations of the 1981 Royal Commission on Criminal Procedure, if accepted, would accelerate this process. The Commission makes a number of suggestions which are designed to make it easier to convict accused persons, such as the extension of police powers of arrest and detention – in the case of 'grave' crimes the police will be able to hold suspects for twenty-four hours and then seek extensions through private hearings in magistrates' courts, thus defeating habeas corpus, that supposedly sacred guardian of the liberty of the individual[17] – and the granting to the police of a discretionary power to refuse access to lawyers in 'grave' cases if they deem that this will impede their inquiries. In addition, the Commission recommends the dropping of the exclusionary rule, and in its place suggests a code of practice for the regulation of interviews that has no external sanction[18]:

> The duty to see that these rules [which themselves are very vaguely defined] are obeyed should rest in the first instance where it does now, with the police service itself . . . Breach of the rules should be regarded as being a breach of the police disciplinary code.

The only remaining external sanction against the police abuse of their powers of detention and interrogation will be through the risk of a civil action after the event, a remedy the cost and complexity of which would make it largely prohibitive, or an appeal on the basis of the European Convention's minimum standards that confessions should not be obtained by torture or inhumane treatment. The Commission's message again is to 'trust' the police and their internal disciplinary procedures, despite the fact that it is the power of the chief constables themselves and the absence of police accountability to *outside* democratic bodies that is the nub of the problem.

What this cursory examination reveals is on the one hand the expansion of police power and on the other a diminution in the accountability of the police to any democratic body. Police authorities and the courts – for all their limitations as organs of discipline over the police – are, in principle at least, open to the public, visible in their operations and function according to rules and regulations the violation of which can be seen to have occurred. The impulse behind the erosion of these forms of regulation is coming from many quarters: the police, the judges, conservative political forces and even some supposedly liberal commentators. The effect of this erosion is to leave police power unchecked, hidden behind the walls of police stations, the corridors of the Home Office and the minds of those new local potentates, chief constables. At no period of British capitalism has popular control of the police been possible in reality. But the fact that the idea that the police are servants of the public has always been a myth should not blind us to the significance of changes in the degree of influence the 'public' can wield over the police. The present period marks a decline of such influence.

POLICE IDEOLOGY

Repression never arrives unpackaged. In capitalist society whatever form repression takes and however severely it is imposed, it comes with a definite ideological wrapping. The increase in police powers is presented as a practical necessity in the light of rising crime rates, public disorder and subversion. The only motive for introducing new draconian measures appears to be to restore law and order, to protect the lives and property of the majority of the citizens, to punish crime and to serve the community's best interests, even when the community itself is not aware of them. Those who openly resist the police are depicted as hooligans or subversives; those who criticize the police are presented as undermining legitimate authority and paving the way for crime and subversion.

The undercutting of police accountability to political bodies, like police authorities, is justified in terms of the imperatives of maintaining police 'impartiality' and 'professionalism' in the face of political pressures – as if the Home Office and the heads of chief constables were free from politics! The undercutting of accountability to the courts is justified in terms of police efficiency and the imperatives of crime control.

It is not the case that moves toward a tougher and less democratic policing are necessarily accompanied by a decline in legitimacy or in ideological appeal (for what they are worth the opinion polls still show the substantial majority of citizens supporting the police and the government's law and order programme). The State's drive to win popular support is as strong as ever. What we witness now is not a switch from rule by 'consensus' to rule by 'repression' as some authors have put the matter.[19] Rather the content of the ideological message is shifting: with greater emphasis on 'order' at all costs; on a re-definition of 'individual rights' in the direction of those 'rights' which run counter to the interests of the labour movement (rights of individuals not to be disturbed by demonstrations, pickets, riots, trade unions, rights of employers to hire and fire at will, rights of tenants to buy their council houses, etc.) and on police autonomy from political pressures. The audience to which the message is addressed is also shifting: away from organized labour and toward a petty-bourgeoisie radicalized from the Right and a section of workers and the unemployed that are disaffected from the labour movement and increasingly mobilized around a racist and authoritarian platform. What is taking place is not just a turn from ideology to repression, but the gradual development of a new kind of ideology and a new kind of repression. There is no ground for supposing that the State will carelessly surrender that legitimacy which socialists have long been striving to remove from it. Socialists have to work to break the ideological grip of the State, in the law and order arena as in any other; the State will not do our work for us.

Thus the ideology of police professionalism and autonomy from politics is not *manifestly* mythical. It needs to be demonstrated by socialists that the 'preservation of public order' involves political decisions about what kind of 'order' is being preserved: that the methods used to control public disturbances involve political decisions about how the police impose their authority on citizens; that police attitudes toward trade union pickets involve political assessments on the character of trade unions and so forth. It needs to be demonstrated that neither are the police themselves apolitical (the right-wing views of many police from chief constables down are clearly documented); nor is the Home Office that directs the police apolitical; nor indeed are the laws which the police purport to enforce apolitical. The issue, then, is not between political accountability and professional impartiality but between democratic and open political control versus an administrative and closed political control. At the same time 'professional impartiality' is not *just* a myth but has its roots deep in the organization and practices of policing (the way they talk, the uniforms they wear, their separation from the military, their apparent role in courts, etc.). The social function of even the most 'professional' and 'impartial' police – e.g. for preserving existing property relations and the order they support – is not self-evident nor does the turn to authoritarianism automatically reveal it.

As an illustration of the ways in which an increase in the power of the police and the insulation of this power from democratic controls can be packaged – and even made to look attractive – by the contemporary conservative consciousness, we can consider the introduction to the Report of the recent Royal Commission on Criminal Procedure. The issue which the Commission poses is that of establishing 'a fundamental balance' between the 'interests of the community' and the 'liberties of the individual' as far as pre-trial criminal procedure is concerned. The questions which the Commission puts concern, first, from which direction this balance has been disturbed since there was last a general overview and, second, what needs to be done to rectify the imbalance so caused. On the former of these issues the Commission, in an apparently even-handed manner, makes reference on the one hand to the threat to individual liberty posed by growth in the power of the State and the police, and declares that 'the need to define and assert the rights of the individual' has become a matter of 'urgency and significance'. On the other hand, it writes of 'the manifestly growing anxiety' about rising crime rates and of the consequent need to grant to the police more powers, that this anxiety might be allayed. However, the apparently open way in which the Commission initially poses the problem soon transforms itself into an exclusive concern with 'criminals getting the better of the law' and with the supposed danger to the public posed by the excessive safeguards enjoyed by defendants. By page 9 of the Report the 'urgent' problem of State power has been laid dutifully to rest. So much for the Commission's initial show of balance. Henceforth, the problem of 'balance' is afforded a new significance. On the assumption that the 'balance' has shifted in favour of 'individual liberty' and against 'the interest of the community', the question is now whether – to rectify the imbalance caused by the growth of crime – it is permissible to encroach upon defendants' existing rights. Do the requirements of 'order' and 'justice' override the protection of the rights of suspects? Or does the protection of such rights override the requirements of 'order' and 'justice'?

The Commission's conception of 'balance' presupposes exactly what it should have been looking into: namely an identity of interest between the community and the police. In the Commission's eyes, to support one is to support the other. But does the 'community' really have an interest in the arbitrary arrests, forced confessions, random searches and so forth that proliferate as police powers are augmented and police accountability is diminished? Further it presupposes an antagonism between the protection of individual rights and the interest of the community. But does not the community have an interest in seeing to it that the 'innocent' are not convicted and therefore that the rights of defendants are upheld? The very manner in which the Commission sets up its 'balance' conceals the dogma of identifying police power with community interest and of counterposing 'individual liberty' to 'community interest'.

The Commission strives to put a silk lining in its argument by situating the problem of 'balance' in a philosophical context. There are two opposing philosophical approaches, it declares, to the issue at hand: 'utilitarianism' and 'libertarianism'. Utilitarians, we are told, subordinate the rights of individuals to their utility for the general interest, and would therefore be willing to rescind defendants' rights, if that were useful for securing the 'right result', i.e. the conviction of the guilty. Libertarians, we hear, treat individual rights as absolute and so would not countenance any interference with the existing rights of defendants. Between the rocks of utilitarianism, that threaten to shipwreck individual liberty, and the rocks of libertarianism, that threaten the survival of the ship of State, the Commission's job is to find a safe, moderate and balanced middle way.

The Commission has got its learned philosophers wrong. Utilitarianism does not pre-empt discussion of the content of the 'general interest' to which individual rights are subordinated. Some like Bentham, showed little interest in, for instance, the right of silence when he wrote of it[20]:

> If all the criminals of every class had assembled and framed a system after their own wishes, is not this rule the very first which they would have established for their security? Innocence never takes advantage of it. Innocence claims the right of speaking, as guilt invokes the privilege of silence.

But there is also a strong liberal tradition (including J. S. Mill) within utilitarianism which argues that the 'public interest' consists precisely in the maximization of individual rights and the minimization of State interference. Similarly libertarianism does not pre-empt discussion on the content of individual liberties; e.g. the defence of the individual right to property has been a basis for the most illiberal defence of the right of the police to shoot tear gas canisters at looters as well as the right of an employer to discipline and dismiss workers at will or the right of scabs to pass the picket line. Nor does it in any way settle the relation between individuals and the State, since in law the State often appears in the garb of an ordinary individual. In such manner did Lord Denning recently defend State secrecy under the umbrella of an individual's rights to privacy. Thus when the legal officer of the National Council for Civil Liberties appealed against her conviction for publicizing Home Office documents about prison conditions (which she had secured through the legal process of 'discovery' when representing an ex-convict against the Home Office, and which had already been read out in open court) Denning declared that the State's right of privacy must be protected[21]:

> It was one of our fundamental rights that everyone had a right to privacy, included in which was a right to respect for his confidential documents . . . the press was not free to publish confidential documents without the consent of the owner.

The libertarian defence of the individual's right against the State thus undergoes a metamorphosis – by the miracle of a legal fiction – into a defence of the State's right against the individual.

The advantage which the Commission gained from its philosophical polarity between utilitarianism and libertarianism was to enable it to 'discover . . . a third road'. The 'third road' turns out to be a kind of deal: the existing rights of defendants will be 'modified' (read lessened) in return for which 'an associated and considered use of checks and safeguards' on the exercise of police power will be introduced. What does this trade-off between 'rights' and 'safeguards' really mean? The rights of defendants indicate, when considered from their reverse side, a definite form of regulation over the police. It provides, in a word, legal controls over police power. Now, as we have indicated, this legal control over the police is already inadequate. The Commission itself cites evidence to show that the exclusion of improperly induced confessions from court does not succeed in inhibiting this police malpractice. But they do provide some sort of accountability, some form of external control over the police.

But what of 'safeguards'? What form of regulation over the police does this term imply? What we find is no more than internal, disciplinary proceedings within the police itself. The move from 'rights' to 'safeguards' in fact means a transition from legal overview over the police to police self-administration. 'Trust' in police honour is to replace accountability before the law. Such is 'balance'.

The point at issue is the identification between the police and the public interest. For this identification to be anything more than empty rhetoric, there must exist some actual form of accountability to the 'public' and not merely an association of ideas. Rights under law are not the only way this accountability can be secured. More representative, more powerful and more open political organs of control (at both national and local level), more public access to the inner sanctuary of police stations, more critical scrutiny from bodies within the labour movement, etc. offer additional means. But the Commission is not offering a substitution of one form of public accountability for another. Rather beneath the rhetoric of 'balance' it proposes the replacement of legal controls by the internal, disciplinary mechanisms of the police themselves. In the name of the 'interests of the community' the Commission proposes measures which set the police yet further above and apart from the community (since most commentators agree that crime detection is largely dependent on public information and cooperation, it even exacerbates the poor record of the police in their performance of this, their basic, social function). The Commission's conceit is that some liberty must be sacrificed for the good of all. What we discover is that this sacrifice is not 'for the good of all' at all, but to place the police on a still higher pedestal above society.

THE SOCIALIST RESPONSE

There are as many views on the nature of the police among socialists as there are currents within the socialist movement. At one extreme there are those who believe that in essence the police are a democratic force, impartially enforcing the law and serving the community. They see what is happening now as a deviation from this ideal, an abuse of powers, a deformation of their proper role in society. At the other extreme, there are those who insist that in essence the police are a repressive force belonging to the dominant class or the State or that they are, as it were, a 'law unto themselves'. They see recent developments as the logical and necessary outcome of the basic character of the police, and one that merely clarifies and brings to public attention just how repressive the police are.

In line with these differing conceptions, we also find distinct strategies concerning what ought to be done with the police. At one pole, we find socialists who fight for the imposition of police accountability both to public, political bodies like police authorities and to public, legal bodies (the courts). They argue that defendants' rights must be protected or reinforced; that police authorities must be given real powers or scrapped in favour of new, popular organs of control with real power over the police; that all major policy discussions on police matters must be debated before parliament; that laws which grant the police excessive discretionary powers (like 'sus' or the Prevention of Terrorism Act or the 1971 Immigration Act) must be repealed; that the most militaristic of police units (like the SPGs) be scrapped, and so forth. If such measures were introduced, it is argued, then the police would become in reality the guardian of democracy that in theory they are supposed to be.

At the other end of the socialist spectrum, socialists argue that the fight for accountability is lost from the beginning, since the police – as the repressive arm of the State and the ruling class or because of their own nature as a 'disciplinary' power – are inherently immune from meaningful popular control. They argue rather that any participation on police authorities or the like would only lead to the incorporation of those that do so; that any committee established to look behind the walls of police stations would become compromised; and that legal rights are a deceptive defence given the record of the judiciary in siding with the police in case of disputes. What is needed, they argue, is a clear exposé of the actual nature of the police and the sweeping away of all democratic illusions, and on this basis the establishment of popular organs of self-defence both to provide the community protection (e.g. against fascists) that the police fail to provide and protection against the police themselves. The general orientation in this case is combative: not to reform the police but to prepare for and organize resistance against police oppression.[22]

Alongside these differences of analysis and strategy there also coexist distinct ideas concerning the long-term goals of socialists in relation to the police. At one end, it is argued that the police are a necessary condition of any democratic society, and at the other that the police, like all organs of the State, must be overthrown and their functions performed by the self-activity of the people. In a socialist society, it is argued in the latter case, there will be no need for a special force above society; anti-social acts will be controlled by the people themselves. The maintenance of a police force appears not as a condition of democracy but as proof that society is not yet democratic, that the people have not yet learnt and fought to rule themselves.

Until recently both these perspectives existed on the fringes of political debate, as conservative orthodoxy on the police ruled the roost; and each pursued its message largely ignorant of and isolated from the other. Now that the conservative orthodoxy has been visibly shaken and the threat of police repression has become pressing, the need for socialists to work out an effective basis for developing and publicizing our critiques, our strategies and our goals has become equally urgent. Let me end by throwing my oar into this debate.

The police are and always have been a class force. That this is so is apparent in their functions, in their control and in the inner relations which characterize them – even in the most democratic of bourgeois societies: in their functions because the impartial protection of private property means in fact the protection of the ownership of the means of production by a small minority of capitalists, and for the mass of the population merely protection of their capacity to labour and to consume (thereby the police defend a system based on the exploitation of the many by the few); in their control because the most accountable systems of policing always have reserved the key areas of control for a State machinery that exists beyond the will of the people themselves; in their inner relations because the very relations of hierarchy and authority the police express are but one aspect of bourgeois domination. It is also evident to me that the struggle for socialism is a struggle for the abolition of all 'special' forces elevated above society and for the performance of policing functions through the self-organization and self-activity of all citizens. Any goal short of this appears to me to be trapped within the narrow horizons of bourgeois consciousness. In that the police represent a restriction on full democracy, the task of socialists is to overthrow that force.

At the same time it is equally clear in my eyes that, first, for the vast majority of the population the police do appear – in actuality or in potential – as a democratic force and that socialists should take their views seriously and act not in opposition to the people but with the people. Consequently the limits of 'police democracy' need to be demonstrated in practice and not presupposed and reformists must be related to and not denounced. Second, within the confines of those societies in which police exist and are necessary, enormously different systems of policing can operate and it is the absolute duty of socialists – both for our own sake and for those whom we wish to represent – not only to defend those who are victims of police oppression, not only to help protect those whom the police fail to protect, but also to fight for as democratic and humane a police force as possible. Third, while it is not really possible to rely on legal rights as a defence against police power, their existence and their enforcement do offer a crucial inhibition on police power. It is imperative in this context for socialists both to resist incursions into existing rights and to fight for specific new rights and their enforcement (e.g. not to be shot at with tear gas canisters or run over by landrovers at demonstrations). Fourth, the overthrow of the police is not an immediate possibility and the optimum condition for securing this end is democratization of the police as well as the self-organization of the working class. It is only when the impartiality and the accountability of the police have been pushed to their maximum that the specifically capitalist character of police oppression will stand out in all its sharpness and that resistance will be directed not only against particular injustices but also against police rule as such.

The practical conclusions I leave to those readers who agree with my observations. My only comment is one that I direct to my comrades on the left of the socialist movement. A struggle is being waged to bring the police under some kind of democratic control and to curb their most outrageous powers. This is not in and of itself a 'reformist' struggle, but one of the crucial ways in which workers' control can be fought for now. Denunciation of the police may in fact serve as a cover for abstaining from this struggle and abstentionism is not the hallmark of socialists. When comrades argue that accountability will only lead to incorporation and compromise, we should reply that this danger does exist, but the fact that it exists is no reason for abstaining from the fight for accountability. Rather it is up to us to ensure that avenues of accountability are not used by the police to draw democrats into their web, but by socialists as a base and forum for pushing ever more democratic demands and for winning new adherents. If the State can be forced to make concessions on accountability, they will do so with the *aim* of strengthening police presence and neutralizing dissent. Socialists should not thereby boycott such concessions or the fight for them, but learn how to use them for our own benefit rather than for the benefit of the State. When comrades argue that the real struggle is on the streets, we should reply that direct action is not counterposed to the political struggle for accountability or the legal struggles for the enforcement of rights. Socialists learn to combine forms of struggle, to move from one to another as circumstances dictate and not to fetishize direct action as the only 'revolutionary' mode. When comrades argue that our task is to overthrow the police and not merely reform them, we should reply that this should not blind us to the immediate task of exercising our influence over the police as they are. We do not counterpose reforms to our larger goals. When comrades argue that the intention of many supporters of accountability is to improve relations between the community and the police we should reply that we must make sure that such improvement is at the expense of police power and not of the community and point out the folly of believing that antagonisms between police and community can be overcome (indeed the hostility of the police and conservatism to accountability is intense). It is not for socialists to sit on the sidelines of a crucial struggle. The fight for police accountability is a fight for all socialists.

NOTES

I should like to thank Glynis Cousin, Sol Picciotto and the CSE Law and State Group (c/o Sol Picciotto, Law, Warwick University) and comrades from Socialist Organiser for their help in producing this contribution. The ideas are of course my own responsibility.

1. For instance, there has been a proliferation of Marxist writings on the law and a renewed interest in the works of classical Marxists. See especially Pashukanis (1978), Beirne and Sharlet

(1980), Fine *et al.* (1979), Holloway and Picciotto (1978) and Thompson (1980)

2. For an outline and critique of these and other such developments, see especially the State Research Bulletins, the State Research Pamphlet, No. 2: 'Policing the Eighties', and Hain (1980)
3. See Scorer (1976) and Scorer and Hewitt (1980)
4. See the discussion documents of the Campaign to Stop the Scottish Criminal Justice Bill
5. See discussion in Thompson (1980)
6. See *Rights*, the journal of the NCCL, 5 (4), Mar./Apr. 1981, special issue on the Report of the Royal Commission on Criminal Procedure
7. Foster, Ch. 2 (1974)
8. Trotsky (1969), p. 23 and my discussion on these issues in 'Law and Class', in Fine *et al.* (1979)
9. For a discussion of the Commission and the Act, see Critchley (1972), Ch. 9
10. For a general critical discussion on the limits of legal forms of regulation, see Picciotto: 'Theory of the State, Class Struggle and the Rule of Law', in Fine *et al.* (1979)
11. My thanks to Nick Blake for a talk and unpublished article in which he surveyed in detail the current threat to the 'right to silence'
12. Royal Commission on Police Powers and Procedures, p. 61 (1929)
13. The Report of the Royal Commission into Criminal Procedure (1981) gives in my view an exaggerated emphasis to the ineffectiveness of the 'exclusionary rule'. See p. 113
14. Criminal Law Revision Committee, 11th Report, p. 16, (1972)
15. R v Sang (1979) 2 All ER, 1222 at 1230
16. Denning, p. 8, (1974)
17. Denning described habeas corpus as 'our great writ which guarantees personal freedom in *The Due Process of Law* (1980) but has been less than zealous in applying this freedom to detained immigrants. See Paul Watchman: 'Palm Tree Justice and the Lord Chancellor's Foot' in Robinson and Watchman (1981)
18. Report (1981), p. 111
19. For an example of the use of the repression-consensus opposition, see Hall *et al.* (1978)
20. This passage by Bentham was quoted favourably in the Report of the 1972 Criminal Law Revision Committee; see Bentham's

Treatise on Evidence, p. 241 for the source
21. Times Law Report, Feb. 6 1981
22. An eloquent defence of the 'rule of law' and attack against 'ultra-leftism' is to be found in Thompson (1980)

SELECT BIBLIOGRAPHY

General background reading

P. Beirne and R. Sharlet, *Pashukanis: Select Writings on Marxism and Law*, Academic Press 1980
Bob Fine, *et al.*, *Capitalism and The Rule of Law*, Hutchinson 1979
J. Foster, *Class Struggle and The Industrial Revolution*, Weidenfield and Nicholson 1974
J. Holloway, and S. Picciotto, (eds), *State and Capital: A Marxist Debate*, Edward Arnold 1978
V. Lenin, *State and Revolution*, Foreign Languages Publishing House, Moscow
K. Marx, 'The Civil War in France', in K. Marx, *The First International and After*, Penguin 1974
K. Marx, 'The Critique of the Gotha Programme', in K. Marx, *The First International and After*, Penguin 1974
R. Miliband, *The State in Capitalist Society*, Weidenfield and Nicholson 1969
E. Pashukanis, *Law and Marxism*, Ink Links 1978
A. V. Sellwood, *Police Strike – 1919*, Allen 1978
L. Trotsky, 'Fascism, Stalinism and the United Front', *International Socialism*, 1969, 38/39, 2–70

Critical writings on contemporary law and order problems

Carol Ackroyd, *et al.* *The Technology of Political Control*, Penguin 1977
Bethnal Green and Stepney Trades Council, *Blood on the Streets*, 1979
Nick Blake, *The Police, The Law and The People*, Haldane 1979
K. Boyle, *et al.* *Ten Years in Northern Ireland*, Cobden Trust 1980
Tom Bowden, *Beyond the Limits of the Law*, Penguin 1978
Tony Bunyan, *The History and Practice of the Political Police in Britain*, Quartet 1977

Campaign to Stop the Scottish Criminal Justice Bill: Discussion documents, 1980

Barry Cox, *et al.*, *The Fall of Scotland Yard*, Penguin 1977

T. A. Critchley, *A History of Police in England and Wales*, Constable 1972

Clare Demuth, *'Sus': A report on the Vagrancy Act, 1824*, Runnymede 1978

Peter Hain (ed.), *Policing the Police*, Vols 1 and 2, John Calder 1980

S. Hall, *Drifting into a Law and Order Society*, Cobden 1980

S. Hall, C. Cricker, T. Jefferson, J. Clarke and B. Roberts, *Policing the Crisis*, Macmillan 1978

Institute of Race Relations, *Police Against Black People*, Race and Class Pamphlet No. 6, 1979

Lambeth Borough Council Report of the Working Party on Community Police Relations in Lambeth, 1981

National Council for Civil Liberties, *Southall, 23 Apr. 1979*, 1980

David Ranson, *The Blair Peach Case: Licence to Kill*, Friends of Blair Peach Committee 1980

R. Reiner, *The Blue-Coated Worker*, Cambridge UP 1978

P. Robinson, and P. Watchman, *Justice, Lord Denning and The Constitution*, Crower 1981

Catherine Scorer, *The Prevention of Terrorism Act, 1974 and 1976*, NCCL, 1976

P. Scorer, and P. Hewitt, *The Prevention of Terrorism Act*, NCCL 1981

State Research Bulletins *'Policing the Eighties'*, State Research Pamphlet No. 2, 1981

Edward Thompson, *Writing by Candlelight*, Merlin 1980

Official reports, judicial and police views

J. Alderson, *Policing Freedom*, MacDonald and Evans 1979

Denning, Lord, *Let Justice Be Done*, Birkbeck College 1974

Denning, Lord, *The Due Process of Law*, Butterworth 1980

R. Mark, *Policing a Perplexed Society*, George Allen 1977; *In the Office of Constable*, Collins 1978

Royal Commission on Police Powers and Procedures: Report, 1929

Royal Commission on the Police, Report 1962

Royal Commission on Pre-Trial Criminal Procedure, Report, 1981

Chapter six

BIAS IN THE MEDIA

Greg Philo

When people are asked to define democracy, one of the things they often mention is the existence of a free Press; and less commonly, the role of that Press in creating an informed citizenry – one that is educated by its exposure to cultural institutions of quality, and one that as a result is capable of making responsible decisions because of its regular access to plentiful quantities of uncontaminated information. That we in Britain possess such a Press, and enjoy a television network of unrivalled neutrality and excellence, are amongst the proudest boasts of those who would legitimate the present distribution of social and economic power. Those seeking to change that balance of power need to know how valid these claims are, and need to be in a position to explain both the character and the origins of the biases which in practice are so central a feature of the presentation of news and entertainment by the media as a whole.

It is common to complain that the general coverage of political and social issues, both in the Press and on television, frequently distorts in subtle ways: with stories chosen to over-emphasize the disruptive and the violent (with editors preferring the sensational to the routine, and the dramatic confrontation to the quiet solution); with too little presentation of essential background information and historical detail, and too great a tendency to trivialize and to over-simplify; with too quick a search for the personal angle that takes public attention away from the wider social processes involved; with too great a propensity to present the official line as self-evidently superior, and to identify with the authorities simply because they possess the trappings of office; with too easy a slippage into a bolstering of the conventional stereotypes of the day (the lazy worker, the devious foreigner, the ignorant black and the subversive militant); with too ethnocentric a preoccupation with local issues and with only the British dimension of events that happen abroad and with too great a silence on the hidden spheres of social power.

We will have cause, in a later section of this chapter, to provide evidence on much of this, but first we need to establish why this pattern of reporting should be so common; and for the Press and commercial television at least, there seems to be three main forces at work: the structure of ownership in the media industry, the commercial pressures to which privately owned newspapers and television companies are subject, and the particular training and conventional practices of journalism as a profession, both in the private sector and also in the BBC.

WHO OWNS THE MEDIA?

In Britain, almost everything we understand as mass communications, such as newspapers, books, records and films, is owned by twelve companies. They include household names like EMI and Rank, and huge combines like British Electric Traction. Just five large companies now control 80 per cent of the circulation of national daily and Sunday newspapers, and those same five, because their interests stretch into every aspect of the media industry and beyond, own 70 per cent of commercial network television and of the output of paperback books as well. In this country Rupert Murdoch owns the *Sun*, the *News of the World*, *The Times* and the *Sunday Times* as well as regional papers. The first and most obvious pressure on what the media produce comes from this pattern of ownership and financial control. Historically, this concentration of ownership gave immense power to a handful of people who used the media for propaganda purposes. The Press is the most striking example. In 1948, Beaverbrook, the owner of the *Daily Express*, quite bluntly told the Royal Commission on the Press 'My purpose originally was to set up a propaganda paper and I have never deviated from that purpose all through the years'. Other press barons promoted their political views by the same means, though not always to such extremes as Lord Rothermere. In the 1930s he used his papers, including the *Daily Mail*, to give support to the Nazis in Germany and Oswald Moseley's Blackshirts in Britain. One editorial proclaimed 'We cannot expect a nation of "he men" like the Germans to sit forever with folded arms . . .' (*Daily Mail* 31 Mar. 34). Readers were also given helpful instructions on how to join the British Union of Fascists.

Papers such as the *Daily Mail* still attempt to orchestrate public opinion. Recent popular themes are campaigns against nationalized industries, attacks on so-called 'scroungers' and the explanation of recent street riots in terms of the activities of 'outsiders'. These themes are obviously not chosen at the whim of individual proprietors – their origins are more complex. It is more accurate to see the journalists and editors and the mass media generally as one part of a society which takes private ownership, social hierarchies and profit for granted – as being the natural ways of organizing economic production and social relationships. Since the mass media have such a critical role to play in the battle of ideas over how such a society is to be explained and how it is to be justified, it is natural for the private owners and senior editors of major national papers to use periodically their position to canvass causes that protect the privileges of the elites from which they come, and with which they identify. In this sense, biased reporting and monopoly private ownership of the national dailies necessarily go hand in hand.

COMMERCIAL PRESSURES?

The corporations who own commercial radio, television, and the Press clearly have a vested interest in a certain kind of economic system. A company such as EMI has owned everything from local radio to steak houses, hotels and yacht marinas. The main interest of such companies on a day-to-day basis is simply to make money. A generalized commitment to the status quo goes alongside the pressure to sell the product. And this pressure to sell is particularly acute in the precarious world of newspapers and television, where profits are low (and for the quality dailies non-existent) and where production and distribution costs are high. The newspaper industry in particular is a microcosm of the general economy it attempts to report, with heavy concentration of ownership, outmoded technology and strong unions; and most newspapers survive only by a degree of subsidization from the non-newspaper parts of the conglomerates to which they belong, and by a bitter struggle for advertising revenue and circulation. Editorial antipathy to unionism is perhaps understandable in such a context; their equally strident opposition recently to the subsidization of ailing industries is less so. But in any case the fact that the media is an industry has a definite and sizeable effect on the shape and content of its output. The pressure of advertising, for example, can be quite direct. The *News Chronicle* and the *Daily Herald*, for example, both folded – to leave the national Press almost entirely Tory in its sympathies – because they could not attract sufficient advertising revenue to sustain them, even though their circulation figures (9.5 million in their last full year of operation) were high. When *The Guardian* opposed the Suez invasion in 1956, it paid a high price in lost advertising revenue for its dangerous lack of patriotism. This case, and the *Sunday Times* pursuit of the thalidomide tragedy in spite of their heavy reliance on advertising from the company concerned, are correctly cited as evidence of the fact that advertisers do no *always* dictate editorial policy. But there is still no getting away from the fact that papers must be sensitive to the need for advertising revenue and for an expanding readership.

Commercial pressures can be seen at their purest in the history of commercial, and particularly American, television. In the 1950s, companies that were sponsoring programmes actually complained about television drama which showed people living fulfilled lives in spite of being poor. To be happy without commodities was regarded as fundamentally un-American. In addition the demand for high audience ratings at the cheapest cost, had led to 'formulae', for producing long-running series with the same basic characters and plots. If one was a 'success' in the ratings then another twenty like it would follow. Single plays were taboo, since anything which 'ended' meant that viewers would change channel and perhaps not come back. Thus we have *Dallas* and *Crossroads* which go on for months or years, with each show having a dramatic 'hook' at the end, so that viewers will turn on next week.

The tedium and repetition of formula westerns, detective stories and comedy shows comes because they have to be basically the same. This is so that people can pick up the plot when they switch from channel to channel as the adverts come on. Central characters frequently repeat what has happened so far, since in America there are very long advertisements about every eight minutes. The idea is to 'catch' people as they move channel. Hence on *Star Trek*: 'Captains log, star date 10/5, we have landed', etc. Such pressures affect British programming, since commercial companies here are also searching for ratings, and more significantly are making major series with the intention of exporting them to the American market. The style and content of programmes is affected when television is run simply as one part of a business conglomerate. At present 'independent' television in Britain is controlled by companies such as Granada. This has extensive interests in television rental, cinema, exhibitions, bingo, and the music industry. Other television holding companies have had interests in theatres, telephone answering equipment, merchandizing, insurance and property. People who are appointed to control channels and make programmes in such a context are unlikely to demand radical alternatives.

JOURNALISTIC PRACTICES?

Although economic interests are important, the institutions of the media, especially broadcasting, cannot be seen as simply relaying ideology from the State or private capital. The media institutions and the journalists they employ do have some autonomy. They usually wish to claim that their reportage is accurate and trustworthy. Programme makers in Britain certainly do not see themselves as being passive mouthpieces, and at times actively dissociate themselves from establishment figures. This may take the form of arguments with individual politicians, e.g. the rows between Harold Wilson and the BBC over how much he was making on his book royalties. But such arguments are likely to be conducted on an individual level. The television may challenge politicians but not the political or economic system. In the same way it may look at 'isolated' abuses in the economy – it may investigate 'pockets of poverty' or the effects of unemployment in a single area but not usually the nature of the economy which produces these.

The pressures on journalists to operate in this way are many. A would-be radical journalist knows that he or she has to get copy past the sub-editor, and the television reporter faces similar sifting mechanisms of editorial control. He or she will know from bitter experience that 'alternative' stories can be lost on an editor's desk, that they can be extensively rewritten on the way to the print room, or even that they can be tolerated this time at the cost of losing that journalist access to resources (of film, programme space and so on) in a period to come – or even at the cost of not having contracts renewed, or actually being sacked. Journalists tend to rely on established sources, both for speedy stories and to give their reports legitimacy before the sub-editor and a degree of protection from the laws of libel; and this relationship to sources restricts journalistic freedom in very important ways. Since official sources are easiest to come by, and serve as the best protection for the journalist in any ensuing row, the relationship of reporter to source gives the profession as a whole a disproportionate tendency to disseminate the views of the elite. It also means that journalists are under pressure not to jeopardize their future access to a useful source by too strident a critique of the institution in which it is situated. Radical journalism survives of course, but it has to battle against a whole training and socialization process and against a work ethos inside the national dailies and television companies that sets tacit limits to what is, and what is not, acceptable. Those limits are invariably narrow, and are no less potent for being generally unspoken, backed up as they are by more conventional senior managerial sanctions of an administrative or coercive kind. And all this serves to remind us that 'news' on television and in the Press is not self-defining. News is not 'found' or even 'gathered' so much as made. It is a *creation* of a journalistic process, an artifact, a commodity even, as manufactured as a motor car or a Cruise missile; and in that manufacturing process strong forces exist to skew its content.

PUBLIC BROADCASTING

People expect the Press to be partisan, but the television is supposed to be impartial. However, the history of these organizations and especially the BBC shows how closely they are linked to the political establishment. The BBC developed in close relationship with the State and under Reith it came to embody in its language and programme content a form of liberal capitalist ideology. In practice this was the belief that the class system was basically sound and that as long as working people 'knew their place' they were capable of improvement by gradual exposure to 'high culture'. This attitude hardened, however, when the working class forgot its place in the General Strike of 1926. Statements by Reith, who was director general at the time, are very revealing about the role of broadcasting when class relations and class antagonisms become overt. A critical issue in the strike was whether the State should commandeer the BBC and run it as a propaganda agency in defence of the 'public' interest. Reith opposed this and sought formal autonomy on the grounds that the BBC could fulfil the required function more effectively as a politically independent body. In the end, the State and broadcasting reached a mutually acceptable compromise which exists to this day. Reith commented in his diaries that 'the cabinet decision is really a negative one. They want to be able to say that they did not commandeer us, but they know that they can trust us not to be really impartial.'[1]

The broadcasting institutions at present, and especially the BBC, are thoroughly hierarchial. The higher up one goes the more likely it is that people will be drawn from the established channels of power and influence. The composition of the BBC Board of Governors in 1981 illustrates a long tradition of appointing men (and occasionally women) from the good and worthy sectors of Britain's upper classes. Amongst the twelve governors are the owner of the Castle Howard stately home and ex-President of the Country Landowners Association, the former editor of *The Times*, an ex-presbyterian minister now director of a university, a former personal secretary (and wife) of a prime minister of Northern Ireland, a former High Commissioner for Canada, a university professor, the director of Littlewood's Pools, and a former Minister of State. Where trade unionists are appointed they tend not to be known as 'radical' – at present we have Lord Allen of Fallowfield. There is also one black woman, recently appointed, who was general secretary of the Campaign Against Racial Discrimination. But overall, the predominant character of the board is white upper middle class with a high proportion from public schools and Oxford and Cambridge. The people who actually make the programmes in both the BBC and 'Independent' companies are also drawn mainly from a narrow section of the population. This is particularly obvious in the recruitment of ethnic groups and women. Black people are under-represented across all areas of recruitment, except at the lowest levels. Women tend to be allocated roles as personal assistants and researchers rather than producers and reporters. A survey of three ITV companies revealed that of the seventy-four producer/directors of *Weekend World*, *TV Eye* and *World in Action*, only ten were women. A similar situation prevails on the technical side of broadcasting: in 1978, of the 360 people recruited by the BBC for technical posts only 10 women were appointed.[2]

There are many pressures which operate to keep television workers in line. Some are quite direct – certain programmes on contentious issues (Ulster being an obvious example) are subject to direct censorship by senior management. Others, as in the Press, fall foul of D-notices, the Official Secrets Act or the law of libel. But more subtle processes are at work too. One very obvious factor shaping journalistic activity and their general life-style is their level of pay. Producers at an Independent company will receive upwards of £26,000 per year plus expenses for hotels and restaurants, etc. Their cultural style is quite different from many of those on whom they report. A high proportion come from public schools, Oxford and Cambridge. Such cultural differences are very important since they create immense problems for journalists as professionals. Most have few experiences outside their own class and culture and are not well placed to speak about what it is like to be unemployed or be scrutinized for co-habitation by social security investigators. In addition, the broadcasting organizations set limits on what their employees are allowed to do or say. Not everyone in these companies wishes to diverge from these limits, and given the background and training of most journalists, this is hardly surprising. But even where individuals are critical it is very difficult to break from normal journalism and the 'acceptable' house style as there are always pressures from the top to conform. No journalist or producer can fight every battle which comes along. In the end the most effective form of control is self-censorship. In the BBC the production of 'correct' journalism is constantly monitored in news and current affairs meeting. These involve the top thirty producers together with the director general and various assistants. The minutes of these meetings show that the news is sometimes subject to quite direct interventions. A complete set of minutes was recently leaked and reprinted in the *Leveller* magazine. In these the top management discuss, for example, how a new phase of economic crisis might mean new restrictions on news output[3]:

The Editor of News and Current Affairs said that at the present juncture stories about this country's currency needed careful handling . . . he was inclined for the first time in his career to suggest that they should always be checked first with the Treasury. . . . It would be wrong in the present circumstances to put out a major news story of which the Government had no warning.

Such direct and overt interventions are comparatively rare in most areas of reporting. The official line is likely to emerge and be changed through much more informal processes such as the routine contacts between journalists and civil servants of the kind we discussed earlier. Journalists are highly dependent on Whitehall as a major source of information, especially on the economy, industry and foreign affairs. Press briefings in this context are likely to be manipulative and journalists who do not toe the line are subject to the ultimate sanction of not being given information. Control as direct as this is again only a rare occurrence, since most top journalists share a similar social and cultural background with the hierarchies of the State. More importantly, the routine working practices of journalists are informed by the class assumptions of the society in which they live, that some people are more important than others and have a greater right to speak.

Stuart Hall, amongst others, has written extensively on this last feature of BBC life, of the way in which the BBC Charter's commitment to 'impartiality' and 'balance' builds into journalistic practices within the Corporation a particular kind of conservative bias.

The search for 'balance' is interpreted in formal elite terms, as requiring only a canvassing of the views of spokesmen from the major political parties, and not the exposure of those spokesmen to the arguments of others who do not share their assumptions.

Television news coverage is informed also by a set of substantive judgements and moral and political choices that slip in unannounced, unexamined and unsubstantiated in much of its reporting. For example, that trade unions are responsible for economic problems or that strikes are unfortunate unless they happen in Poland. But it does not follow that broadcasters present the world simply from the point of view of a 'ruling class' or the State, and are totally against labour. Neither do they hold to some form of 'middle' ground between all the contending political positions. They occupy and largely defend a distinct political position. The world which they prefer is a form of liberal capitalist democracy. In such a society the working class knows its place, but receives definite rights and privileges – consequently it is hoped that there may be a high degree of consent in the basic system. In such a world, the BBC would then feel able to speak on behalf of 'one nation' and the 'community'. It was never very easy to presume that such a consensus really existed. But with the onset of the present economic crisis it is becoming increasingly difficult. The broadcasters have now to make sense of new and difficult social and economic trends like unemployment, investment collapse and inflation. The change in government to the Conservatives in 1979 is a good illustration of the problem that they face in maintaining a coherent, consensual view. This was difficult enough with the economics of the last Labour government, but at least the Social Contract had a semblance of being an 'agreement' with something for everyone. But the BBC is distinctly unhappy with the politics of the new right and the rise of Thatcherism. However hard they try (and *Nationwide* probably tried hardest of all) they cannot work out how to say 'we are all pulling together' in the face of 3 million unemployed. Their natural territory is the right-wing of the Labour Party or the Social Democrats. These offer once again the prospect of an economy, with an orderly working class, whose leadership negotiates with government for the appropriate concessions. The popularity of the Social Democrats with the broadcasters comes from a heart-felt desire for a return to such politics. The policies of the new right, by contrast, are awakening political agitation and raising demands for an alternative politics that the BBC had long ago pretended does not seriously exist.

WHAT EVIDENCE IS THERE OF BIAS?

There are now a number of detailed research studies showing systematic bias in Press and television accounts of the economy, industrial relations, Northern Ireland, and in the general coverage of women and ethnic groups. The Glasgow University Media Group analysed television news programmes over a period of six years and concluded that news coverage was thoroughly imbalanced and partial. This analysis of economic and industrial coverage showed that journalists compressed their accounts of the world into a series of narrow and limited descriptions. The basic assumption underlying these was that the normal workings of our existing social and economic system were supposed to operate for the benefit of everyone involved. The news did not take account of any fundamental division between capital and labour, or between employers and those who worked for them. Phenomena such as strikes were analysed largely in terms of disruption and trouble which they caused to the community. Most significantly of all, there was no routine examination of the disruption and chaos that can 'normally' be produced by an economy organized around private interest. In Britain manufacturing industry has been starved of investment because it has been possible to make more money in other areas such as speculation in land or food. This has encouraged stagnation, inflation and unemployment. One other effect of these 'normal workings' is that capital is simply moved between countries, depending on where it can receive the best return. For example, when the Conservative government removed exchange controls in 1979, over the next two years £4,500 million was moved out of this country to be invested abroad. Much of this has gone into property, or has gone to countries such as South Africa where very high returns can be made from cheap, controlled labour. But such information is hardly prominent in the news. Where are all the headlines which could read:

We Wus Robbed – Three Million Unemployed As Capital Flows Abroad?

There is no routine reporting by the news of this form of 'damage to the economy'. The lack of investment means that machinery and plant become more obsolete and industry becomes more uncompetitive. But there are no outraged consumers on the news being asked about the movements of high finance. There is no comparable analysis of this sort of problem in the way that strikes are endlessly and routinely reported – we are offered a view of the world from the 'top downwards'. There is a reluctance to scrutinize the actions of the middle or upper classes as a source of 'trouble' and even more of a reluctance to examine the economic system on which this class structure rests. Instead, the activities of the workforce become the focus of the news. There is a search for stories of pig-headedness, wreckers, reds under the bed, exorbitant wage claims, strikes, and people who are workshy, think the country owes them a living, etc. There is no comparable list relating to the activities of management or the owners of capital – there are no routine references to management intransigence, incompetence, expense account lunches, perks, fraud, manipulation of wage deals, lock-outs, or tax avoidance. Most importantly, the economic mechanisms which regularly produce basic conflicts and decline are not routinely discussed as an explanation of problems such as unemployment and inflation. The world economy is presented as a kind of omnipresent force and movements in it (balance of payments, exchange rates, cheap imports, etc.) are the problem, but these movements are rarely explained for what they actually are – simply people making money in the best way they can. A multinational firm may be reported as regrettably being forced to close a factory in the North of England because it is uneconomic, but will not usually be spoken of as having made a *decision* to move its capital somewhere else because it can make more money there.

Where explanations are given they tend to focus simply on the latest problems that have been generated by trade unions or working people. In this example from BBC *News* a variety of quite different groups and situations are simply lumped together in the general theme of trouble, rumblings and unrest from the working class[4]:

The week *had its share of unrest. Trouble in Glasgow* with striking dustmen and ambulance controllers, short time in the car industry, no *Sunday Mirror* or *Sunday People* today and a *fair amount of general trouble* in Fleet Street and a *continuing rumbling* over the matter of two builders' pickets jailed for conspiracy.

Trade unions tended to be blamed for basic economic problems such as inflation and economic decline. Other causes were largely played down as the news focused on the favoured views of the 'authorities' and a variety of 'official' and 'acceptable' spokesmen. The Glasgow Media Group's research shows that this distortion was systematic. The Group found, for example, that:
* In January 1975, a widely reported speech by the prime minister which referred to 'manifestly avoidable stoppages of production'

caused by management and labour was transformed in twenty-nine later references and made to apply to the workforce *alone* as part of the general view that 'the ills of British Leyland' could be laid substantially at the door of the labour force.

- In the coverage of a strike by engine-tuners at Cowley in January 1975, as against BBC1's twenty-two references to Leyland's 'strike problem', there were five references to 'management failings' and one to the company's investment record. On BBC2 there were eight references to strikes as against three to management and two to investment; on ITN thirty-three to strikes, eight to management, and none to investment.
- In the first four months of 1975 there were seventeen occasions when views were given on the news against the government's policy of wage restraint and lower wages as a solution to the economic crisis. There were 287 occasions when views were expressed in favour of these policies.
- In the thirteen weeks of the Glasgow dustcart drivers' strike (1975) which was reported in 102 bulletins and included *twenty interviews*, not once was a striker interviewed to state his case nationally.
- In the same story from Glasgow, the causes of the strike were mentioned only eleven times out of forty items on BBC1, six times out of nineteen on BBC2 and nineteen times out of forty-three mentions on ITN.

DRAMATIC PICTURES AND THE SHORTAGE OF TIME?

It is sometimes argued that distortions in the news arise from the technical constraints on producing. Shortage of time and space are often pointed to as well as the need on television to go for dramatic visual images. But these arguments are not borne out by the evidence produced through analysing television programmes.

There were two main conclusions from the analysis of visual material. Firstly, the visual aspects of news presentation do not normally determine whether stories are run or how much attention or importance they are given. Many of the most important stories are not very 'visual' anyway and consist largely of 'talking heads', (shots of people talking directly to camera or being interviewed). This is especially true of political, industrial and economic coverage. Secondly, what happens in practice is that the news will look for the most visually interesting shots within the limits that govern the particular story and what will 'normally' be said about it. The real question is, what determines these limits? Why, for example, are the cameras outside the factory filming pickets, with a journalistic commentary on the need for 'law and order', rather than inside the factory filming graphic evidence of management mistakes? Obviously journalists look for the dramatic and the sensational angle on stories, but the question is, *which* drama and *which* sensation to tell what kind of story?

The same might be said of the arguments over time and space. The suggestion here is that the shortage of these necessitates tight, routine formulae which become the bases of news production. All this begs the question of why some formulae are developed rather than others. It takes no longer to run a headline on a strike of capital, than it does on a strike of labour. But where are the tight routine formulae giving us stories such as:

Capital Strike Devastates Industry

or

Dividends Payouts Threaten Jobs

The argument on the limits of time and space looks even thinner in the face of the saturation coverage given to stories such as strikes at Leyland. These have become a staple diet for television news over the last ten years, yet journalists have still not managed to give coherent alternative views of what is happening there. It is hardly the shortage of time that has prevented it.

DOES IT REALLY MATTER IF THE NEWS IS BIASED?

It is sometimes argued that people simply 'make up their own minds' and are not influenced very much by what they read or see. Our own view is that television cannot simply tell people how to think or act. Nonetheless it has a profound effect, because it has the power to tell people the *order* in which to think about events and issues. In other words it 'sets the agenda', decides what is important and what will be featured. More crucially, it very largely decides what people will think *with*, in the sense that it controls the information with which we make up our minds about the world. For example, people who work in car plants might know that there are many reasons why their industry is in decline and why production is lost. But those who take their information from television are likely to focus on a narrower range of causes. There are many who have never worked in a factory who are sure that the main problem is strikes. When the Glasgow Group analysed the coverage of BL the news persistently presented strikes as the main cause of lost production and stoppages. Yet in that period, half of the total stoppages were caused by factors *other* than strikes at Leyland, such as machine breakdown or mistakes by management. Yet the television account used the word 'stoppage' and the word 'strike' as if they were the same thing. If viewers heard 'another stoppage at Leyland' or 'more trouble today' they would be likely to hear these as a reference to strikes.

In the same way we found that wages rises were treated as the main cause of inflation and the two words 'wages' and 'inflation' became almost synonymous on the news. Yet there were many other causes of inflation in the period which we analysed. People were forced to pay higher prices for land, houses and rents as a result of the speculative boom in property in the early 1970s. Yet property speculators were not consistently pilloried on the news or their actions held up as one of the causes of rising prices. This role was reserved for trade unionists, and month after month the figures for wage increases were compared with price rises as if the one was automatically causing the other. Without the *information* that there are other causes of inflation it would be difficult to reach conclusions other than that wages and unions were to blame. When we showed our results to trade union schools and conferences we found that people believed that wages had shot up and had caused inflation. This was so even where this had not happened to them as individuals, and their own wages had fallen in real terms. This apparent contradiction was resolved time and time again by each group of trade unionists saying that while *their* wages had fallen other people's must have gone up. They tended to believe the news account even where it differed from their own immediate experience. While the wages of a few groups such as the miners had indeed risen and were the focus of a great deal of news coverage, the mass of working people had actually taken a cut in their real wages. While strikes and wages are routinely referred to on the news as the cause of economic problems there is no systematic examination of other areas which may cause difficulties, such as private investment. References to this as creating problems, if they occur at all, appear only as fragments. Unless we are informed what under-investment means, what it causes and what has happened to the money that might have been invested in industry, then it is difficult to 'make up our minds' about what is really wrong.

WHAT NEXT?

There are a number of groups organizing at present for change in the Press and broadcasting. The Campaign for Press Freedom has brought together a large number of different groups and unions, in the demands for the setting-up of a Labour Press and the 'Right to Reply' to material published in the privately owned papers. The campaign is now turning its attention to broadcasting as well, and the extension of the Right to Reply to television and radio will be an important first step. It is important that the organizations of Labour and the trade unions press for a balanced and accurate television service. Pressure from the outside lends support to those who are working for better television within the organizations. There is already much going on inside – the television technicians union (ACTT) is pressing hard for change and has re-established its committee to monitor bias in television. Recently we have been seen how the tacit threat of strikes by the NUJ changed the attitude of the BBC management to the Carrickmore incident and persuaded them to show the *Panorama* programme on the security services.

It is crucial that local organizations and trade unions keep up a steady contact with journalists. Where specific issues arise, such as a strike, then Press handouts and prepared 'copy' should always be provided. This can go on alongside the development of 'alternative' local media and news sheets etc. It is probably not worth bothering with the very right-wing press, but those journalists who will try to use material properly should be kept informed. A very good book giving advice on this and on how to contact the press, television and radio is Denis MacShane's *Using the Media*. In 1981, the *Changing Television Group*[5] was set up. This was an *ad hoc* group of television producers and researchers who met to discuss possible reforms. Their main demands are as follows.

1 *Aims of broadcasting.* Broadcasting should be required to represent fairly and accurately the divisions within our social world resulting from class, race or sex and programmes should be made from the perspectives which result from those divisions.

2 *Control.* To put the new aims into practice, the present Board of Control should be made more representative of the class, racial and sexual composition. Ultimately, boards should be elected at local and regional levels.

3 *Access.* A major part of the output should be given to forms of access programming, with proper budgets allocated to these. Material from non-professional sources should also be featured,

and broadcasting authorities should encourage the development of resources in the community to produce this.

The background and affiliations of the professionals who at present make programmes, should be broadly representative of the outside society. There must be positive discrimination in the recruitment of women and ethnic minorities to rectify existing imbalances.

Finally, we must realize that the media will not change until it is pressured to do so. There are some who work within it who are unhappy with its organization and content. But they will remain isolated unless the demand for change is voiced loudly by the unions, and through political parties. Broadcasting is at present required by law and convention to be balanced and impartial. As such it should be the subject of immediate criticism. It is foolish to wait for changes in other parts of society before pressing such basic arguments. Neither television nor the press will change until the population who are misrepresented and who suffer the effects of these biased media demand instead that the media be truly democratic and representative.

NOTES

1. E. C. Stuart (ed), *The Reith Diaries*, Collins 1975, p. 96
2. Mary Holland in an Edinburgh Television Festival Programme 1980
3. *The Leveller*, Jan. 1978, 15
4. BBC News, 18.55, 19 Jan. 75 (our italics)
5. Information and copies of their document *Changing Television* can be had from Changing Television Group, 14 Rosaville Road, London SW6

FURTHER READING

Glasgow Media Study Group, *Bad News*, 1976; *More Bad News*, Routledge and Kegan Paul 1980; *Really Bad News*, Writers and Readers 1982

P. Beharrell and G. Philo (eds), *Trade Unions and the Media*, Macmillan 1977

J. Curran et al. (eds), *Mass Communications and Society*, Arnold 1977

S. Hall et al., *Policing the Crisis*, Ch. 3, Macmillan 1978

J. Curran and J. Seaton (eds), *Power Without Responsibility: the press and broadcasting in Britain*, Fontana 1981

D. McShane, *Using the Media*, Pluto 1981

Chapter seven

INCOME, WEALTH AND THE WELFARE STATE

John Westergaard

There is a widespread view that socialists are barking up the wrong tree when they call for radical measures of social reconstruction to reduce inequality.

That argument usually has two prongs to it. First, it is said, full equality – or anything close to it – is a snare and a delusion: it is neither desirable nor possible. The very most that can be asked of any complex industrial society is a state of 'moderate inequality', where economic differences are tempered by rights of social citizenship open to everyone.[1] This would provide the means of secure livelihood for all (or at least for all prepared to 'contribute') at a standard fair enough to allow their common participation in the normal life of the society. It would also provide the opportunity for each individually to add to that according to personal ability and initiative – although, so many reformers would say, the result should not be so marked an accumulation of wealth and influence as to create unmanageable social tension or to defeat the aim of open opportunity.

The second common prong of the argument is to the effect either that we have already achieved such a state of affairs, or rather more modestly, that we are well on the way to doing so. Certainly, so this line of conventional wisdom runs, the trend has been fairly steadily towards mass conditions of no more that 'moderate inequality'; and this by means of measures and pressures of events – through welfare reforms, economic growth and the bargaining power of organized labour – falling well short of the radical institutional changes demanded by socialists. Indeed, it is now often added, the wheel has already turned too far towards equality: social security guarantees have been extended, taxation has been stepped up, differentials (as inequalities tend to be called in this vocabulary) have been eroded, to such a point that both individual effort and so also national economic enterprise are at risk of collapse.

Of course the two prongs of this argument cannot, in the end, be separated. An assessment of what has – and has not – been achieved towards reduction of inequality requires a judgement of what might, and what should, be achieved. But I shall concentrate in this chapter first, and for most of the way, on the issue of fact. My purpose is to set facts against the fiction – for this, summarily, is what it is – that Britain is now a significantly more equal society than it was a generation ago. I shall try to test against the record the postulate that public policy, economic change and trade union pressure have combined to shift the distribution of resources substantially away from the once privileged, in some steady trend which is claimed to leave remaining deprivation as a problem affecting only minorities of the population and to leave socialism without a plausible target.

This postulate needs a little more elaboration. There are several strands to it, expressed as assertions or implicit as assumptions in both political commentary and common parlance. *First* is the notion that overall inequalities of income have progressively narrowed, especially from the Second World War onwards. That is commonly coupled, *second*, with a view that remaining wealth and privilege now are little more than 'frills', a thin gloss of icing on a cake the solid substance of which is common citizenship for all but a few; and, because the rich are now so small in number and their wealth in aggregate is so limited, that any further redistribution to alleviate remaining poverty can come only from the broad 'middle mass' of the population. *Third*, and close on the heels of this point, comes the proposition that most people now belong to that broad 'middle mass'. Wage-earners, professionals, officials, business managers, executives and even directors – we are most of us 'middle class' (or alternatively 'working class') today; the old class labels, it is said, have lost their meaning except as reflections of a kind of 'cultural lag'. Once indeed produced by sharp inequalities of income and wealth – and associated inequalities of security and opportunity, influence and power – class divisions now survive only as peculiar differences of everyday manners, child-rearing habits and social outlook, and otherwise as pernicious figments of socialist and trade unionist imaginations lamentably trapped in memories of a vanished past. *Fourth*, and in further pursuit of this proposition, we are told that such poverty as can still be found is not a consequence of the simple class-formed injustices of earlier times. Poverty is no longer a sign of labour's subordination to capital, of property's concentration of wealth and power in few hands, of a corresponding dependence of the many on the vagaries of labour markets geared to the business of yielding a good financial return to capital. Indeed, it is said, poverty such as it is today is only superficially a single phenomenon. The poor may have their lack of means in common, but not the causes of it. They are therefore neither a 'class' nor members of a larger 'working class'. Many are poor because they are old; some because they are chronically sick, or handicapped, or 'unemployable' through deficiency of personal character or capacity; others because they live in families with only one parent or many children; others again because their skins are black or brown; many women, it may or may not be added, because as women they suffer discrimination against their sex both within their own households and in the larger economy. So, to summarize this strand of common belief, the poor today are a diverse assembly of victims of this, that or another particular 'handicap'. If more help is due to some of them – e.g. 'help to self-help' – we are told that it should go to meet, in carefully discriminating fashion, the specific needs of specific groups at risk. Once again, the inference runs, socialist measures for wholesale transformation of the economy are beside the point.

Of course there are, and have been different versions of this bundle of conventional thought, varying in their emphasis on this or that strand of argument or in their evaluation and diagnosis of causes and prospects. In the 1950s and into the 1960s, for example, something like a consensus of establishment opinion welcomed the allegedly inexorable trend towards a quasi-equality of citizenship as a triumph for policies of 'mixed economy' moderation and as portending the end of ideological divisions in politics and industry. From the mid-1960s so sanguine a view found less strident expression. It was harder to maintain at full voice, not only or even mainly because accumulating statistical evidence on economic distribution told against it; but because events – new popular militancy, incipient signs of 'stagflation', uncertainty of profits – began to shake establishment confidence. But if, for example, orthodox opinion now acknowledged the 'rediscovery of poverty', it also came to terms with it by denying, as outlined before, that its existence signified a persistence of economically embedded class inequality. Faith in the inexorability of the assumed trend towards a state of common citizenship – if at a slower pace than postulated before, and with a little more reform needed to help it along – remained firm. The countercurrent of the 'new right' – politically represented in Britain by Heath in the guise of Selsdon-man before Thatcher took over in monetarist dress – has again not questioned the 'facts' as conventionally conceived; only their positive evaluation by adherents of a Keynesian mixed economy. The trend, so the argument now comes from authoritarian liberals who challenge the 'settlement' of the 1940s, has indeed been one of creeping equalization. But, they say, because the effect has been to generate ever-rising popular expectations of something-for-nothing and neglect of the discipline of markets and differential incentives, the trend must be reversed. So old centre and new right alike take socio-economic levelling to be a fact of recent history, the former for good and the latter for ill. Yet there is little in the evidence to give substance to this assumption which they hold in common.

TRENDS OF INCOME DISTRIBUTION

It makes sense to look first at the trends of income distribution over many years – back to the Second World War – because the prime article of established faith is that income inequality has been more or less steadily compressed over the past three or four decades. True, the evidence relevant for such a long-run view presents some special difficulties. It comes mainly from information about taxation, so that a variable mixture of supplementary sources and guesswork has had to be added to fill at least some of the gaps left in respect of income which, legally or illegally, was not reported to the tax authorities. Moreover, even when for realism we concentrate on 'disposable' income after payment of direct taxes, the picture is still crude in other ways. It takes no account of further deductions from real income by indirect taxation; no account of additions to it from use of public services in kind as distinct from cash, as well as from enjoyment of private welfare benefits in the form of all manner of 'perks' to privileged employees; and no account of variations in household composition among the 'tax units' (broadly speaking married couples and unmarried adults) for whom estimates of income are given. Nevertheless, handled with caution, the record provides a reasonable base from which to start.[2]

Measures of policy and less deliberate economic changes during and immediately after the Second World War did indeed produce quite a significant shift in income distribution away from the wealthy. Thus the ostensible share of the richest 5 per cent of the population dropped from just under a quarter of all post-tax income in 1938 to around a sixth by the end of the 1940s. Though these figures exaggerate, as we shall see, they reflect some real moderation of inequality; and there has been no subsequent return to the pattern as it was before the war. But if the disparity of incomes has actually narrowed further since the immediate postwar years, this has been to a small degree at best. On the face of the official tax-based information, the share of the richest 5 per cent – to take them again – fell from some 16 per cent of total personal income after direct tax in the early 1950s to about 13 per cent or a little more in the late 1970s; that of the richest 10 per cent in all from 25.5 per cent to 22.5 or 23 per cent of the total. But even this modest apparent shift benefited those already fairly comfortably off at least as much as the poor: thus the 30 per cent of people with the lowest incomes had their recorded share of all income after tax boosted only from 11.5 to barely 13 per cent over the entire period from the early 1950s to the late 1970s.

A glance behind the face of the figures, moreover, suggests that even this slight further compression of inequality registered since the aftermath of the war may be illusory. Econometricians have made various adjustments to the first-order data up to about 1960, to allow for certain kinds of effective income not assessed for tax (such as some unreported income from capital). The results point not only to a greater concentration in the hands of the very wealthy than appeared from the formal record, but also to a conclusion that the real drop in their share of the total was smaller in the 1940s than the original figures would have it, virtually nil during the 1950s. It seems from this that the use of devices to dodge taxation – available especially to business people and some professionals – was almost certainly stepped up during this period, to the effect that the official record increasingly understated the full extent of income inequality. Corresponding adjustments have not been made to the figures after 1960. But it is plausible, and supported by some evidence from supplementary sources, that since then 'perks' of greater variety and sophistication have grown still more in their importance as real additions to the recorded incomes, particularly of directors and executives: this not only to keep taxation at bay but also to reduce the impact of the incomes policies pursued by governments at various times over the past twenty years. If account were taken of that, the modest apparent drop in the shares of the well-to-do in total post-tax income since around 1950 would be still slighter and might even vanish. Certainly their real shares are larger than they seem.[3]

Though employment at high levels of business management provides very effective opportunities to convert part of real income into unrecorded forms, a good deal of money-spinning takes place lower down the socio-economic scale which is similarly invisible. Nobody accurately knows the size of the 'black economy', with its petty tax-fiddling to complement refined measures of tax avoidance at the top of the tree, its 'moonlighting' jobs, its building-and-decorating operations paid in ready cash, and so on.[4] It may, all in all, add some 8 per cent or even more to recorded national product, though by other estimates less than half that. But while the distribution of benefits from this clandestine economic activity is as difficult to determine as its size, there can be little doubt that its pay-off is small on the whole for those who are low also in the formal economic pecking order: for the unskilled, the elderly and the sick as well as for women, for example; perhaps also for workers in industrial areas by contrast with those in areas of 'mixed class'. So adequate allowance for invisible gains and earning of all kinds would boost the incomes recorded both for the very wealthy and, though in all probability far more patchily, for quite a lot of people in the middle range; but a good deal less, if at all, for the poor and the near-poor. On all scores, then, inequality of income is still sharper than it looks at first sight.

Whether all the same it has been mildly reduced in recent years – as the tax-based information suggests before a pinch of salt is taken to it – is a question for which some check against other sources can be made, though no further back than the early 1960s. For the period since then official estimates of income distribution have been published which come, not from tax records, but from regular sample surveys of 'family expenditure'. For various reasons (including inadequate sample coverage of the very wealthy and of some groups among the poor) these data also understate the full extent of income inequality; and changes in the form of the figures make for difficulties in precise comparisons over time. But they provide a useful supplement to the tax-based record, just because their source is different and because they add important refinements – separate analyses of the circumstances of households of different composition; and estimates of income both before and after 'State intervention' to take away taxes (indirect as well as direct) and pay out welfare benefits (in kind as well as cash), though again without adequate account of private 'perks'.

Calculations from this information – for all types of household taken together and for most of them taken separately – show that in the 1960s (and not least, ironically, during the period of Labour government then) overall inequality of real incomes, allowing both for taxation and for public welfare benefits, tended to widen rather than to narrow.[5] There was, however, some reversal of that trend during the 1970s when, despite a further increase of inequality as measured by reference to 'original incomes' (which exclude all State benefits and take no account of taxation), this was outweighed by a rather more progressive trend in the effects of taxes and public welfare. The result, in the end, was a very slight compression in the range of 'final income' over this last decade.[6] Technicalities obstruct any attempt to put these contrary indications from the 1960s and the 1970s neatly together. But overall, it is safe to conclude, they more or less balanced out.

The weight of this evidence, then, goes to reinforce scepticism about the hint of slight 'equalization' offered by the first-order tax-based information. Yet there is neither room nor need for dogmatism. The data to hand are all imperfect; and some mild changes in income distribution, in this period or that, would hardly be surprising anyway. But over the full span of years from the immediate aftermath of the Second World War to the late 1970s – which is as far as we can go as yet – at best income inequality in Britain became just a little less acute; no less plausibly, it stayed on balance very much as it was. The period of and just after the Second World War indeed showed shifts of income that, rather modest though they were, helped to make Britain a fairer society. But that in no way signified the beginning of a growing trend. On the contrary, the range of inequality has been more or less stable since then: not entirely frozen, but so broadly constant in pattern as to make nonsense of the view that continuous and substantial equalization has been at work.

WEALTH AND POVERTY

It is just as much nonsense to claim that only modest 'differentials' are involved, unworthy of description as inequality. Take as a preliminary indication the most recent evidence from the 'family expenditure' sample material – useful for this purpose because it provides adjustment for differences in household composition (on assumptions that children count for much less towards living costs than adults, and that couples can live more cheaply than two single people each on their own). After such adjustment of the figures, the poorest tenth of all households in 1979 were calculated to have, between them, only about 4.5 per cent of total 'final income' in cash and kind at their disposal; the best-off tenth, by contrast, some 20 per cent of the total – well over four times as much.[7] The disparity, plainly, is large even on this basis; but the gap between rich and poor is far greater in reality.

The trouble with this first indication is that, though the figures have the advantage over others of allowing both for variations in household composition and for the incidence of taxes and public welfare, they sizeably understate inequality for other reasons. They do so because the 'best-off' tenth here are quite a mixed group, comprising many people who are 'just' very comfortably placed as well as a few extremely rich whose share grossly exceeds their small numbers; and because, moreover, it is the real incomes of the latter that are especially under-estimated in all official data. To get closer to reality on these scores, we can turn to the attempts made to correct the tax-based records – which do distinguish the very rich in a way that the sample-based figures do not – for some of the unreported income-boosts available at the top of the financial tree. With allowances of this sort for 1959–60, for example, it was likely that the richest 1 per cent of the population – a very small group in concentrated privilege – between them then enjoyed at least 10 per cent of all real personal income after direct tax: twice the 5 per cent share officially recorded for them; and, notably, little if anything short of the probable real share then taken by the entire poorest quarter or more of the population.[8] Corresponding adjustments for unreported effective income are not available to correct the tax-based records since that time. But if only a prorata allowance were made in the comparable official figures for 1976–77,[9] the share of the richest 1 per cent in all real post-tax income would come out then at about 8 per cent – rather more than the aggregate share of the poorest fifth of the population; and this without regard for the possibility that increased resort to tax-and-incomes-policy-avoiding devices in the 1960s and 1970s might make a larger adjustment reasonable.

Precision is impossible here. Unrecorded real income and relatively low exposure to indirect taxes may boost the share of the very rich more than allowed; consideration of other factors (family size among the wealthy by comparison with the poor whose households are generally small, for example, and the proportional distribution of public welfare services in kind) will tend to pull the other way. On balance the rough guess just made could be quite realistic. But whether the highly privileged 1 per cent have a share of all real income as large as that of the entire sixth, or the entire fifth, or even the entire quarter slice of the population in the poorest circumstances, makes no significant difference to the conclusion. The concentration of current resources for livelihood in the hands of a tiny minority is enormous; the gap between them and the poor yawns wide; and there is wealth enough piled up at the extreme top to eliminate mass poverty in the low reaches of the scale, if will and radical measures were directed to that. The figures, for all their margin of error, give no substance to the notion that redistribution now can come only from 'the middle'.

True enough, poverty is not in this country what it was – or what it still is for hundreds of millions outside the old and the new industrial nations. While in relative terms the range of inequality has hardly shifted in Britain since the early 1950s, absolute levels of living have risen fairly steadily until the last few years. The poor have taken part in that growth of material comfort: their poverty is no longer the poverty of rags, gross malnutrition and early death. But if poverty is defined – in some way, whatever the detail – by reference to common contemporary standards, it persists in such relative terms on much the same scale as a generation ago. An elaborate study a few years ago, for example, used 'family expenditure' sample material to check on the size of the gap, over time, between the incomes of households at average levels of living and those of households, similarly composed, among the poor. Had expanding 'affluence' from the early 1950s to the early 1970s narrowed the gap, and thus given to people at the bottom of the economic pile that special boost which politicians so often claimed it would? The answer, quite in line with other evidence of the persistence of inequality, was 'no'. The poor had just about kept up with others as overall living standards rose; no more.[10]

This answer was resoundingly confirmed by a recently published monumental enquiry into the subject.[11] That showed very widespread poverty by a variety of definitions – with 9 per cent of the population living on real incomes actually below the official supplementary benefit level in 1968–69; another 23 per cent dependent on 'near-poverty' incomes less than 40 per cent above this minimum standard set by the State; and about one person in every four lacking the means likely, from evidence collected in the study itself, to be necessary for ordinary life by common current standards.[12] Comparison with both earlier and later information, moreover, gave no reason to believe that the scale of poverty in such relative terms had declined in the years up to the enquiry, or has declined thereafter during the 1970s. Indeed the effect of recent acute recession must have been to make for still more poverty.

Of course any 'poverty line' is rather arbitrary. It does not mark off a distinct group of the population from the rest; and, wherever it is drawn within reason, there will be much movement across it from one time to another. Conservative opinion tends to find consolation in that, because it means that many people who are below the line today will be above it a week, a month or a year later. But it also means the converse; many who are not 'in poverty' now will be so in future and/or have been so in the past. In short, the risk of poverty extends far more widely than is shown by its incidence at any one time. That risk, moreover, is very unevenly distributed. It is considerable for those many people whose lives, and those of their families, are tied to wage-earning in manual or low-grade non-manual work; and especially so if the work, as often and irrespective of individuals' ability, involves little skill.

It is true that many poor people are old, and many old people poor. But ageing does not, by itself, bring severe financial hardship with it. It does so for those who have little or nothing from occupational pension schemes, 'golden handshakes' and property income to add to basic State provision when they retire. Managers, executives, directors and professionals in fact carry much from their privileges in working life with them into retirement; but even with the extension of occupational pension arrangements to others, effective coverage and the terms of such extra pensions worsen the further one looks down the occupational scale. Even before retirement, moreover, it is the members of wage-earning households who are especially at risk of poverty. They are at risk as adults because unemployment, short-time working and ill-health – the latter usually with little of the protection of normal earnings against sickness provided for salaried staff – are all more common among people dependent on the lower reaches of the labour market. They are at risk also because those who remain wage-earners without achieving promotion to more secure and better-paid work generally reach the peak of their earnings fairly early in working life, and do not enjoy automatic annual increments in pay thereafter. From middle age onwards, moreover, they may find themselves forced down the ladder of earnings – off bonus-paid or lucrative overtime work, for example, or from more skilled to less-skilled jobs – and then into early retirement through poor health or politely phrased redundancy. Their children, of course, are similarly at risk of poverty while growing up. The evidence to these effects – both from the monumental study of poverty quoted before and from a wide range of other enquiries[13] – is massive. It leaves the proposition that poverty is now for all practical purposes a consequence of special 'handicaps' unrelated to the larger workings of markets and property – unrelated to continuing inequality of 'class situation' – without a leg to stand on.

155

Socialist arguments

LABOUR MARKETS, PROPERTY AND PUBLIC WELFARE

The ways in which labour markets work obviously play a large part in the making of economic inequality, because most people are employees for many years of their lives: men usually for some forty years or more of full-time work; women too now very extensively, though still with conventional interruption of their working lives by child-rearing, and often in part-time jobs when employed. Evidence on the long-run trends of inequalities in earnings between jobs of different kinds shows some compression of the range of disparity in pay: especially, it seems, during and shortly after the Second World War and again, perhaps as a side-effect of rising inflation, in the course of the 1960s.[14]

A pinch of salt needs, once more, to be taken to some of these signs of diminution of 'differentials'. An apparent continued fall in the – still pronounced – advantages of pay enjoyed by 'higher professionals' over others during the 1960s, for example, may reflect the special boom in recruitment to work of this kind during the period, with consequent temporary depression of the average by the fairly low starting salaries of young people newly admitted to 'higher professional' jobs. A downward trend in the continuing premium of 'managerial' salaries over most other pay since the mid-1950s – and the overall figures here in any case gloss over very large differences between many in quite humdrum management posts and a small richly rewarded elite of top executives – may mask relative stability maintained through increased use of invisible 'perks' in place of cash salary increases. A narrowing of the gaps, level for occupational level, between women's and men's earnings in full-time employment during the 1970s seems to point to some positive effect of legislation for equal pay. But this is to look aside from the marked disadvantages still suffered by women through their common relegation to subordinate levels of work even when full-timers, and through the fact that so many women can take only ill-protected part-time employment. One long-standing trend has gone to accentuate labour market inequalities rather than to reduce them. This is a gradual decline since the 1930s in the relative earnings of male (but not of female) clerical workers – from a level once about the same as those of skilled manual workers, to a point now on average below semi-skilled manual earnings though still for shorter hours. It is doubtful, however, how far this can be seen as a firm sign of 'white collar proletarianization'. There is, from other evidence, much movement into and out of such low-grade non-manual work – some upwards by promotion of young clerks to managerial posts, for example, some by recruitment into 'dead-end' routine office work of elderly men once in blue-collar jobs – to confound any conception of clerical employment as a single kind, or of clerks as a single social group.[15]

For all these qualifications, the net effect first of wartime mobilization of resources and later of bargaining pressures in the boom conditions of the 1960s was probably to compress the broad range of occupational disparities in earnings somewhat.[16] But if the labour market contribution to income inequality has thus been cut back a little, demographic changes – a rise in the proportion of old people in the population especially – and mounting unemployment since the 1960s have increased the numbers not at work who live on very sparse means; and overall inequality of incomes has changed little if at all. Moreover, the gross differences in earnings between different broad bands of employment remain very marked; and the order of the occupational hierarchy in this respect is, except for the relative fall in male clerical earnings, just as it was. 'Higher professionals' and the very mixed group of 'managers' are at the top, with average earnings two to three times as good as those of unskilled workers even before one takes the pinches of salt necessary to the current figures in their case. 'Lower professionals' follow well below them, though like the more privileged groups – and unlike manual wage-earners – they typically move on an 'upward curve' during much of their working lives, because they enjoy annual increments of salary and significant opportunities for promotion. The gradations of manual wage-earning – skilled, semi-skilled and unskilled – are still firmly at the lower end of the scale, with only supervisors (and, in the case of women, large numbers of routine clerical staff) to fill the wide earnings gap above them to 'lower professional' level.

Step for step on the occupational ladder, women continue to earn less than men even in full-time work; and, in very broad terms, their disadvantages in earnings increase *down* the ladder. The few women in 'higher professional' jobs in 1978, for example, earned on average 20 per cent less than their male counterparts, but women in manual work 40 to 50 per cent less than men in corresponding wage-earner grades. This point needs emphasis. Discrimination against women does not negate the 'class' hierarchy of the labour market. It extends and sharpens it: even taking the unqualified figures at face value, women in full-time manual jobs earn only about a quarter of the average for 'higher professional' men.

There is a risk, however, of staring oneself blind by concentrating on labour market inequalities. Property ownership makes a large contribution to the total inequality of income, because it accounts for a substantial part of the share of the very rich. I suggested earlier that, after adjustment of the first-order tax-based figures to allow for 'invisible' gains, the richest 1 per cent of the population in the late 1970s may have had as big a share of all real income after direct tax as the entire poorest fifth. At least a quarter or so of the income thus in the hands of a tiny minority came from investments – a far higher proportion than just a step or two down the scale[17]; and with the qualification 'at least' because invisible income added into the adjusted estimate is likely to include a good deal from capital, and because among the very rich there are many – directors and top executives of business corporations – whose earnings from employment are more in the nature of profits arising from control of capital than they are labour market salaries. So property ownership, *de jure* and still more *de facto*, plays a crucial part in creating that extreme concentration of privilege in few hands which continues to mark the overall inequality of incomes in Britain.

This is not surprising, because property of all kinds is very unequally spread; and property of a kind that yields disposable income – shares and other securities especially – is yet more so. Ownership of assets in some form, it is true, has become more widespread over time. Until the 1960s this had little effect for the great bulk of the population, because such diffusion of wealth as the estimates suggested involved mainly redistribution among the very rich to reduce the impact of death duties; since then it has had some real effect for many people, because owner-occupation of housing has become more common.[18] Even so, in 1976, still a quarter of all 'marketable wealth' was officially estimated to be owned by only 1 per cent of the adult population; little short of half by a 5 per cent minority; and altogether just over 60 per cent by no more than 10 per cent.[19] Conversely, the nationwide study of poverty a few years earlier had found nearly one in every three households to be without assets of any kind to more than a total value then of £200.[20] What matters even more, for the effect of property on income distribution, is that individual ownership of securities which yield money in dividends and interest – and can readily be sold – is a massive resource still confined to very few people. Thus in 1976 again, probably more than half the total value of personally owned company securities was in the hands of a minority comprising about 0.5 per cent of the adult population, nine-tenths of it in the hands of some 5 per cent. Ownership of land, similarly by reference to its value and excluding dwellings, was almost as heavily concentrated.[21]

In short the weight of private capital accounts, in very direct fashion, for much of that extremity of privilege which is to be found at the top of the income scale. Capital, as an influence on labour markets to gear them towards ultimate profit-making, also plays a large part in shaping the hierarchy of earnings from employment. But the role of government, so common belief would have it, is now sizeably to modify the resulting pattern of inequality through progressive taxation and public welfare provision. There is something to that belief, but not very much.

For a start, taxation by itself makes for little redistribution between wealthy and poor, if indeed any. While direct taxes – income tax in particular – do fall proportionately rather more on the broader shoulders, effective rates of tax on that score rise only quite gently above the lowest steps of the income ladder. This is so – even without regard for the ways in which portions of high income can be converted into non-reported form to avoid tax – for several reasons: because, for example, allowances reduce real tax rates up the scale below their nominal levels; and not least because governments have refused to adjust the tax threshold sufficiently over time to counter inflation, so that liability for income tax now starts very low down on the ladder. What is more, the limited progressive effect of direct taxes is more or less neutralized by the regressive effect of indirect taxes – especially of rates, duties on tobacco and beer, some other charges, and probably VAT – which fall proportionately more heavily on the weaker shoulders.[22] Calculations from 'family expenditure' sample material allow the combined impact of *all* taxes assignable to individual households to be estimated.[23] Over most of the income range for most types of households, direct and indirect taxes together in 1979 took away rather more than 40 per cent of 'original incomes'. But they took away somewhat less, in fact, among the best-off 20 per cent of households; and more, in some cases much more, among the worst-off 20 per cent. Measured this way the incidence of total taxation was thus actually regressive: softest on the wealthy and hardest on the poor.

We can use another measure, if we add to 'original incomes' State cash benefits – old age pensions, dole, supplementary benefit and other cash payments in fact financed from taxation. A very slight progressive effect then appears, though only at the bottom of the ladder. On this basis, in the case of most types of household, direct and indirect taxes together in 1979 took away about a third of the gross money incomes of the poorest 20 per cent; a little more (up to about two-fifths) by and large from everybody else – but that almost irrespective of income, and indeed with a tendency for the best-off 20 per cent to pay a notch less than those on 'middle' incomes. Whichever set of calculations we take, the belief that taxation hits the wealthy hardest – and 'penally' – is in flagrant contradiction to the facts.

The State's services nevertheless make for some redistribution from rich to poor – not through progression in the incidence of taxes, because there is virtually none of that when the effects of all taxes are added together; but through allocation of the benefits which some of the tax revenue goes to fund. Cash benefits, in particular, have a necessarily progressive effect. Old age pensions, dole, supplementary benefit, family income supplement and the like lift many incomes originally nil or negligible to somewhere near the official 'poverty line' – if often, as noted earlier, still short of it. The impact of direct payments of this sort is concentrated at the bottom of the economic hierarchy. The value of State services in kind is spread more widely; and in some cases – education especially – the well-to-do draw more from the services in absolute terms than do those lower down the scale. Yet in relative terms the boost to real incomes from State benefits in kind is also greater for the poor than for the rich, because the poor have so very little to start with.

All in all, therefore, with the impact of taxation broadly neutral and the impact of public welfare broadly progressive, government activity does, at the end of the day, reduce the range of inequality. By one summary estimate (incorporating detailed adjustments for variations in household composition), the general effect in 1979 was to raise the real income share of the poorest tenth from nil to 4.5 per cent and to reduce that of the wealthiest tenth from 27 to 20 per cent, with smaller shifts at other levels of the hierarchy.[24] That overstates the real shift and understates final inequality, because the figures fail to capture slices of high income – including private welfare benefits and other 'perks' – that fall outside the sample record. For many types of household, moreover, even the recorded shifts were far more modest: for married couples with one or more children, for example, and for adult-only households with no retired members. Redistribution through the 'welfare state' in fact benefits primarily public pensioners – the working-class old in particular – and single-parent families. Some of the money thus shifted comes from the wealthy: not because they pay proportionately more tax than most others; but because their high incomes yield more at a near-even real rate of tax, and gain proportionately little from State benefits because they are so large to start with. Much of the money comes – by 'horizontal' rather than 'vertical' redistribution – from ordinary wage-earners at work. As near-even rates of taxation show, it is not least their purses which keep the welfare state going.

CONCLUSIONS: MYTHS, FACTS AND PROSPECTS

In short, conventional wisdom proves false when set against the facts. Income inequality has *not* substantially and progressively diminished since the step in that direction which came in the 1940s. Wealth at the top has *not* been so trimmed that alleviation of hardship today could come, in bulk, only from a broad 'middle mass'. A state of common 'social citizenship' is *not* near achievement, when poverty cuts off many millions of the population from participation in ordinary life by current standards. Such poverty, moreover, is *not* of a new kind, a product of diverse and discrete 'handicaps' unrelated to class circumstances: it is now, as before, mainly a risk of wage-earning life. Taxation does *not* hit the wealthy hardest. And though 'welfare state' benefits and services have indeed helped to reduce inequality below its prewar level, funding them is *not* a burden that falls chiefly on the well-to-do: very much of the money comes from the pockets of wage-earners at work.

It is a matter of speculation rather than straight fact to answer the question why, nevertheless, it is widely believed that equalization has been in steady progress. The point that such a belief serves strong vested interests cannot go all the way to an answer: even propagated by the mass media, the belief needs some contact with observable reality to make it plausible. One feature of reality has been rising average 'affluence', until quite recently. For a fair time at least, this probably helped to mask continuing inequality; and politicians have indeed wanted economic growth just because it offered a chance of keeping discontent about distribution at bay. Inequality may also have become less visible both because maintenance of privileged wealth now involves more subterfuge, to evade taxation and sometimes government restraint of incomes; and because money can no longer buy domestic servants, or therefore the upkeep of palatial homes, on the same scale as earlier. Here is one reason, too, why the rich themselves feel that they have lost out. Again, slippage of some differentials in employment earnings – perhaps notably those of men in routine office jobs by comparison with manual workers, because this shift affects an old line of cultural division – can have been misread to signify a larger change in income patterns. Above all, both the rhetoric of 'welfare state' provision and the increased presence of organized labour in industrial and political affairs have hinted a promise of equalization: it seemed natural for a time to assume fulfilment of the promise, though little in fact happened to bring that about.

But if welfare rhetoric, stronger labour representation in industry and State bodies, past economic growth itself and, on top of that, government pretensions to regulate incomes against inflation – if these have all, even will-nilly, served to suggest a prospect of fairer shares, they have also thereby served to raise popular expectations. In turn the clash between such heightened expectations and the reality of little distributional change – veiled but not permanently concealed – can probably account for much of the flow and ebb of new militancy from the 1960s. There has been a history since then of volatile action and demonstration – in workplaces, about housing and in the streets – in waves of discontent which even at their peaks have generally lacked clear and common political focus, yet have shown widespread loss of faith in the status quo and once-tolerated authority. From this has come establishment anxiety that the country may be 'ungovernable'. Two lines of official policy have emerged in response to that, and to that complex of associated issues which include the need perceived to restructure a vulnerable British economy in the face of international crisis. One, the preference of the broad political centre, is designed in essence to restore the equilibrium of the socio-economic settlement of the 1940s. It seeks accommodation – some form of moderate 'social contract' – with the union movement as the main organized force for disruption. The other, for which Thatcherites speak in Britain today, hopes to take apart the 1940s settlement; to reduce the scale and scope of State activity; and, by so curtailing 'public promises', to defuse popular expectations and 're-educate' people to set new store by the virtues of private thrift and market discipline.

Neither line of policy offers a prospect of radical distributional change towards equality. The second, neo-liberal line most clearly does not. Its advocacy is for sharper inequality to reward initiative, this to be made palatable both by eventual prosperity and by open opportunity. But whatever the promise of prosperity, the consolation of opportunity – something like equal opportunity to achieve wealth or poverty according only to talent – rings hollow when, as much research has conclusively shown, entrenched inequality of condition itself makes equality of opportunity a will o' the wisp.[25] The first, more orthodox line of policy offers hope, it is true, of some modest shift to fairer shares as a lubricant for 'social contract' making; but no more, in all likelihood, because its Labour-right and Social Democratic–Liberal protagonists adhere to the rules and mechanisms of a 'mixed economy' where the prime moving forces will still be those of capital and commercial markets. Those moving forces set limits to redistribution.

Broad persistence of relative inequality since around 1950 is not a phenomenon peculiar to Britain: evidence from other Western countries points to much the same there.[26] This is hardly a result of accident. More likely it goes to show – if only in rough outline – the nature of the limits set to redistributive reform and collective bargaining, so long as private capital is in first place and, be it noted, gives a right to high income irrespective of its owners' 'contribution' or 'need'; so long as employment earnings vary widely under pressures directed partly to profit optimization for capital, partly to protection of professional and other sectional employee interests well placed in the diverse markets for labour, never towards a pattern of distribution that makes plausible moral sense; and so long as public welfare provision, whether skinflint or generous, is designed to mitigate the effects of property and market distribution, not to set those mechanisms of distribution aside. A transformation of the economy into socialist shape would not of itself guarantee much greater equality: it could well be open to inegalitarian manipulation and abuse of new power. But it is one necessary precondition for much greater equality.

NOTES

1. This view has been argued in sophisticated form by T. H. Marshall, especially in his *Citizenship and Social Class*, Cambridge UP 1950, Ch. 1. See also his *Social Policy in the Twentieth Century*, Hutchinson (4th edn) 1975
2. The main sources used for the next two paragraphs to describe long-run trends are a series of estimates by H. Lydall, J. Utting, R. J. Nicholson, A. J. Walsh and J. E. Meade, summarized in J. Westergaard and H. Resler, *Class in a Capitalist Society*, Heinemann Educational Books 1975, Penguin Books 1976, pp. 39–43; and reports of the Royal Commission on the Distribution of Income and Wealth, No. 5 (HMSO 1977, Cmnd 6999, Ch. 3 and Appendix C) and especially No. 7 (HMSO 1979, Cmnd 7595, Ch. 2 and also pp. 51–3)
3. Other things being equal, some drop in the share of income going to the very rich would have been expected from some time

during the 1960s onwards (though not earlier), if the proposition were true that, under powerful bargaining pressures from labour, profits then began to be so squeezed that capital's share of income in relation to labour declined. This proposition was first presented in comprehensive form, and from a Marxist perspective, by A. Glyn and R. Sutcliffe in *British Capitalism, Workers and the Profits Squeeze*, Penguin Books 1972. But the proposition is open to unresolved doubts on grounds concerning: the adequacy of the measures of profit available; the difficulties in determining the allocation of 'benefits', as between capital and labour, of the large and increased share of product represented by government revenue and expenditure; the question whether a decline in apparent pre-tax *rates* of profit was translated into a decline of effective post-tax *shares* of profits; and of course the very uncertainties referred to in the text whether, with allowance for probably rising unreported gains at top business levels, any shift in the distribution of real personal income indeed occurred in the 1960s and 1970s

4. On the 'black economy' see, for example, *Twelfth Report from the Committee of Public Accounts*, HMSO 1981; J. I. Gershuny and R. E.Pahl, 'Work outside employment', *New Universities Quarterly*, Winter 1979–80; S. Henry, *Can I Have It in Cash?*, Astragal Books 1981

5. See J. Westergaard and H. Resler, op. cit., pp. 45–8

6. For this point I have made calculations from the data in G. A. Stephenson, 'The effects of taxes and benefits on household income, 1976', *Economic Trends*, Feb. 1978 (which includes information for 1971 as well as 1976) and Anon., 'The effects of taxes and benefits on household income, 1979', *Economic Trends*, Jan. 1981. Some summary data to the same effect, though only for 1973–78 and without distinction between households of different type, are given in *Social Trends*, 11 HMSO 1981, 102 Table 6.27

7. *Economic Trends*, Jan. 1981, op. cit., 112 Table T

8. See the summary of the effects of this adjustment (by J. E. Meade) and of earlier corrections to the tax-based record in J. Westergaard and H. Resler op. cit., pp. 42–3

9. The tax-based record (Royal Commission on the Distribution of Income and Wealth, Report No. 7, op. cit., p. 15) gives the 1976–77 post-tax share of the richest 1 per cent as between 3.5 and 4 per cent (the latter figure incorporating an allowance for tax-deductable mortgage interest and the like). This would be

doubled (i.e. up to some 8 per cent) if correction for untaxed property income were to produce the same proportionate effect as estimated by J. E. Meade (see note 8. above) for 1959. The post-tax share of the poorest 20 per cent in 1976–77 was about 7.5 per cent according to the tax-based record; but the true figure would be lower after upward adjustment at the top of the scale

10. See G. C. Fiegehen, P. S. Lansley and A. D. Smith, *Poverty and Progress in Britain 1953–73* (Cambridge UP 1977, p. 28). For this analysis the 'poor' (in two categories) were defined as households at such a point of the scale that their incomes were exceeded by 90 per cent, and by 95 per cent of all households. After adjustment for household composition, income in the first of these two categories (10 percentage points above the very bottom) was shown to have been 57.9 per cent of 'median' income in 1953–54, 57.4 per cent in 1971; in the second category (5 percentage points above the very bottom), 48.8 per cent of 'median' income in 1953–54, 48.5 per cent in 1971 – if anything, a slight deterioration in the position of the poor relative to average circumstances

11. P. Townsend, *Poverty in the United Kingdom* (Penguin Books, 1979). The results of this very large report are summarized and discussed in its two final chapters, 26 and 27

12. This third measure of poverty (as a matter of 'relative deprivation') can be questioned on both conceptual and technical grounds; see, for example, the exchange between a stridently voiced critic, David Piachaud, and Peter Townsend in *New Society*, 10 and 17 Sept. 1981. But while this no more any other measure of poverty can claim the simple 'objectivity' ascribed (say) to a temperature scale, Townsend's 'relative deprivation' standard deserves full credit as a pioneer attempt to put flesh onto a notion of 'social citizenship' – possession of the means to a reasonably all-round share in ways of life currently within the common expectations and practices of ordinary people. And the broad nature of his conclusion is not in doubt – that very many people (whether one in every four, or rather fewer or rather more) do not have the means for 'citizenship' in such a sense

13. See the summary of differential risks of poverty in P. Townsend, op. cit. pp. 895–902; and for some other digests of evidence for these points, for example: A. C. Walker, 'Towards a political economy of old age', *Ageing and Society*, March 1981;

Inequalities in Health (Department of Health and Social Security, Report of a Working Group chaired by Sir Douglas Black, 1980, especially Chs. 2 and 3); J. Westergaard and H. Resler, op. cit. (e.g., pp. 80–92, 122–6, 131–3)

14. The main evidence discussed in this and the following paragraph is drawn from G. Routh, *Occupation and Pay in Great Britain 1906–79* (Macmillan 1980, especially pp. 119–32): updated from an earlier edition (1965) mainly by material from the official annual New Earnings Survey initiated in 1968

15. See especially A. Stewart, K. Prandy and R. M. Blackburn, *Social Stratification and Occupations* (Macmillan 1980, Part 2); also J. H. Goldthorpe, *Social Mobility and Class Structure in Modern Britain* (Clarendon Press, 1980, e.g. pp. 140–1); and J. Westergaard and H. Resler, op. cit. (pp. 82–3, note 4, the point of which evidence, however, I myself underrated in otherwise arguing too simplistically that male clerical work was in process of 'proletarianization' – e.g. pp. 75–6 and 292)

16. Contrary to common belief, however, incomes policies do not seem in the long run to have diminished 'differentials'; see, for example, J. L. Fallick and R. F. Elliott (eds) *Incomes Policies, Inflation and Relative Pay*, Allen and Unwin 1981

17. Royal Commission on the Distribution of Income and Wealth, Report No. 7, op. cit. (p. 39, unadjusted figures on this point for 1975–76)

18. On long-run trends and avoidance of death duties see, for example, A. B. Atkinson, *Unequal Shares: Wealth in Britain*, Allen Lane 1972, especially pp. 126–38, an analysis which also firmly disproved the notion that concentration of property reflects little more than a 'natural' accumulation of wealth in the hands of middle-aged and elderly men (pp. 49–52). See also A. B. Atkinson and A. J. Harrison, *Distribution of Personal Wealth in Britain*, Cambridge UP 1978, and note 19, below. The recorded share of the very rich in total propertied wealth is also subject to fluctuation with the state of the stock market – downwards when company share values are depressed, as during several years of the 1970s, but liable to rise again if and when the market recovers

19. *Royal Commission on the Distribution of Income and Wealth, Report No. 7*, op. cit. (Ch. 4 these figures from p. 93)

20. P. Townsend, op. cit., p. 201

21. Royal Commission on the Distribution of Income and Wealth, Report No. 7, op. cit. (pp. 148 and 151). I have translated the

figures given there into estimates for the entire adult population on an assumption that the nearly 50 per cent of the population excluded from the Royal Commission's figures (as having insufficient wealth to be assessable for probate or tax on death) owned no securities or land

22. Anon., 'The effects of taxes and benefits . . . 1979', *Economic Trends*, Jan. 1981, op. cit. (110–1). While this puts VAT among the regressive taxes, another analysis using similar data for 1977 concluded that VAT then had a mildly progressive incidence, though changes due in 1979 were likely to reduce this effect: D. W. Adams, 'The distributive effects of VAT in the UK, Ireland, Belgium and Germany', *Three Banks Review*, Dec. 1980

23. The following analysis is from Anon., 'The effects of taxes and benefits . . . 1979', op. cit. (note 22. above) supplemented by my own calculations from the data there. For an analysis of comparable data for 1976 to the same effect, see J. Westergaard, 'Social policy and class inequality', *The Socialist Register 1978*, Merlin Press 1978. The nature of the material, the assumptions incorporated and limitations involved, are discussed in Chs. 2 and 3, by G. Stephenson and M. O'Higgins respectively, of C. Sandford, C. Pond and R. Walker (eds), *Taxation and Social Policy*, Heinemann Educational Books 1980

24. Anon., 'The effects of taxes and benefits . . . 1979', op. cit. (Table T, 112). Calculated in the same way, the shares of the poorest fifth were 1 per cent of 'original income' but 11 per cent of 'final income'; of the richest fifth 45 per cent 'originally' but 34 per cent 'finally'. (The composition of the 'fifths' and 'tenths' referred to is not identical 'before' and 'after' because the effects of taxes and benefits are, besides some overall compression of inequality, also to change the positions of some households in the rank order)

25. For the most recent large-scale research on 'social mobility' in this country (though confined to the experience of men), see J. H. Goldthorpe, op. cit. (e.g. Ch. 9) and A. H. Halsey, A. F. Heath and J. M. Ridge, *Origins and Destinations*, Clarendon Press 1980, (e.g. Ch. 11). The results show that, in respect of both occupational and educational achievement, *overall* opportunity has increased (as more 'middle class' jobs have become available and educational provision has grown); but that in *relative* terms disparities in opportunity between men (boys) of different social origin have remained the same, and marked, over several generations

26. See, for example, V. George and R. Lawson (eds) *Poverty and Inequality in Common Market Countries*, Routledge and Kegan Paul 1980; and summary references to relevant work for the USA in S. M. Miller and D. Tomaskovic-Devey, 'Poverty', *British Journal of Sociology*, June 1981, and for some other countries including Sweden in J. Westergaard and H. Resler, op. cit. (pp. 119–22)

FURTHER READING

N. Bosanquet and P. Townsend (eds), *Labour and Inequality: A Fabian Study of Labour in Power 1974–79*, Heinemann 1980

F. Cripps *et al.*, *Manifesto: A Radical Strategy for Britain's Future*, Pan Books 1981

F. Field, M. Meacher and C. Pond, *To Him Who Hath: A Study of Poverty and Taxation*, Penguin 1977

P. Townsend, *Poverty in the United Kingdom*, Penguin 1979

J. Westergaard and H. Resler, *Class in a Capitalist Society: A Study of Contemporary Britain*, Penguin Books 1976

Chapter eight

FRAUD AND SCROUNGING IN THE WELFARE STATE: A SOCIALIST ANSWER

Frank Field

'Every day that goes by I am being bombarded with letters and telephone calls from people backing my campaign and pointing out examples of social security fiddles,' Mr Sproat said.

Mr Sproat gave the following examples of alleged swindles on the social security:

An unemployed Liverpool man was drawing full State benefit but earning £180 a week driving a hot dog stand on wheels around the city . . .

A woman from Guyana came to Britain with four children, claimed benefits for them and continued to claim even after they had returned to Guyana and one had died . . .

A Nottingham man obtained a colour television set on social security, the local office paying for the set because as it had doors it was classified as furniture.

'The sad fact is that today you can get practically anything on the State if you convince the local pay out offices,' Mr Sproat said.[1]

The fear of fraud has always been present in our social security system. Since the war, however, the preoccupation with the nature of fraud has altered as the economic situation fluctuated. The significant changes since the major Welfare Acts in 1948 have been the rise in unemployment, the growth of groups in need outside the contributory national insurance scheme and, consequentially, the increasing importance of the supplementary benefits as a system of first rather than last resort. And this transition has meant that the issue of fraud has changed from the initial fears of workshyness to concern with people living on benefit and working – or at least being capable of self-support.

This chapter examines the way in which these fears have been raised, the extent to which they are true, and the policies which have been devised to deal with them. It also records a fundamental change in the temper of the debate. Under Labour governments fraud was always a legitimate but marginal issue, which was picked up and put down as and when the political climate allowed. Under the present government, action against fraud has become much more part of a central aim of policy. This priority was reflected in the Conservative Party's election manifesto, and this change should be seen as part of their party's fundamental assault on the frontiers of the mixed economy and the welfare state.

In contrast, the argument in this chapter is that fraud and abuse, where it exists, has been shown to be significantly less than was assumed in every campaign; that it is in response to poverty, unemployment and powerlessness that most people get involved in fraud; and that the whole question of fraud has been exploited out of all proportion by the media. In addition this chapter aims to show that in relation to tax fraud, social security fraud is far less significant both morally and economically; in human terms it exacts a personal price that no tax dodger ever pays; and that what is required is not further spurious and expensive drives against fraud but a closer examination of why people are drawn into this practice and what might be done to prevent this happening.

In covering these points the first section looks at the extent of known social security fraud and examines the main areas where abuse occurs. The second section contrasts this information about known social security abuse with the extent of tax fraud. As social security abuse is judged mainly to be an issue in the Supplementary Benefit Scheme, the third section looks at the reasons why large numbers of poor people are dependent on supplementary benefits and outlines how a socialist government can move from a means-tested to a universal provision of social security.

SOCIAL SECURITY FRAUD

The extent of fraud

In 1978–79, £15.2 billion was paid out in social security payments, rising a year later to a little over £18 billion. For these two years the government has released figures on the total amount of overpayments of benefits which the Department of Health and Social Security (DHSS) decides in that year it has no prospect of recovering. Part of this total includes fraud on behalf of the claimant although

Table 8.1 Irrecoverable overpayments of benefits 1979/80

	Total (£)	Fraud on the part of the claimant or other person not being a servant of the Department (£)
Family Benefit	698,210	78,763
Unemployment Benefit	3,000,257	385,257
Sickness and Invalidity Benefit	2,976,089	437,535
Maternity Benefit	82,856	5,684
Widow's Benefit	315,717	125,392
Retirement Pension	799,565	58,297
Industrial Injury Benefits	247,199	24,905
Others	349,882	14,779
Supplementary Benefit	12,756,162	3,633,084
War Pensions	107,227	30,243
Total	£21,333,164	£4,793,939

Source: Department of Health and Social Security

the present government argues these totals are not an accurate gauge of fraud (see the appendix) (p. 191). In 1978–79 the total amount of irrecoverable overpayments stood at £19.5 million and a year later at £21.3 million. Table 8.1 details how these irrecoverable overpayments of benefit were spread between the different benefits. Overpayments occur because of errors within the DHSS itself, claimants unintentionally failing to inform the DHSS of a change in their circumstances, as well as by fraud.

It is also important to relate the extent of known fraud, rather than the overpayment figure, to the total amount paid out in benefits. Once these two sets of figures are related we find that the ratio varies greatly according to the benefit claimed – e.g. from each £670 paid in supplementary benefits £1 is written-off as fraudulently claimed. For war pensions the figure is £1 in every £12,000 and on industrial injuries the ratio is £1 in every £13,000 paid out in benefit. The fraud ratio for maternity benefit is £1 in every £25,000, for family benefits (child benefits and Family Income Supplement) £1 in £36,000 and in retirement benefit £1 in every £150,000 paid out in benefit. While to many people this might suggest that fraud is a small issue, the DHSS is fairly vigilant on behalf of taxpayers. For example, in 1978–79, almost 38,000 claimants had their circum-

Table 8.2 Special investigations: Number of investigations and number of benefits reduced or withdrawn

| | *1977–78* | | | |
	Investi-gations (No.)	*Allowance withdrawn /reduced*	*%*	*Investi-gations (No.)*
Undisclosed income	21,925	8,008	36	22,782
Earnings as employees	14,108	5,143	36	14,642
Self-employment earnings	7,498	2,748	37	7,801
Other income or capital assets	319	117	37	339
Fictitious desertion	2,150	975	45	2,097
Undisclosed cohabitation	9,916	3,987	40	9,920
Other cases	249	114	46	202
Contributory benefit cases	1,847	440	24	2,847
Total	36,087	13,524	37	37,848

Sources: *Hansard*, 12 June 1979, col. 205–6 written; 21 May 1981, col. 165–6 written (corrected)

stances investigated as part of the drive against fraud. By 1980–81 the number of investigations had risen to a little under 53,000. Throughout recent years the DHSS has had a 98 per cent success rate in bringing prosecutions against those suspected of fraudulent claims.

It is possible to break down the range of special investigations and the numbers of benefits reduced or withdrawn as a result of the DHSS's anti-fraud drives. The information for recent years is presented in Table 8.2.

The figures in the Table show that anti-fraud investigations are heavily concentrated in two areas; primarily against those claimants whom it is thought are drawing benefit as well as working (whether as employees or in self-employment), but also against single mothers who might be cohabiting or claiming fictitious desertions on behalf of their husbands. In examining the evidence of fraud in respect to the first category it is important to determine how the nature of the debate has changed from one concerned with workshyness to one which now heavily concentrates on working while drawing benefit. And in looking at the political response to public campaigns against the 'scrounger' it again is crucial to distinguish between a general political response which has resulted in a reduction in the benefits paid to all unemployed claimants and their families, and more specific measures – or control procedures – which have been aimed

1978–79				1979–80				1980–81	
Allowance withdrawn /reduced	%	Investi-gations (No.)	Allowance withdrawn /reduced	%	Investi-gations (No.)	Allowance withdrawn /reduced	%
8,712	38	23,196	9,446	41	30,316	12,263	40
5,471	37	15,472	6,063	39	27,159	10,958	40
3,125	40	7,323	3,230	44	2,686	1,087	40
116	34	401	153	38	471	218	46
926	44	2,259	1,115	49	2,756	1,482	54
3,936	40	11,476	4,973	43	15,166	7,005	46
96	48	387	174	45	1,097	801	73
682	24	3,105	806	26	3,605	1,079	30
14,352	38	40,423	16,514	41	52,940	22,630	43

against unemployed claimants who might be in a position to commit fraud or abuse of the system.

'Workshyness'

Since 1951, and the first detailed study by the National Assistance Board, successive reports issued by the Board and the Supplementary Benefits Commission have stressed consistently first how difficult it is for the layman to judge whether a claimant is workshy – as opposed to suffering from a mental or physical disability or condition which makes the undertaking of work difficult and, second, how small the number of workshy actually is. In 1951, after completing their enquiries, the National Assistance Board recorded: 'In all, out of nearly 60,000 recipients who were classified as 'unemployed' at the beginning of December, the Board's officers were not prepared to say that more than 7,000 persons could be working if they really wanted to work.'[2]

A much more detailed investigation on unemployed claimants was carried out in 1956 and the Board reported similar findings.

The results disclose many problems, but do not support any suggestion that workshyness is extensive, since three out of four of those interviewed, and more than four out of five of those who had been out of work for three or more years, were found to be under some sort of physical and/or mental handicap.

Interviewing officers regarded 7 per cent of unemployed claimants as workshy, although on closer examination it was found that over three-fifths of these claimants had physical disabilities or ill-health. Moreover, a considerable number of claimants, handicapped or not, whose attitude to work was considered unsatisfactory 'would probably have been unable to obtain employment even if they had been enthusiastic in seeking it', and the Board went on to observe 'and in some cases lack of success over a long period may perhaps have contributed to a previous loss of enthusiasm'.[3]

Similar studies by the National Assistance Board, giving rise to almost identical conclusions, were carried out in 1958, 1961 and 1964. In 1973 the Department of Employment (D.E) initiated its first survey on the attitudes of unemployed claimants. The interviewers were not requested to judge whether a claimant was workshy, but they were asked to collect information on the unemployed's attitude to work. Although, on the assessment of the local office staff, a third of unemployed men appeared 'somewhat unenthusiastic' for work, this did 'not mean that those men would in practice refuse a job if one had been offered them'. The report noted that they would be in danger of losing benefit if they did. Moreover, on closer examination the vast majority of these men lived in areas where the D.E thought that job prospects were bleak for all unemployed workers.[4] It is therefore difficult to judge to what extent the unemployed claimant's enthusiasm had waned after repeated failure to find work. Nor can we judge to what extent this response given to interviewing officers was a cover for men who feel rejected by a society unable to offer them worthwhile full employment.

General control procedures

Despite the evidence from these surveys on the relative unimportance of workshyness as a form of social security abuse, a whole battery of control procedures has been built up and reinforced during the postwar period. Unemployed claimants may be eligible for two kinds of benefit. The first is the national insurance benefit which is conditional on a claimant being available for work as well as fulfilling the contribution conditions. Claimants who qualify may be eligible for the flat rate unemployment benefit and, until it is phased out, an earnings related supplement. Second, there is the means-tested supplementary benefit. The following control procedures are applied to supplementary benefit unless otherwise stated.

A claimant may be refused benefit at the outset of his claim. No figures have been collected on the number of claimants so treated but experience from welfare rights agencies suggests that the numbers are not inconsiderable.

Unless a claimant heads a single-parent family, is registered sick, or is over retirement age, benefit is payable conditional on registering for work (although this condition is about to be changed). Furthermore, those claimants who it is judged have left or lost their previous jobs 'without good cause', or who refuse suitable employment 'without good cause', are suspended from unemployment benefit for up to six weeks, and on top of this will lose 40 per cent of their supplementary benefit entitlement. A claimant may also be suspended indefinitely for unemployment benefit if he places unreasonable restrictions on the kind of work he will take. Again, welfare rights organizations find that many claimants are wrongly penalized for allegedly leaving their work without good cause. In 1970, 274,000 claimants were suspended from unemployment benefit for allegedly leaving their job 'without just cause' and a further 44,000 lost benefit on the grounds that they had refused employment 'without just cause'. By 1980, after a massive rise in unemployment, this latter number had fallen to 7,900 but the numbers being suspended because they had left their employment without giving a good enough reason to the D.E had swelled to over 344,000.

Elaborate procedures exist for checking up on the unemployed, and the chief agents are the unemployment review officers. The first ten officers were appointed in 1961 because:

> It was found that an officer who had sufficient time to conduct long and repeated interviews with the man concerned, to arrange for him to receive offers of employment through the Ministry of Labour (now Department of Employment) to make sure he went after jobs, to question him closely about the results of his application – confirming his story with the employer where this seemed desirable – was often able to bring about greater and more decisive results than an officer who had normal area office duties to carry out at the same time.

Today there are 984 unemployment review officers and the number of interviews they conducted with unemployed claimants for each year since 1976 is presented in Table 8.3.

The number of unemployed claimants sent for by the review officers rose from around 148,000 in 1976 to almost 340,000 in 1980

Table 8.3 Unemployment review officers' interviews with unemployed claimants

Year	Number invited to interview	Number who ceased drawing benefit shortly before interview	Number * interviewed	Number who ceased drawing benefit shortly after interview
1976	147,635	19,595	109,387	38,015
1977†	136,270	17,978	104,684	39,863
1978	165,102	28,418	116,181	43,739
1979	219,000	40,000	307,000	84,000
1980	338,000	42,000	593,000	97,000

* Some claimants were interviewed more than once
† Covered 11 months only (1 Jan. 77 to 30 Nov. 77) due to change in statistical year
Figures for 1979 and 1980 are rounded to the nearest 1,000
Sources: *Hansard* 11 June 1979; 21 May 1981

and the numbers who ceased to draw benefit before their interview rose from a fraction under 20,000 to 42,000. Similarly, the numbers who ceased to draw benefit after their interview rose from 38,000 to 97,000. Dramatic as some ministers find these figures they do not provide evidence for a causal relationship or indicate the extent of workshyness amongst unemployed claimants. The dole queue is not made up of a static number of people and it is important to visualize the 'movement' behind any unemployment total; in May 1981, for example, unemployment stood at over 2.5 million and yet in the same month 280,000 claimants left the unemployment register – largely because they had jobs, although some others became sick and others retired. It would be surprising therefore if some of those unemployed claimants sent for interview were not to be found amongst those who had left the roll as jobs became available for them.

Two further control procedures operate against the unemployed. First, it is standard procedure that those claimants on benefit for more than six months and under the age of 55 who claim they are suffering from some sort of physical or mental disability, are referred for medical examination. In 1960, when this procedure was started, 46 per cent of claimants requested to attend medical examinations during the year found employment either before or shortly after the examination. The government does not now release figures on claimants whose benefit was made dependent upon attending a DHSS medical. The official explanation is that no benefit is paid out on these terms.

Claimants may also be paid benefit conditional that they attend a re-establishment centre where we are told they will be 'reintroduced to a work routine'. In 1977 2,374 unemployed claimants attended a re-establishment centre and by 1980 the number had risen to 2,935. In 1977, 606 claimants were discharged from the centres into employment, but by 1980, despite the increase in the number attending the courses, the total had fallen to 478.

Blanket disenfranchisement

All these control procedures continue to apply today, unlike what was known as the 'four-week rule' which operated from 1968 until 1973. It was in response to the considerable Press and television coverage of social security abuse that the Supplementary Benefits Commission carried out in 1967 a special inquiry into 1,900 claimants made in three London offices. 'These analyses did not show any substantial group of claimants, for example in particular occupations, who had been unemployed very much longer than others, but the inquiry indicated some weakness in the control system.'[5]

On the basis of this survey the government introduced what became known as the four-week rule. In areas where it was 'thought' by local offices in the DHSS that work was available, all single, fit, unskilled men aged under 45 were told on claiming supplementary benefit that their entitlement would cease after four weeks. Married men, skilled workers and women were allowed three months before the same rule applied. Men between 45 and 60, and those not fully fit were given six months if necessary before their supplementary benefit was curtailed. Men over 60 were granted up to a year.

Over the five years during which the four-week rule was in operation almost 330,000 claimants lost benefit. As the rule was only applied in areas where the government alleged work was available for those who wished to find it, no official surveys were carried out on the fate of those claimants who lost benefit under this control procedure. However, an independently conducted follow-up survey was carried out by Molly Meacher who reported that if her small sample was at all reflective of claimants penalized under the rule then something like[6]:

Socialist arguments

* 137,000 claimants deprived of benefit remained unemployed
* 55,000 claimants who lost benefit were mentally- or physically-ill claimants
* 25,000 men with criminal histories were driven back to old habits when their benefit was withdrawn
* 27,500 men resorted to crime for the first time after losing benefit
* 88,000 men 'probably' had no income whatsoever when their benefit was terminated
* a further 49,000 men probably had only a small amount of unemployment benefit.

Despite the growing public and parliamentary criticism the rule was not finally abandoned until the three-day week in 1973.

Group discrimination

It has also been in response to the fear that large numbers of the unemployed are potential malingerers or workshy that the social security system discriminates *en bloc* against all unemployed claimants and their families. From soon after the start of the National Insurance Scheme in 1948 until October 1972 the standard rate of 'long-term' and 'short-term' national insurance benefit was the same. (The long-term benefits are, essentially, the continuing benefits, such as retirement and widows' pensions; 'short-term' by definition, are the intermittent benefits, chiefly unemployment, maternity allowance and the like.) A year later, the long-term benefit for a single person was increased by 15 per cent but the short-term benefit was increased by only 9 per cent. This discrimination has continued and at the present time a single claimant and a married couple drawing the long-term national insurance benefit gain benefits of 31 per cent and 30 per cent above single and married claimants drawing the short-term rates. Unemployment benefit is paid at the short-term rates for up to a year of unemployment. After that, many unemployed claimants and their families become dependent very quickly on supplementary benefits and join many of their colleagues who draw supplementary benefit often as soon as they join the dole queues.[7]

Since 1966 the supplementary benefit rates have also made a distinction between long- and short-term rates. In the first place the difference in benefit came about by the payment of what was called a 'long-term addition'. The rationale for this addition was that claimants being on benefit for any length of time had expenses over and above the normal day-to-day needs of supplementary benefit claimants. In 1973 the Supplementary Benefit rates were divided into two sets of rates: the ordinary and long-term rates. So since 1966, then, the difference in income between long- and short-term beneficiaries has widened and today a single person and married couple on the long-term rate receive 27 and 25 per cent more respectively than their counterparts on the ordinary rate. But as the unemployed are officially classified as short-term claimants, and are only eligible for the short-term rate – no matter how long they have been on benefit – the supplementary benefit system also discriminates against the unemployed.

Cohabitation

The cohabitation rule is designed to prevent single people claiming benefit while living as a common-law partner of a person ineligible for benefit and while the rule applies to both sexes it is enforced overwhelmingly against women. Interest in how the rule operates was initiated by the campaigning work of Tony Lynes at the Child Poverty Action Group.

The Supplementary Benefit Act (since refashioned as the Social Security Act) lays down that persons in full-time work and their dependants are ineligible for supplementary benefit. In order to maintain equity between the poor family in full-time work and a claimant cohabiting with a full-time worker, the Supplementary Benefit Commission is required by law to enforce the cohabitation rule as it was known. In order to determine whether a common-law marriage existed the old guidelines for supplementary benefit officers stipulated:

It is generally accepted that the question of whether a woman is cohabiting with a man as his wife within the meaning of the statute, requires an examination of three main matters:
1. their relationship in relation to sex;
2. their relationship in relation to money, and
3. their general relationship.
Although all three are as a rule relevant no single one is necessarily inclusive.

The cohabitation rule also covers those claimants who have been deserted. Families where the working breadwinner has left home may be eligible for supplementary benefit. The number of cases where the DHSS alleged that the desertion was fictitious and claimants fraudulently claimed benefit is given in Table 8.2. In 1980 the circumstances of over 15,000 single parents were investigated on grounds of undisclosed cohabitation while over 2,700 other single parents were suspected and investigated on grounds of fictitious desertion.

Guidelines for investigating officers on how to establish fictitious desertion or cohabitation are laid down in secret codes. The difficulties of building up the information on whether or not a common-law marriage exists are fairly obvious. Not surprisingly, therefore, many of the cases which came to the Child Poverty Action Group in the early years of the campaign appeared to centre on the officers' attempts to establish that there was a sexual relationship between the claimant and another person.

The question of cohabitation caught the media in a somewhat ambivalent mind. While public money had to be protected from abuse, this concern began to take second place to reports on the supposed activities of the 'sex spies' – the name quickly given to the investigating officers. Reports of officers spying through letter-boxes and similar antics were enthusiastically reported by the media and particularly the popular Press.

The public exposure of the policing of the cohabitation rule led the Supplementary Benefits Commission in 1976 to publish a discussion document in which it proposed that the Supplementary Benefit Act should be amended to substitute the term 'living together as husband and wife' for the present expression 'cohabiting as man and wife'. With the change in name came a change in emphasis; officers were once again told to take into account all the different circumstances which would substitute a common-law marriage, and not to concentrate on sexual matters. These new rules continued to operate until the 1979 Thatcher government changed the whole tempo of the anti-fraud campaign.

Changing gear

A foretaste of what was to come was outlined in the Conservative Party's manifesto which declared: 'We shall act more vigorously against fraud and abuse', and in early 1980 the government announced a major new drive against social security abuse. The minister who was then responsible, Reg Prentice, reported: 'Efforts to control fraud and abuse have been inadequate for several years. Excellent work has been done by the staff working on these problems, but their numbers are insufficient'. The minister went on to report[8]:

We have insisted that the prevention and detection of fraud and abuse should be given higher priority, and despite our general policy of reducing staff numbers we are providing the extra staff needed to boost prevention and detection efforts. Another 1,050 – 450 this financial year and 600 next – are being employed on this work. They will include a further 470 staff, doubling the existing number, to work on unemployment review in relation to supplementary benefit claims, and a further 60 who will work on unemployment benefit claims in co-operation with the Department of Employment. There will be an extra 170 liable relative officers and a further 270 fraud specialists.

The government estimated that this tightening of the control procedures by the appointment of additional staff would save £50 million.

The main thrust of the new anti-fraud drive has been organized under what is called the Specialist Claims Control operation. Under this procedure officers work in small teams – usually of four members – and sift through the papers of claimants registered at their local office. In guidelines leaked to the Press these small teams have been instructed what to look for in countering abuse amongst the unemployed and single-parent families and these guidelines show how widely cast is the shadow of fraud suspicion. In picking out unemployed claimants for visits by the control teams, officers have been told to select 'by reference to the following criteria'[9]:

(c) the claimant has a skill – e.g. typing, car repairs, some building trade etc. – and local knowledge indicates that there are local job opportunities for him;

(d) the claimant has a record of self-employment;

(e) there is evidence that the claimant has worked in a significant money-earning occupation which could nevertheless be followed on a casual or spare-time basis (e.g. bar staff);

(f) the claimant is apparently fit and in good health (i.e. is not in receipt of any of the incapacity/disablement benefits and no report by a Visiting Officer contains reference to the claimant's poor health);

(g) (unless there is some clear indication of fraud) current unemployment has lasted for more than 4 months.

The guidelines for selecting single-parent families who may be committing fraud include the following criteria[10]:

(a) a 'fraud awareness' report by a visiting officer e.g. (indicating signs of a man's presence) which has not yet been followed up by the local office fraud section;

(b) the liable relatives officer has advised that SCC [Specialist Claims Control] action might be desirable;

181

(c) no information is held regarding the identity of the liable relative or his whereabouts are not known;
(d) the claimant refuses to take proceedings for maintenance;
(e) the claim has been made on the grounds of desertion, and it is alleged that the reason for the desertion was the family's economic circumstances;
(f) there is evidence of debt, e.g. rent/rate arrears, unpaid electricity/gas bills, etc;
(g) (unless there is clear indication of fraud) the claim has been current for more than 4 months (this will allow time for an initial liable relative activity to be carried out);
(h) the child(ren) is/are of an age which would enable the mother to take up work.

The guidelines for the new small anti-fraud units also suggest other actions that should be taken by officers other than interviewing the claimant. The guidelines for officers say[11]:

These may involve any of the techniques normally used in fraud work – e.g. checks of other Departmental records, discreet enquiries of employers, business associates or neighbours or, if time allows, approved special investigative methods such as observation, shadowing liaison with police and checking of vehicle numbers.

In May 1981 the DHSS published a survey on the savings resulting from its special anti-fraud drive and the information is presented in the Table 8.4. This government report claims that an additional

Table 8.4 Savings achieved by the 1,050 extra staff: 1980/81

Activities	*(£m.)*
Unemployment review	22.5
Unemployment review (UB only)	1.3
Liable relative officers	4.9
Fraud	3.0
Special investigation	7.6
Child benefit increase	1.0
	40.3

Source: The Government's campaign against social security fraud and abuse, mimeograph DHSS, May 1981

1,050 fraud staff saved £40.3 million and that the full complement of staff – over 5,500 – prevented £171 million worth of fraud.

How reliable are these figures? It is probably too early to answer this question in anything like a definitive way, but the evidence gained as a constituency MP throws a disturbing light on the current practices. As the minister indicated, much of this extra effort against abuse has been concentrated against claimants who the DHSS assumed were drawing benefit as well as undertaking paid employment. Thus, in practice, DHSS officers have concentrated on interviewing claimants who have skills which might have allowed them to work on the side, and those with training as motor mechanics, holding public service vehicle licences, and those possessing painting and decorating and similar skills have been singled out for special interview. If what has happened to some of my constituents is typical of what has happened elsewhere, the new procedure works in the following fashion.

The first move is for a couple of officers to call on the claimant's house. Each of the claimants is then requested to attend an interview at the local DHSS office. The claimant is interviewed by the two officers in a locked room – although the DHSS claim that the rooms are not locked, that the lack of a handle on the outside is to prevent people interrupting the interview, and that at any time the claimant can leave. Each of the claimants reported that the questioning by the two officers was more in the style of an interrogation than an interview. The claimants reported that they were told that their benefit would cease which is a frightening prospect for claimants with families to support and without any other income. At some stage in the interview it was suggested to the claimants that their benefit would continue for a short period if they agreed to sign a statement. Copies of the statement were not provided to the claimants but each of the claimants asserts that they were asked to give an undertaking to spend part of their benefit advertising for work in return for its short-term continuation.

If the operation of the new fraud drive in Birkenhead is anything like what is happening in other parts of the country it is surprising that the government has announced a 'saving' of only '£40 million in benefit'. The net has been cast so wide, the army of claimants interviewed and threatened so extensive, and the numbers so great where benefit was terminated on grounds that the person had the skills to be working, that 'savings' well in excess of the £50 million might reasonably have been expected.

TAX FRAUD

The different status afforded to the poor in our community is illustrated when we contrast the controls against social security abuse
with the measures operated to prevent tax fraud. Not only is the size
of known tax abuse larger than the known social security abuse, but
the resources given over to tackle social security fraud are way in
excess of that afforded to the Revenue, despite the latter's plea for
an increase in specialist staff.

The most recent report from the Inland Revenue shows that over
£60 million was remitted or written-off as irrecoverable. Almost £40
million of this related to income tax and a further £15 million to
corporation tax. A little over £1 million of the £60 million was written-off due to the hardship which would be caused to the taxpayer
if the Revenue enforced collection. Something over £32 million in
tax liability was written-off to the insolvency of the taxpayer but
almost £19 million was lost to the Treasury because the taxpayer had
gone abroad or was untraceable. Britain remains one of the few
countries where people can emigrate without presenting a tax-
clearance certificate.[12] Had such a reform been brought in in
1969 then the extra tax gained by this small reform would have
amounted to almost £125 million. The lack of such a measure is
just one contrast with the battery of anti-abuse measures on the
social security front.

It must be stressed that these revenue figures are similar to those
given by the DHSS: they are the sums written-off as irrecoverable
by the Treasury. And just as guestimates are made about the true
total of social security fraud, so too are guesses made about the true
extent of tax fraud. One such estimate was made by the then chairman of the Inland Revenue who estimated that the black economy
(i.e. undisclosed earnings) is in the region of £14 billion with a cost
to the Treasury (or the community) of £3.5 billion in lost tax
revenue.

According to some experts this total may only be the tip of the
iceberg. Anthony Christopher, the general secretary of the Inland
Revenue Staff Federation (IRSF) – the taxman's trade union – has
said of the £3.5 billion of lost revenue: 'We are only guessing at the
figures – the real amounts are probably much higher.' The Inland
Revenue Staff Federation's newspaper has put the matter more
bluntly. 'The truth of the matter is: if you decide to cheat the system, the chances are that you will get away with it. That is unless
you are greedy, stupid or just plain unlucky!.'

The difficulties of detection are considerable. Anthony Christopher takes up the story again:

If a man is self-employed, doesn't get too ambitious, works alone, advertises carefully and moves occasionally – we haven't got a hope in catching him. We just don't have the manpower to track down people like that. We can't investigate companies – so how can we spare the time on one man?

Reacting to the government's announcement of an additional 1,000 anti-fraud investigators for the social security system, Anthony Christopher observed: 'With an extra 1,000 staff the Inland Revenue could return ten times more than the £50 million a year lost through fraudulent social security claims.'[13]

There are three areas where the IRSF believes tax abuse to be considerable. The first centres on business accounts. Since 1977 tax inspectors have been selecting a few business accounts with the aim of achieving a detailed investigation of 5 per cent of non-company accounts each year. Despite the fact that this results in the vast majority of business accounts going unchecked, the restrictions on the numbers of Revenue staff has meant that this modest target has never been achieved and the coverage in the last year for which figures are available (1979) was only 2.5 per cent. For company accounts the coverage was a mere 0.25 per cent. Yet of those cases selected, 82 per cent of the businesses concerned were found to have understated their profits. The additional tax recovered from these cases where it was not appropriate to seek interest and penalties was £14.1 million in the year ended 31 October 1979. In addition, the yield from cases where interest and penalties have been sought rose from £14 million in 1976 to £40 million in 1979.

A second area where tax abuse has been located is in the PAYE system. For most employees and directors tax is gathered through the PAYE system and part of this work in the PAYE system centres on the fringe benefits given to employees and for which the employee is liable for tax. The Revenue has difficulty in persuading employers to fill in and return these forms. And yet those which are filed back at the Revenue 'are all too rarely verified though they are often incorrectly completed'.[14]

Another example of PAYE abuse arises for the use of employers as agents to collect tax on employees' earnings. The Revenue reports some employers deduct the tax but hold onto the revenue, and sometimes falsify the returns to cover their tracks. The evidence is that such irregularities are on the increase. For example, while between 1963 and 1973 just a quarter of visits to employers to check on PAYE operations threw up something unsatisfactory, by 1980 more than half of such visits showed something wrong. Part of this growth reflects the better selection of cases to investigate, 'but much of it must be put down to increasing fraud by employers'.

A third area of possible tax fraud comes from the tax returns from directors. A sample of 10 per cent of director cases in a selection of tax offices showed that 45 per cent had the potential to yield significant amounts of additional tax if pursued, although seven out of ten of these cases had not been pursued. Even a minimum increase in staff was likely to bring a significant increase in tax revenue. One office managed to produce an additional £3.75 million in tax by making sure that the directors just filled-in the returns while accepting the answers given on the forms without any questions being asked.

The different attitudes to tax and social security abuse is again illustrated by the differences in the resources devoted to anti-fraud work. Within the Inland Revenue not only has the size of the staff been cut – 10,000 since 1979 – but a limit has been placed on the growth of special offices. These were first established in 1976 to look at any area where the Revenue is at risk and where careful and detailed work is required over and above that which can be given by the district office. The offices have been highly successful. A special office's investigation into practices at Smithfield Market resulted in an additional £800,000 profit per annum. Very substantial settlements were made in individual cases in addition to the considerable success in countering losses of tax in certain industries. A recent drive in Fleet Street resulted in an additional £2 million of tax.

Despite the recommendation that there should be a network of special offices covering all Inland Revenue regions only six are in existence. The yield from the first four is quite spectacular: it has risen from £6.4 million in 1977 to £20 million in 1980. Cases presently under investigation by the special offices are likely to bring in tax of more than £80 million.

A further difference in moral attitudes becomes apparent in reaction to the way some rich and poor groups try to maximize their income. When the Child Poverty Action Group produced a leaflet which helped claimants claim their full entitlement, and also reminded claimants of the Fisher Committee's recommendation that they should not be pressed into taking jobs which gave them a lower income than the dole or supplementary benefit, some Tory MPs and part of the media attacked this action as a new form of abuse. In contrast, richer groups are able to maximize their income by working the tax regulations to their maximum advantage. Such action is usually known as tax avoidance and one of the more recently notorious examples of this practice concerns the Vestey family.

The extent of the tax loss by this one family alone was highlighted by reports in the *Sunday Times*. Writing under the heading 'They made £2.3 m in profits . . .They paid just £10 in tax. Why?'[15] the *Sunday Times* went on to explain that because of major loopholes in the tax law, the Vesteys have avoided 'paying enormous amounts of income tax for more than 60 years'.

The way the Vesteys planned to minimize their tax bill is not untypical of some very rich groups in this country and is therefore worth looking at in a little more detail. The *Sunday Times* picks up the story again.

No one knows how much altogether the Vesteys have collected in Britain free of income tax. The Vestey trust accounts are kept in Uruguay and the Commissioners of the Inland Revenue had to issue a legal notice under the 1970 Taxes Act to compel the Vesteys to produce them. Their reluctance is understandable because the figures are astounding.

In 1942 the trust's capital fund's assets were valued at £18 million – worth today at least £150 million. The two income funds, one for each branch of the family, had a total income for one year, 1966, of about £600,000, easily £2 million at today's values. If this income had been received in Britain then tax on it would have been at least £1.4 million. Between 1962–66 the Vesteys received £2.6 million from the income funds, tax-free.

Commenting on the House of Lords ruling that a Vestey family trust, through which the family draws income on its international meat and other trading interests, was outside the scope of the Inland Revenue, Lord Thorneycroft, a former chancellor of the exchequer, and then chairman of the Conservative Party, remarked, 'I would not criticise the Vestey family',[16] – a rather more charitable view than is offered to many poor people trying to maximize their low income from the means-tested welfare state. Moreover, there is no reason to believe that the Vestey operation is unique.

A SOCIALIST ALTERNATIVE

To argue, as this chapter has, that the extent of social security fraud is less than the wild allegations made with increasing rapidity in the media is not to say that there is no such thing as social security fraud. It would be amazing if there were not, for there is no reason why the poor should have a higher moral standard than any other group in the community. Indeed, by their poverty they may well be excused for being less rather than more honest than the rest of us. What this chapter has tried to do is to set the issue of social security fraud within the context of the amount paid out in benefit and the considerable battery of measures which are undertaken to control the extent of any fraud. What is required, therefore, from a socialist alternative to the present system is the building of a system of social security which by its equity and relative generosity automatically minimizes the extent of fraud.

We have seen that most detected social security fraud occurs within the supplementary benefit system and it is against this group of claimants that the most stringent anti-fraud control measures are in existence. A further increase in the anti-fraud armoury would no doubt bring forward some gains in public funds, partly from uncovering further abuse but also from claimants who, in seeing claimants dubbed as workshy and scroungers in the public debate, decide not to draw benefit. The most recent figures (for 1977) showed that £340 million went unclaimed in supplementary benefit. In the present system a balance ought to be kept between the two goals of preventing abuse and ensuring a claimant's right to benefit. In the longer term there is the need for a socialist alternative to the present system which would guarantee a minimum income free of means tests.

The key to any immediate reform which guarantees a national minimum income is a large injection of funds into the Child Benefit Scheme. The reasons for such a first move are as follows. First, an overall reform of the welfare state without significantly increasing the level of child benefit is likely to undermine public support for the programme. In the 1920s, when unemployment benefit was cut, additional payments for children of the unemployed were made in an attempt to stave-off widespread political unrest. From that day since, the payments for the children of the unemployed have been more generous than the support given to working families with children. The result is that while only a small number of families are better-off on the dole rather than working, many more working families find themselves only marginally better off in work. Failure to act on child benefits will therefore continue to place the working poor at a disadvantage to the poor who are unable to work.

Second, an increase in child benefit is the most immediate and effective means of tackling the problem of family poverty amongst those who work, and it does so in a way which increases incentive to work rather than the reverse. Child benefits are paid to all families but are deducted from many other social security benefits for children. The larger the child benefit, therefore, the greater the difference in income between a family when it is at work and when it is dependent on benefit.

Third, child benefit changes are an important way of maintaining tax equity. In 1977 we saw the phasing out of child tax allowances to coincide with the introduction of the Child Benefit Scheme. With the abolition of child tax allowances in April 1980 child benefits took on a dual function. On the one hand they are the most effective way of channelling resources to families on low incomes. On the other they are the only mechanism by which chancellors can increase the tax-free income of taxpayers with children when making regular revisions in the tax threshold for other taxpayers.

The introduction of a really generous system of child benefits, together with a second major reform – the scrapping of the contributory conditions for national insurance benefits – will make it much easier for helping the other two main groups of claimants now dependent on supplementary benefits – the unemployed and single parent families – and against whom most of the anti-fraud control procedures are aimed. While the most effective way of helping the unemployed is to provide jobs, the level and kind of benefits available to those out of work is of key importance.

We saw earlier that claimants are eligible for flat-rate unemployment benefit and for an earnings-related supplement. A major restructuring of the welfare state would allow the unemployed to claim a flat-rate unemployment benefit for twelve months at the end of which they would become eligible for an unemployment benefit paid at the higher rate of national insurance benefits. Similarly, unemployment benefit should be paid for as long as need lasts and this change in the eligibility rules and the value of unemployment benefit ought to be tied-in with the government's retraining programme.

Until the recent record increase in the numbers of unemployed the fastest-growing group of poor people were single-parent families and their children. The introduction of a generous system of child benefits will not only have an immediate effect on the livelihood and aspirations of many single-parent families, but will also make the introduction of a single-parent family allowance much more politically acceptable. Most of the discussion up until now about a non-means-tested benefit for single-parent families has been built on the assumption of an inadequate system of child support. The result was a formation of policies which suggested the payment of generous benefits to the mother (or father) so as to cover her and her children's needs. A generous system of child benefits means that the children of single-parent families will be treated equally with other children, and the more generous the level of child benefit going to all children, the lower will be the proportion of the single-parent family's income coming from a non-means-tested single-parent family allowance.

The third group of people in conspicuous poverty are the sick and disabled, for despite the introduction of invalidity benefit large numbers of the sick are poor. The reasons for this are that some long-term sick and disabled never become eligible for insurance benefits, or, if they do, are only able to draw the non-contributory invalidity pension. The abolition of the contributory principle will allow the non-contributory invalidity pension to be used as the entrance into the Invalidity Benefit Scheme. Claimants could serve a six-month probationary period on the non-contributory invalidity pension (as do others claiming sickness benefit) before becoming eligible for invalidity benefit.

A second stage of reforming benefits for the disabled should centre on the introduction of some kind of disability allowance. The introduction of this benefit should build on the existing arrangements which already go some way in compensating people for the extra costs of disability, and would replace the present capricious and confusing arrangements with a coherent and adequate system of income maintenance.

How could this major reform of the welfare state be paid for? The answer is also relevant to offering a socialist alternative to the present fiscal system. Since the war the direct tax burden has shifted in two directions, vertically on to those on lower incomes and horizontally onto households with children. And yet, judging by the public debate, the impression is one of an increasing tax burden for those on high incomes.

In one sense both images are correct. The tax burden on the poor and those with children has risen in real terms while the nominal rates of tax for the well-off increased. But the rates of tax for those on high incomes are substantially reduced by the ever-increasing generosity of tax allowances – or what is perhaps more accurately called the tax benefit welfare state. Over a hundred such tax benefits are listed in the current public expenditure White Paper and they range from the personal allowances – such as the single-person's allowance – to those which go under the title of the allowance on mortgage interest relief. Each of these tax benefits disproportionately benefits those on high income, while at the same time lessening the amount of personal income subject to tax – or as it is called – narrowing the tax base. As the tax base narrows, new groups have to be brought into tax to widen it and the nominal rates of tax are pushed higher in an attempt to recoup some revenue.

A major reform of this tax benefit welfare state has been set out elsewhere.[17] This involves the return to a tax exemption scheme in place of the personal allowance system with a policy of cash ceilings on the non-personal tax benefits. Both policies will result in a reduction in real value of the tax benefit welfare state. Such a reform of the tax benefit welfare state will have to be embarked upon if greater equity is to be created in our direct system of taxation while at the same time releasing the resources necessary to embark upon a restructuring of the traditional benefit welfare state.

APPENDIX

Extract from 'The Government's campaign against social security fraud. A statement by the Secretary of State', 6 May 1981.

Criticisms of the government's campaign

13. Since the statement in February 1980 a number of criticisms have been made of our new measures. One was that the deployment of an extra 1,050 staff on anti-fraud and abuse measures was excessive given that a previously published figure relative to fraud and abuse was only '£4 million per annum'. In order to dispel that criticism, it is necessary to spell out just what the figure of £4 million signified. In effect, it was a figure prepared for accountancy 'writing-off', and bears no real relationship to the total size of the fraud and abuse problem. Firstly it relates only to *fraud*, and not to abuse such as voluntary unemployment. Secondly it relates only to *discovered fraud*, not to the total loss to public funds. Thirdly it refers, not to *total discovered fraud*, but to the amount written off as 'irrecoverable' when all the Department's efforts to recover overpayments have failed. Finally, it has no regard to *the benefit that would have been paid* if our specialists had not detected and stopped the fraud. Hence the figure of £4 million is irrelevant to the question of how much effort we should put in to tackling fraud and abuse. Our current extra efforts alone have turned up ten times that figure as preceding paragraphs have indicated.

NOTES

1. *The Daily Telegraph*, 16 June 1979
2. Report of the National Assistance Board, HMSO 1951, Cmnd 8632, p. 8

3. Report of the National Assistance Board, HMSO 1957, Cmnd 181, p. 15
4. *DE Gazette*, Mar. 1974
5. *DHSS Annual Report*, HMSO 1968, Cmnd 4100, p. 251
6. M. Meacher, *Scrounging on the Welfare*, Arrow 1974
7. The rate of unemployment benefit paid to some claimants is below their Supplementary Benefit entitlement and these, together with those claimants with exhorted or incomplete insurance records, may draw supplementary benefit from the outset of their claim.
8. *Hansard*, 13 Feb. 1980, col. 711
9. *Specialist Claims Control*, mimeograph, DHSS, n.d. para. 11
10. Ibid., para. 12
11. Ibid. para. 16
12. Board of Inland Revenue, Report for 1980, HMSO, Cmnd 8160, Tables 9 and 10
13. *Assessment*, Inland Revenue Staff Federation 2 (4), Apr. 1981
14. Ibid
15. *Sunday Times*, 5 Oct. 1980
16. *The Daily Telegraph*, 7 Oct. 1980
17. F. Field, *Inequality in Britain: Freedom, Welfare and the State*, Fontana 1981

FURTHER READING

A. Deacon, *In Search of the Scrounger*, Ball 1976
F. Field, *Inequality in Britain*, Fontana 1981
M. Meacher, *Scrounging on the Welfare*, Arrow 1974

Chapter nine

IMMIGRANTS, RACISM AND BRITISH WORKERS

Barry Munslow

'Why don't they stay in their own country? They are a burden on the British taxpayer and they don't integrate even when they come over here. We only live on a small island and the place is getting overcrowded. Look how many unemployed there are – send back the blacks and you would solve the problems . . . .' We have all heard talk about immigrants taking 'our' jobs and houses, living on the dole, bringing down the neighbourhood and spreading crime and disease. What all the arguments have in common is that they blame the problems of British society on an easily identifiable group, the immigrant community, reflecting an underlying prejudice against the non-white and former colonial minorities who live among 'us'.

Racist scapegoating is an increasingly common explanation being given for unemployment, the decline of the social services and Britain's economic and social misfortunes in general. The reason that these arguments have found such currency is the underlying racism in the society, which has its origins in a history of slavery and empire. The colonization of Africa, Asia and the Caribbean by Britain's ruling class was accompanied by the myth that the peoples inhabiting these areas were sub-human. It was this 'inferiority' of the subject races which was used to justify the robbery and pillage of empire-grabbing, neatly dressed-up at the time in a garb of 'civilizing the natives'. The racism born of empire helped create a sense of superiority among the British working class which still remains with us, and given the multi-coloured nature of the present workforce in Britain, this racism can only serve to weaken the unity and strength of working people.

At a time of massive recession when attacks on trade union power, the welfare state and standards of living generally are the order of the day, racism provides a powerful weapon in the armoury of all those opposed to a strong working class able to defend its interests. The failure to confront racism has been and continues to be a major weakness in the British labour movement and not only because of the internal divisions that it creates. It has limited geographically and racially the scope of class identity which in the new phase of global capitalism will have disastrous consequences. Increasingly, companies operate in more than one country and racism hinders the ability of workers to resist these transnational firms in the only effective way possible – by organizing across national boundaries. This is undoubtedly a difficult goal to achieve because workers in many Third World countries are still struggling to build trade unions nationally and coordinated international action by organized labour has barely yet begun. But the *international* organization of labour is the only way to confront *international* employers and the difficulties involved do not alter this fact.

A politicization of racism has reinforced prejudices and moved the debate nationally further to the right. On the far right are the National Front and the British Movement who advocate repatriation of immigrants, and their members and sympathizers have been responsible for a massive wave of physical attacks against the black community which surfaced in the early 1980s. Bareen Khan and her three children were burnt to death in a racist arson attack in the summer of 1981. This was the most serious of fifteen 'suspicious' fires on Asian property occurring in Walthamstow in two years.[1] In the northern town of Oldham, twenty cases of violence and vandalism directed against the immigrant community were reported in one year alone.[2] Even in mainstream politics, whilst differing in degree, both the Labour and the Conservative Parties have supported immigration controls. Anti-black tub-thumping by the far right has produced a chain reaction along the political spectrum. As one commentator has observed: 'What Enoch Powell said one day the Tories say the next, and the Labour Party passed legislation on the third.'[3] This has led to the present ludicrous situation where it is now generally accepted that good race relations are best served by racist immigration laws. Fears of appearing unpopular with the electorate have played a big part in pushing the major political parties into a tacit acceptance of racism and thereby they reinforce it. One writer has commented, 'It is like some fearful auction, with the Conservatives relentlessly raising the racialist bids, and the Labour and Liberal Parties fruitlessly trying to secure the lot on the same terms.'[4]

We will examine why racism is so powerful in British culture, then turn to see why immigrants come to Britain rather than stay in their own countries. We will try to demonstrate that an insular racism can never be the defence of British workers' interests it purports to be. The firms which dominate the economy are multinational, and depending on their particular interests they can employ foreign labour here in British factories or take those factories to the pools of labour abroad. The irony is that racism and anti-immigration sentiment is now running high when the second rather than the first of these two options is increasingly being employed.

Much is still made of the numbers game, with blacks being portrayed as a burden as well as a threat to British workers. The race issue is defined in terms of the numbers of black people in the country and the entirely false conclusion is drawn that the more the numbers are restricted the less the racial problem will become. The public debate about race relations has all too frequently been conducted in these terms, leading inevitably to the absurd situation of governments passing racist immigration laws to reduce racism! We will show that the hard evidence goes against the claim that black immigrants destroy the health, education and welfare services generally. In fact, as we will show, their labour subsidizes it.

A CULTURE OF RACISM

To combat racist arguments it helps to know the origins of these prejudices. The widespread racist beliefs and assumptions held in British society are intimately tied-up with a massive wave of illegal immigration which turned the world upside down in the eighteenth and nineteenth centuries. We refer, of course, to the founding of the British empire. An uninvited entry into a third of the world's countries based not on peaceful coexistence as a minority ethnic group but everywhere as conquerors, landlords, mine owners and exploiters who wreaked havoc on the indigenous populations. The depopulation of Africa with the slave trade and the setting-up of slave plantations in the American South and West Indies, the massacres carried out with the Gattling gun on the peoples who dared to resist and even total genocide in certain areas of the world, such as Tasmania, were only some of the results of this illegal wave of British immigrants who came to conquer and not just to work as our present immigrants do.

Racism was used to legitimize colonialism on the basis that it's all right to do these things because after all the 'natives' aren't human beings like us. In this way, the English manufacturers could justify a system of slavery to grow the cheap cotton which fed the northern textile mills and made British capitalism grow. An early accumulation of capital from this trade in human flesh gave an essential start to such modern-day multinationals as Unilever, which made an easy transition from slaves to soap powder. Pseudo-scientific arguments about a hierarchy of races provided a convenient garb for the pillage and plunder of empire-grabbing. But, worst of all, it had a disastrous effect on the development of working-class consciousness, as it created both material and psychological privileges among British workers. Cheap food produced by slaves contributed to improving living standards in Britain and even the lowest ranks of British society could feel superior to the highest members of the colonial societies. Although the British working class was internally divided by a hierarchy based on sex, status and skill level, *it was united with the capitalist class* in relation to black workers. The history books and the comics, Empire Day and the schoolmaster, the State and the Church preached a simple message of racial superiority, and the crude economics of cheap labour, raw materials and markets was convincingly portrayed as a mission of enlightenment and civilization. Patriotism, the myth of empire, nationalism, social Darwinism[5] and scientific racism[6] blended together to create one important strand in modern British culture – its underlying racism. Television comedy programmes with stereotyped Indian voices which are meant to be funny, racist jokes heard every day in the pub and at work, all continue to reinforce racist beliefs in a subtle and insidious way: 'It's only a joke after all.'

From the Second World War onwards, not only did Britain lose her colonies but the natives came to live next door. The racial superiority of empire was to create divisions among an increasingly multi-coloured British working class. But this was not the only legacy. Riots against the police in a score of major cities in the early 1980s must be understood not only in terms of increasing State oppression and racism against the immigrant community but also as a direct legacy of empire: 'It is precisely because the role of the police in the colonies was that of an occupying force – and not that of the "friendly bobby" – that the traditional "immigrant" view of the police is one of distrust.'[7] Having said that, we should note the relation between a popular morality which defines black people out of society as an 'alien wedge' and the police who no longer just reflect that morality but also recreate it 'through stereotyping the black section of society as muggers and criminals and illegal immigrants'.[8]

STATE RACISM

The riots in the cities were clearly directed against the police and according to community representatives 'were the climax to a long history of police harassment, provocation and brutalization'.[9] Arbitrary arrests, indiscriminate use of the 'sus' law to pick-up youths on grounds of suspicion alone (deterring many young blacks from going out on the streets), and police brutality were some of the more immediate grievances of the rioters. The ideology of racism created over decades becomes institutionalized in the State itself. There are three components to this State racism: government policies, administrative practices and generalized prejudice (with a complex inter-relation occurring between the three). Racist measures such as the 1981 Nationality Bill and successive Immigration Acts, coupled with full-cost charges for overseas students and foreigners using the health service, legitimize racism and reinforce racist attitudes in the country at large. Enforcing white cultural norms on the non-white population and the assumption that all non-whites are 'foreigners', hence are liable to be raided for being illegal immigrants, are just some of the institutional practices which help constitute this State racism. Finally, the widespread racist attitudes found among State employees, particularly in the police and prison services, are the sharp end of State racism, being encountered in the day-to-day contact blacks have with the State. Racism in the police force has many different manifestations, one being the seeming unwillingness to investigate racist murders and attacks. Of twenty-seven murders claimed by Asian groups between 1976 and 1981 only three were solved and the police described the cases as 'motiveless'.[10]

It would be wrong to paint a picture of an unqualified and all pervasive State racism, however. The situation is far more subtle and complex than that. An early reliance on overt nationalism and racism to help create a capitalist hegemony[11] over the working class has been replaced by the present-day concentration on notions of the 'free society' and 'liberal democracy', allegedly based on equality for all. Many of the benefits are real enough and to be treasured, but this should not obscure the hypocrisy and cant associated with this ideology. Certainly, there are laws against racial discrimination in Britain. But the laws have no teeth and the number of prosecutions has been derisory. Blacks still remain at the bottom of the accommodation and work piles. Proclaimed equality for all, when economic inequality and much of the underlying culture of racism remains unchallenged, explains why the immigrant community remains unconvinced by the rhetoric. Racist laws and laws against racial discrimination lie happily side by side in the statute books. Who can, therefore, take seriously protestations of government good faith? In 1974, after two Race Relations Acts had already been passed (in 1965 and 1968) there were only three men in the Race Relations Department of the Home Office compared with 1,500 in the Immigration Department. The scales of racial justice were rather unevenly balanced. The racist culture in Britain may help explain why black immigrants are discriminated against and the emergence of State racism, but it does not explain how and why a large immigrant population came to be here.

THEY ARE HERE BECAUSE WE WERE THERE. WHY CAPITALISM NEEDS IMMIGRANT LABOUR

Colonial occupation created a total distortion in the living patterns of the peoples concerned. Self-sufficiency was destroyed and a pool of unemployed and underemployed was generated; therefore, when a labour shortage occurred at home, in the metropolis, the colonial workforce was available to meet the demand. There were the sugar-cane cutters receiving a pittance on the plantations in the West Indies, poor peasants and landless in Africa, Asia, southern Europe and Ireland, obliged to leave their countries when their livelihood was no longer viable. The uneven growth of capitalism created the conditions whereby labour migrates from poor underdeveloped countries to the rich developed ones. The colonies were assigned to be agricultural and raw-material producers for the industries of the metropoles and the gap in per capita income between the two continually grew, fueling the migrant flow.

The uneven development of capitalism is also to be found inside a country, with certain regions being relatively advanced and others underdeveloped. This is clearly the case in modern Britain if we compare the south-east of the country with the remainder. However, the starkest differences are to be found between countries: the poor southern European states compared with the rich northern ones, the destitute Third World compared with the rich First World. But this is not by itself sufficient to explain why immigration occurs. For within both rich and poor countries there are rich and poor people. Even after gaining their independence, the legacy of colonialism was such that the interests of the transnational corporations and the local ruling classes continued to dominate and put the squeeze on the peasantry and urban workers, creating unemployment and an increasingly mobile reserve army of labour driven by poverty to migrate. The terms of trade between the underdeveloped and the developed world continued to worsen. More sacks of peanuts, coffee or bananas had to be sold to purchase the same amount of industrial goods and the volume of debt owed to American and European governments and banks grew to astronomical proportions.

Capitalism has always needed a pool of potential workers to draw upon. Here in Britain this was first provided by the peasantry. Later, when Britain's industrial revolution was in full swing and most of the peasantry had been absorbed, the colony of Ireland provided the unskilled labour to build the canals and railways. The arrival of 700,000 Irish immigrants in the last century was spurred on by the potato famines, disasters greatly exacerbated by the cumulative effect of British colonial occupation. But it was not always Britain's colonies which provided the immigrant labour. Part of the 'democratic' banner waved at home included a welcome extended to political exiles and those persecuted in other countries. The Huguenots came from France in the sixteenth century and Jews and Ukranians between 1875 and 1914, victims of pogroms by Tsarist and other despotic eastern European states. The latter provided cheap immigrant labour, especially in the East End of London, until the Tories whipped-up racist fears among the electorate and the first Immigration Act was passed in 1905. Faced with the male working class having the vote, the Tories were quick to beat the nationalist and racist drum and portray themselves as defending the poor British worker from unfair immigrant competition. Needless to say, there was little evidence of concern by the Tories for workers' interests in any other sphere. The 'land of the free' only keeps its doors open for the persecuted when this meets the needs of the economy and the politicians, a fact to which Britain's East African Asians will attest.

Between the two world wars the depression removed the need for importing labour, since there were sufficient reserves created at home to be drawn upon should the need arise. After the defeat of fascism in 1945 the tap had to be turned once again, with full employment now politically essential and with millions of the workforce killed in the war. Politicians were arguing that Britain's prospects for growth depended on securing a sufficient supply of labour. One young Labour Party MP summed up the situation at that time in a speech to the House of Commons. He said[12]:

We are turning away from the shores of this country eligible and desirable young men who could be adding to our strength and resources, as similar immigrants have done in the past . . . we ought now to become a country where immigrants are welcome . . .

This same MP, Mr James Callaghan, was later to remove the passports of the British Asians from East Africa,[13] but that was *after* the labour shortage had been met and when the Labour Party had reversed its policy on opposing immigration controls under pressure from its right wing.

Capitalism has endemic booms and slumps and labour is taken on or discharged according to the requirements at different periods. In the postwar Keynesian boom there was a labour shortage which only finally came to an end in the 1960s. From then onwards there was a long-term recession and 'surplus' labour had to be shed. Immigrant labour was drawn upon in time of shortage and racist immigration laws were established to switch off the flow when it was no longer required.

It is not only in Britain that immigrant workers are employed, as they are vital to the functioning of all capitalist economies. In northern Europe as a whole, 15 million immigrants arrived in the postwar period, coming either from the Mediterranean countries or from former colonies. Greeks, Turks and Yugoslavs went to West Germany; Algerians, Portugese, Spanish, Italians and West Africans went to France; and citizens from their former colonies – as well as southern Europeans – were employed in Holland and Britain. Indeed, by the mid-1970s, Britain had a smaller proportion of immigrants in the workforce with 7 per cent than either Germany (11%), France (11%) and Switzerland (37%). Immigrants in the USA comprise an estimated half of the entire unskilled labour force. The great success of our competitors has much to do with the important contribution made to economic growth by migrant labour. This point cannot be stressed enough, *Britain's problem was a shortage of such labour. It is not that too many immigrants are responsible for the slump in Britain, rather that there were too few to fuel the boom.*

It is clear that migrant labour has always been important, but the question remains why this is the case. Capitalist development depends upon the availability of workers. For capital accumulation to occur, there has to be labour to exploit and the cheaper the labour the greater the accumulation. Two factors can weaken the power of labour in its struggle against employers. The first is a large pool of available but unused labour and the second is a disunited labour force. Migrants provide the cheap labour pool and a racist culture ensures the potential for a divided workforce. Nothing disciplines and saps the power of organized labour as much as a huge pool of unemployed. Every woman and man then fears that they may be replaced and will have to join the dole queues.

This has led some to argue that the labour movement should oppose immigration as it would thereby reduce the supply of labour. The fascists go even further and propose repatriation, on the basis that the number of unemployed equals the number of blacks, hence to solve the problem send them all back. This argument holds no water because in the last Great Depression in the 1930s, there were no blacks or major immigration of any kind. Who was to blame then? Areas of high unemployment today such as the north-east of England, Wales and Scotland have no significant black population. There is no evidence, therefore, that immigration *per se* causes unemployment. If we look closely at the labour market we find that British workers have generally *benefited* because the immigrants took the lower-paid and less desirable jobs which white workers increasingly did not want and hence they became relatively privileged. This was confirmed by a survey carried out by the Unit of Manpower Studies at the Department of Employment, who found that thirty-three out of forty-three employers interviewed gave difficulties in recruiting other workers as a reason for employing immigrants.[14]

The division of labour has all too frequently taken on a racial aspect. With immigrants being assigned the lower-paid jobs with the worse conditions this reinforced racism, dividing and inevitably weakening the working class further. Marx saw this clearly in relation to Irish workers in England last century. He wrote[15]:

Every industrial and commercial centre in England now possesses a working class divided into two hostile camps, English proletarians and Irish proletarians . . . The antagonism is artificially kept alive and intensified by the press, the pulpit, the comic papers, in short by all means at the disposal of the ruling classes. This antagonism is the secret of the impotence of the English working class, despite their organisation.

Last century, as now, cheap immigrant labour did the jobs that under existing conditions and wages, indigenous workers were unwilling to take. In the Lancashire textile industry, Asian men worked a permanent night shift but only at daytime rates of pay. These were also, of course, the first jobs to disappear with the recession. Nearly a third of the workers in the foundries and mills of west Yorkshire are black. Immigrants provide much of the fodder for the

Socialist arguments

most brutally dehumanizing and deskilling work of modern capitalism. In the massive car assembly plants of Ford, for example, the fettling shops and foundries in England are manned by West Indians and Pakistanis, whilst in Germany it is Turkish workers.

THE GUEST-WORKER SYSTEM

We have seen how capital accumulation is served by having a large reserve army of labour and by keeping the workforce divided, and the way capital tries to use migrant labour to this end. Immigrants provide yet another advantage to employers, however. Because their families live in another country, their labour can be bought more cheaply. A wage normally has to cover the cost of the food, clothing, housing and general sustenance of a man and his family, it has to pay for the upkeep of the present and the future generations of workers. The migrant labour or 'guest-worker' system found commonly in Europe and pioneered in South Africa, is ideal, because only the male worker is allowed in, hence he is more mobile and the cost of rearing the family is borne by the woman's labour in the home country, supplemented by the man's savings sent home. Not only can the employer pay less, the receiving country does not have to bear the burden of paying for the rearing and education of the labour. When the worker is worn out or sick he is sent home and the old age and welfare burden is thereby avoided. Capital benefits, therefore, if the social wage can be met elsewhere. Britain has been moving steadily over to this more cost-effective, but socially disruptive 'guest-worker' system, on which the West German 'economic miracle' was based. For some time now no new immigrants have been able to bring over their families to settle. On the contrary, everything done by the Thatcher government was aimed at sending back women and children who had failed to observe each dot and comma of the immigration laws, and we will later be examining this in more detail.

The advantages to the employer of a migrant labour force are that it is cheaper, has lower expectations, is less well organized and is easier to hire and fire. Only a trades union movement which is both open to immigrants and willing to fight for them and give immigrants an equal voice will be effective in combating the employers' strategy. Only the unions can combat the divisive strategy in the workplace and it is to this topic that we must next turn our attention.

202

TRADE UNIONS AND IMMIGRANTS

Most immigrants are members of the working class, so the only logical policy for trade unionists to adopt is to welcome immigrants into the trade union movement. No other policy makes sense, because if left outside, employers can always use migrants to lower wages and weaken the power of the unions. But there are a number of problems which have to be overcome if trade union solidarity between immigrant and indigenous worker is to be achieved. Some trade unionists may oppose immigration yet realize that their own interests are best served by encouraging migrants to join the unions when they are in this country. They will find that the immigrants are understandably reluctant to do so given the obvious hypocrisy in the two positions. Immigrants may well be employed in different kinds of work, hence there can be a lack of contact with domestic workers and a possible conflict of interests may emerge between them.

The situation of immigrants *per se* and black second-generation British may sometimes be different with respect to the trade unions, although the racism to which both are subjected unites them. For the second generation in work, there is the difficulty of getting active union involvement and representation. There are few black shop stewards, for example, mainly as a result of racism found in the workplace. Many young blacks refuse to accept the appalling jobs which society has assigned to them, hence they have never entered the organized working class. The collective who run the *Race Today* journal argue that this refusal by black youth to fill the same work roles as their parents is a revolutionary position. This raises the question of how trade unionists should relate to this section of Britain's youth. An awareness of their situation and the nature of their struggles is clearly important for combating racism within the labour movement and in the community as a whole.

Some new immigrants may lack knowledge or experience of trade unionism and the undoubtedly weak legal position of immigrants reinforced by Home Office and police harassment may hinder their union involvement. Others, however, bring a valuable experience of organization and struggle which can be most useful. Many of the areas in which black men and women work are generally poorly unionized and are likely to have little industrial muscle. Tightening up on immigration laws may reduce militancy because immigrants may fear that being active in the union will attract the law's attention. Language and cultural differences also play a role in creating

barriers to communication and may contribute to a lack of understanding and a reinforcement of racial prejudice. But most important
of all is to define the key problem. This is not the immigrants but
the racism which exists among British workers.

What has been the record of the trade union movement on facing
these problems? The general policy of the TUC has been to play
down the subject, stress the need for immigrants to integrate and
oppose special provisions. This dominant mood of complacency has
been periodically challenged by those who point to the need actively
to oppose the discrimination which obviously does exist. It was not
until the 1958 TUC Conference that the issue of racial prejudice
among British workers was first raised. The following year a delegate
of the Clerical and Administrative Union highlighted the key issue
when she questioned whether the delegates were doing all they could
to confront racism in the movement. She said[16]:

It might even mean that for a time we have to be temporarily unpopular
with certain sections of our members, but if leadership means anything at
all – and this goes for the individual on the shop floor and for the trades
union official – we have to be courageous enough to give this leadership
. . .

Unfortunately, precious little has been done in the subsequent decades to meet this challenge head on and confront the problems. The
recent TUC Black Workers Charter has gone some small way forward, but much more active campaigning is required.

Some argue that immigrants are passive and not interested in join-
ing trade unions. But the important contribution made by immigrant workers to the spread of trade unionism and the fight-back
against employers, has not received the just recognition that it
deserves. Even given the frequent failure of British trade unions to
represent the interests of immigrant workers, lack of independent
immigrant unions (with few exceptions) demonstrates the awareness
of the politically conscious immigrant workers that the unity of
indigenous and immigrant labour is essential for the interests of the
working class as a whole. Grunwick will remain a permanent mile-
stone in the history of the British labour movement, showing how
a section of workers[17]:

. . . totally unorganised, totally ignorant of trade unionism, totally insecure
in a foreign land, can yet develop – in response to autocratic treatment –
such militancy, attract in a few months such solidarity, that all the forces
of the state, the media, the police, the courts, employers' organisations,

racial prejudice and women's inequality can be swept aside by the freshness and dynamism of determined struggle.

Far from being too passive, immigrant workers have been in the forefront of workers' struggles in recent years. Mention need only be made of strikes by the catering staff at Garners, assembly line workers at Ford and others at Imperial Typewriters, the Shotton Bros foundry, Mansfield Hosiery Mills and Howard Cash. Some 61 per cent of male employed blacks belong to a trade union compared to 47 per cent of white employed males, which gives the lie to those who say that blacks will not join the trade unions.[18] Unfortunately, as with the Imperial Typewriters strike, black workers have frequently had to confront hostile white workers as well as employers.

For the British trade unions, the failure to represent the interests of the immigrants also means a failure to represent indigenous workers. The struggle against State racism is important for all trade unionists, it is a vital part of creating working-class solidarity. The trade union movement cannot '. . . simply expect black workers to take part in its activities without acting on their terms too'.[19]

Similarly, internationalist support for workers' struggles in other countries has a vital role to play. Bowaters' papermill in Ellesmere Port produced 70 per cent of the pulp paper in Britain but was being shut down at the same time that the *Daily Mail* was reported to be buying its newsprint from South Africa. As the general secretary of the trade union SOGAT said, 'I am not prepared to see our members in places like Liverpool put on the street while paper is coming into Britain from places like South Africa.'[20] Only support for, and solidarity with, workers' struggles in other countries can help to remove the cheap labour guaranteed by repressive governments on which the multinationals thrive. It is this which creates capital export and unemployment here in Britain. Increasingly the new policy for capital is to replace migrant labour to the factories over here with new factories based in the Third World itself. This is the so-called New International Division of Labour.[21] New 'world market' factories are being set up in enclaves, such as those in Singapore, Taiwan and South Korea, where there are no restrictions concerning tax, export or import controls, profit repatriation and above all, employment and health and safety legislation, to hinder the operations of the multinational corporations. An internal racial division of labour is being complemented and some would argue replaced by a new international division of labour. The attraction for employers is the 300 million unemployed of the Third World with no social security or unemployment pay, desperate for any work in order to survive.[22] In the same way that incorporating immigrant workers into the trade union movement in Britain is helping to defeat the employers' strategy to undercut the cost of labour power here, so supporting the struggles for trade union rights in the Third World will achieve the same effect. Only an anti-racist and internationalist stance can defend British workers' long-term interests – this much is clear.

THE NUMBERS GAME AND IMMIGRANTS AS A BURDEN ON THE SOCIAL SERVICES

Not all immigrants are black and all blacks are not immigrants contrary to the assumptions which are widely held. In fact, nearly two-thirds of those people born abroad but living here are not by origin from the New Commonwealth,[23] and 40 per cent of blacks in Britain were born here and not abroad. Alarmist scaremongering about blacks 'swamping' British culture hides the real truth which is that only four out of every hundred inhabitants are black, under 2 million in total. Although the average number of births is slightly higher among the black population, a recent statistical study concluded that the '. . . difference is probably entirely a result of social class differences'.[24] Moreover, the decline in the birth rate of blacks is greater than the overall decline in birth rate in the population as a whole. As for the argument that Britain is only a small country and is getting rapidly overcrowded – *emigration from the UK has consistently been higher than immigration* and over a large part of the 1970s, the total population of the country was actually falling. Between 1971 and 1976 under a million people entered as immigrants and 1.2 million left to live elsewhere.

The need to control the number of immigrants is the rationale given by politicians for an increasingly harsh series of racist laws passed in Britain. Many people who argue that the immigration laws are a good thing would do well to consider their impact. Very soon after the passing of the 1962 Commonwealth Immigrants Act which was the first restriction on immigrants from the empire, only skilled workers on a limited voucher system were allowed in. The need for unskilled labour had by then been met. From India's allocation of under 4,000 vouchers in 1966, 90 per cent went to doctors, teachers and technology and science graduates – a free brain drain to the British economy and social services. The 1971 Immigration Act, however, brought a complete halt to any new settlement by Commonwealth citizens and henceforth it was only dependents who could be brought in. Since then, the extent of the State's repression and harassment of black people has escalated. To bring families in is an extremely difficult, bureaucratically complicated and frequently humiliating procedure which has kept many families disunited for years. Immigration officials have been responsible for detaining people for long periods of time at airports, doing virginity tests on prospective brides and in collaboration with the police, carrying out raids on black families under the guise of tracing 'illegal' immigrants. At any one time, 200 people are in prison without trial under the powers of the 1971 Act. To be black is to be an immigrant in popular mythology, hence all black people are subject to possible harassment on suspicion of being here illegally. New rules to charge overseas visitors for the use of Health Service facilities have similarly led to demands for black nationals to produce their passports, including on one notable occasion, a member of the Commission for Racial Equality who attended a London hospital.[25]

Immigration laws are racist even though they are framed in terms of nationality rather than race because they are written in such a way that blacks are the ones to be persecuted. The 1981 nationality law follows in this tradition by creating three categories of British citizenship, with those born in British dependent territories suffering a severe curtailment of their rights. Departing from seven centuries of legal tradition, the Bill removes the automatic right of people born here to be British citizens.[26] They must have parents who have British nationality. The laws are also sexist because women can only come in as dependents of men, whilst women cannot bring in fiancés and husbands. One consequence is that many Asian women and their children have found themselves threatened with deportation should their marriage break down. Campaigns were launched around the cases of Jaswinda Kaur from Leeds, Nasreen Akhtar from Rochdale and Nasira Begum from Manchester which exemplified the human suffering caused by such laws and this cannot be ignored by all those who argue in their favour. Attempts were also made to deport West Indian women like Cynthia Gordon, but concerted campaigns forced the Home Office to retreat on many of the cases highlighted – though many more went unheard.

These discriminatory laws do little to control the influx of foreigners because since Britain joined the EEC all its members citizens have right of entry and work in this country (although an EEC citizen unemployed for six months will not have his or her permit renewed). The defence of the 'British way of life' and Mrs

Thatcher's expressed fears that 'we' might be 'swamped by an alien culture' give a clue to part of the reason for such laws. They are a cheap vote-winner for politicians[27] who can draw on the strong strand of racism in British society which the education system and media do precious little to combat. This sentiment is summed-up in the words of the former Conservative MP for Louth, Sir Cyril Osborne, 'This is a white man's country and I want it to remain so.'[28] Adolf Hitler took the cultural and racial preservation argument to its logical conclusion and physically eliminated 20 million Slavs, 6 million Jews and an indeterminate number of others who might contaminate the Aryan population. The hard-core British fascists in the National Front argue in their journal – *Spearhead* that 'if Britain were to become Jew-clean she would have no nigger neighbours to worry about'.[29] And we are left to wonder how they would achieve this.

Apart from the nucleus on the extreme Right, there are many ordinary people who express their fears about the 'decline' in British culture. In response, it must be pointed out that Britain is a nation of immigrants. Over the centuries Celts, Anglo-Saxons, Danes, Normans, Flemings, Hugenots, Irish, Jews, Poles, West Indians, Chinese, Africans, Indians and Pakistanis have arrived and settled in this country. The resulting melting pot of races that we call 'the British' have in their turn provided migrants and citizens to the USA, Kenya, Canada, Australia, India, etc. Each group has made their contribution to the richness and diversity of British life, hence we find that young people now dance to West Indian bands and most people eat Chinese takeaways and Indian (Bangladeshi or Pakistani) curries. Responsibility for the decline of British culture has to be found elsewhere, among other things with the commercialization of virtually every sphere of life, a recession cutting the living standards of millions and a mass media in the hands of a few unrepresentative and unelected individuals and companies. The arguments about numbers and preserving the culture are all too often a cover for a naked racism. In the days before Britain joined the Common Market, Mr Greene, a former MP for Worcester, put the point in a straightforward if somewhat colourful way[30]:

It is absolutely essential to preserve the purity of our race and to prevent contamination with the riff-raff of Eastern Europe, the stiffs of the Mediterranean and the dead beats of the World.

Immigrants as a 'burden' on the welfare state is a commonly heard argument which the facts can soon dispel. Turning first to the health sector, we need to be reminded that when Enoch Powell was Minister of Health, he continued recruitment drives for doctors and nurses in the West Indies, India and Pakistan. He even praised in Parliament '. . . the large numbers of doctors from overseas . . . who provide a useful and substantial reinforcement of the staffing of our hospitals'.[31] Foreign medical staff subsidize the national health service by performing the less lucrative hospital work which others are not prepared to do. A third of hospital doctors and a quarter of GPs are from overseas.[32] In one London hospital alone, four-fifths of all qualified and ancilliary nurses are migrants.[33] From the African surgeon to the West Indian cleaners and porters, immigrant labour (both the highly skilled and the unskilled) heavily subsidize Britain's National Health Service. Given this situation, it is even more incredible that non-scientific and purely racist ideas about black people spreading disease should exist even at the highest levels of the medical administration. Ted Gang, the Civil Servant in charge of health at the DHSS for example, has been quoted as saying that, 'deafness among Asian and African children is probably associated with factors such as lack of hygiene, spitting, etc'.[34] In terms of their use of the Health Service facilities, a report by the National Institute of Economic and Social Research concluded that[35]:

. . . largely because of their age structure (they tend on average to be younger), immigrant families make smaller demands on the Health Services than other families.

When it comes to the social services, a lack of information, communication barriers and the fear of State bureaucracy mean that many immigrants who are entitled to welfare benefits fail to claim them. Migrant workers not allowed to bring their families into the country are the first to be expelled in a time of recession and they are sent home without recourse to any welfare benefits. Settled immigrants also suffer heavily and unemployment among black youths is running particularly high. In Birmingham in 1980, only 26 per cent of school and college leavers classified as being of ethnic origin found work compared with 60 per cent of the white population.[36] It has been estimated that 60 per cent of all social security payments go to the elderly but under 3 per cent of the black population compared to 16 per cent of the total population are of pensionable age[37] hence they are substantially less of a 'burden' in this area. A study done in the *Economic Review* concluded that the average immigrant received about 80 per cent as much in social benefit as the average member of the total population in 1961, whilst the estimate for 1981 was still only 80 to 85 per cent.[38] Because most of the black population are concentrated in the run-down inner-city areas they tend anyway to receive the poorest health, education and housing facilities. The irony of this is that it is the low wages received by blacks from working in many of these services which subsidizes the rest of the population. Cuts in welfare services in times of recession naturally cause a greater proportionate harm to the black workers.

If we turn to housing we find it is certainly true that blacks tend to live in poorer-quality housing. But just as black immigrants were prepared to take on the jobs that whites refused so they were also willing to take the houses not acceptable to whites. The major reason for their generally poor-quality housing is the low wages they receive. To those who say that bad housing conditions are the fault of immigrants, the Milner Holland report on London housing stated quite clearly that, 'The plight of the immigrant is the outcome, and too often an extreme example, of London's housing difficulties; it is not their cause.' Capitalism's inability to deliver the goods of housing and a minimal social security for all, cannot be blamed on the immigrants; their situation is a symptom not the cause.

In the education system racism, language differences, the absence of a multi-cultural curriculum and categorizing a number of Afro-Carribbean children as being ESN have all impaired the chances of black children achieving the same results as whites. Overcrowding and poverty for many of the children does little to facilitate their studies. Those proponents of racially derived intelligence such as Eysenck and Jensen have been totally discredited by both the volume and the quality of the arguments and research findings which disprove their theories.[39] As Noam Chomsky has pointed out[40]:

A possible correlation between mean I.Q. and skin colour is of no greater scientific interest than a correlation between any two other arbitrarily selected traits, say mean height and colour of eyes.

Correlation does not denote cause and it is the other reasons we have indicated which account for the under-achievement of black children in schools.

To those who claim that blacks are a burden on the welfare state, we have produced the evidence to refute their case. One final point, however, needs to be made in response to their 'moral' indignation. What hypocrisy – to speak of those people being a 'burden' on the welfare state who carried the truly odorous burden of the British empire, gross exploitation, slavery and continuing low-wage labour under harsh conditions over the centuries and up to the present. Where is the morality in this?

CONCLUSION

In answer to the questions raised at the beginning of the chapter, we can now summarize our arguments in reply. Immigrants are over here because originally we were over there. The British empire disrupted colonial societies and created a potential pool of labour to be drawn upon. Because capitalism develops unevenly, a situation guaranteed by the military and political might of those who received the early advantage, the gaps in wealth and poverty grew and the need for the poor to travel abroad in order to survive grew with it. When immigrants arrived in this country, they were consigned to the lowest paid and the least attractive jobs, those which generally, at a time of full employment, British workers did not want.

The reason for Britain's present unemployment is not the immigrants but the crisis in capitalism, and repatriation and immigration controls cannot possibly solve that crisis. Employers use immigrants to divide the workforce and thereby weaken it. By employing migrants, they hope to get cheaper labour and thus greater profits. Only by welcoming immigrants into the trade union movement and fighting with them not only in the battles over wages and conditions of employment but also against racism, will an effective counter to this strategy be met. But making common cause with immigrant workers here is not enough. Employers in the era of multinationals can roam the world in search of the most lucrative and exploitative wage labour relations. As never before only a truly internationalist working-class response which opposes repression of trade union rights, civil and political liberties wherever they occur can counter global capital's game. The task is not small but no other response on the part of workers can hope to be successful. This policy needs to be pursued in tandem with a campaign at home for a planned rather than the present anarchic economy to create full employment policies.

The 'numbers' argument we have shown to be fallacious on several grounds, not least being the excess of emigrants over immigrants and the relatively small percentage of black British out of the total population. The arguments about preserving British culture can be seen as spurious because the mass media and a packaged commoditized society under capitalism have already done the damage. Culture is anyway a dynamic, developing and diverse phenomenon. The richness of the tapestry can only be improved and not diminished by having a new weave along with the old. Immigrants are neither a burden nor a threat to British workers but are a necessary ally in the struggle against exploitation. The racism in British society must be tackled head-on if this alliance is to be achieved. As the delegate to the TUC Conference said a generation ago, it might even mean temporary unpopularity among certain sections of the membership, but 'we have to be courageous enough to give this leadership'. Eliminating racist jokes, opposing immigration controls and actively supporting anti-racist campaigns are just some of the ways to meet this challenge. Resolutions and legislation cannot do the job alone.

NOTES

Lou Kushnik, Jane Black, Ong Bie Nio and Gus John provided, in many different ways, much help in the writing of this chapter – some unbeknown to them. A special word of thanks also to the editors David Coates and Gordon Johnston, for asking the right questions.

1. *Observer*, 20 Sept. 1981. The information on the fires was provided by local firemen
2. *The Times*, 6 Feb. 1981
3. Sivanandan, a WEA Lecture on race and racism, Manchester, Oct. 1980
4. P. Foot, *Immigration and Race in British Politics*, Penguin 1965, p. 234
5. A theory which sees the inhabitants of the colonies as being further back along an evolutionary scale and that the principle of the survival of the fittest exists amongst peoples as well as amongst animals.
6. Scientific racism is the belief that black people are genetically less intelligent than whites.
7. An excerpt from evidence given by the Institute of Race Relations to the Royal Commission on Criminal Procedure, April 1979, in *Race and Class*, **XX** (4) (Spring 1979), p. 415
8. See 'Police against black people' in *Race and Class*, **XX** (4) (Spring 1979)
9. The Moss Side Community Action Group, quoted in *Mancunion*, Sept. 1981. For the description of one, perhaps typical case, see 'The Toxteth Family Who Would Take No More' in *New Statesman*, 10 July 1981
10. *Observer*, 20 Sept. 1981

11. The term is explained and explored in further detail in Chapter 4 by Bob Jessop.
12. The speech was made in June 1946 and is quoted in R. Cohen, *Migration, Late Capitalism and Development.* Address to the Annual Conference of the Development Studies Association, Swansea 1980, mimeograph
13. James Callaghan was then Home Secretary
14. See Department of Employment, *Manpower Studies No. 10 Hotels: The Role of Immigrants in the Labour Market,* HMSO 1971
15. K. Marx in a letter to S. Meyer and A. Vogt, April 1870, in K. Marx and F. Engels, *On Britain,* Moscow Foreign Language Publishing House 1962, pp. 551–2
16. R. Miles and A. Phizacklea, *The TUC, Black Workers and New Commonwealth Immigrants 1954–1973,* Working Papers on Ethnic Relations, No. 6, SSRC 1977, p. 13
17. J. Dromey and G. Taylor, *Grunwick: The Workers' Story,* Lawrence and Wishart 1978, p. 199
18. Counter Information Service, *Racism. Who Profits?* Report No. 16, Russell Press 1976, p. 20
19. *Black Workers and Trade Unions,* Report of a conference organized by the Trades Union Basic Education Project, WEA Northwestern District, Oct. 1980, p. 5
20. See *Links, No. 6,* Bulletin of the North-West Trades Union Anti-Apartheid Liaison Committee, Oct.–Nov. 1980
21. The best study so far available refers mainly to Germany, see F. Fröbel, J. Heinrichs, O. Kreye, *The New International Division of Labour,* Cambridge UP 1980
22. T. Hayter, *The Creation of World Poverty,* Pluto Press 1981, p. 18
23. The New Commonwealth excludes the older white settler states of Australia, New Zealand and Canada and refers basically to Africa, India, Pakistan and Bangladesh.
24. The Runnymede Trust and the Radical Statistics Group, *Britain's Black Population,* Heinemann 1980, p. 15
25. *The Guardian,* 28 May 1981
26. *The Times,* 22 April 1981
27. One study suggested that the identification of Enoch Powell's views with the Tory Party gave them an estimated increment of 6.7 per cent in votes in the 1970 election. See D. T. Studler, 'Policy voting in Britain: the coloured immigration issue in the

1964, 1966 and 1970 General Elections', *American Political Science Review* 72, (1), Mar. 1978

28. *Daily Mail*, 7 Feb. 1961
29. See D. Edgar, 'Racism, Fascism and the Politics of the National Front', *Race and Class*, XIX, (2) (Autumn 1977), p. 120
30. P. Foot, op. cit., p. 110
31. *Hansard*, 8 May 1963
32. Third World First, *White Student Black World*, 1977, p. 30
33. L. Doyal, *The Health of Underdevelopment and the Underdevelopment of Health*, a paper given at the BSA Medical Sociology Conference, University of York, Sept. 1981
34. Brent Community Health Council, *Black People and the Health Services*, Brent CHC 1981
35. K. Jones, 'Immigrants and the Social Services' in *Economic Review*, National Institute, Aug. 1967 (our insertion in the brackets)
36. *Financial Times*, 23 Mar. 1981
37. Counter Information Service, op. cit., p. 34
38. K. Jones, op. cit
39. See L. J. Kamin, *The Science and Politics of I.Q.*, Halsted Press 1974
40. Quoted in M. Billig, 'Psychology, Racism, and Fascism', Searchlight 1979, p. 34

FURTHER READING

The journals *Race and Class*, Institute of Race Relations, 247–9 Pentonville Road, London N1 9NE; *Race Today; Searchlight; State Research Bulletin*, 9 Poland St, London W1; and the *Race Relations Abstract*, Sage Publications cover much of the ground on racism, immigration, the police etc. They are essential sources for further reading.
Useful books include:

S. Castles and G. Kosack, *Immigrant Workers and Class Structure in Western Europe*, Oxford UP 1973
A. Sivanandan *Race, Class and the State*, Pluto Press 1982
A. Phizacklea and R. Miles, *Labour and Racism*, Routledge and Kegan Paul 1980
P. Foot, *Immigration and Race in British Politics*, Penguin 1965
Counter Information Service, *Racism. Who Profits?* Report No 16, Russell Press 1976

The Runnymede Trust and the Radical Statistics Group, *Britain's Black Population*, Heinemann 1980

J. Berger, *A Seventh Man*, Penguin 1975

L. Kushnick, 'Racism and class consciousness in modern capitalism' in B. P. Bowser and R. Hunt (eds), *The Impact of Racism on White Americans*, Sage Publications 1981

M. Castells, 'Immigrant workers and class struggles in advanced capitalism: The Western European Experience' in R. Cohen, P. C. W. Gutkind and P. Brazier (eds), *Peasants and Proletarians*, Hutchinson 1979

Chapter ten

ARGUMENTS AGAINST SOCIALISM

Gordon Johnston

In this concluding chapter I want to consider three arguments which are frequently canvassed, to discount the possibility and desirability of society being organized on principles other than those informed by a capitalist ethic, and to suggest that the consequences of socialism and the presumed means of its realization would entail an unjustifiable amount of human suffering. The first of these arguments is the accusation that socialism can only be achieved and maintained by the systematic use of violence. The second focuses on the claim that the ideals and principles which inform socialism are contrary to human nature. And finally I want to consider all that is implied in that despairing yet ever popular catchphrase, 'why don't you go to Russia?'. Although it is comparatively easy to explode the cruder variants of these arguments they all involve real problems for socialists. This is hardly surprising given that they all make claims about the processes and consequences of a revolutionary transformation which they are designed to obfuscate and which we have yet to witness, and for which there are no cast-iron guarantees as to what will and what will not transpire. For socialists to argue otherwise, as they sometimes do, is politically naive and intellectually dishonest: and with this in mind I want to consider the arguments outlined above in some detail and suggest how socialists might respond to them.

SOCIALISM AND VIOLENCE

I do not think that what we call 'crimes of violence' are anything like as severe a threat to the maintenance of tranquillity in this country as the tendency to use violence to achieve political or industrial ends. As far as I am concerned, that is the worst crime in the book. I think it is *worse than murder*.[1]

Discussions about violence in general and political violence in particular are plagued with three problems: the tendency to consider violence outside the social and historical context in which it takes place, the apparent reluctance to define what violence is and the assumption that victims of violence suffer to a greater extent than victims of other forms of human suffering. Yet these problems immediately become more comprehensible when one considers that the starting point for so many discussions on violence is the view that it is always and automatically wrong, that it can never be justified and that nothing is ever achieved by it. For these problems are indicative of a presumed and widely shared agreement on the question of what violence is, and of the need to combat it, and are canvassed now at a time when it is generally regarded that Britain is becoming a more violent society than it has ever been before. Indeed the presumption of such an agreement on the question of violence is but one theme in a more general and increasingly urgent appeal to maintain those political institutions, values and procedures which are regarded by defenders of capitalism at least as essential for the survival of 'civilized' life. The character and origins of this appeal lies not only in the claim it makes for the moral efficiency of the market economy but also in its particular interpretation of Britain's political development, one that has been admirably summarized by Peter Shipley[2]:

Britain is renowned among nations for its high degree of constitutional stability and the absence of violent political conflict. Since the upheavals of the seventeenth century, when Parliament triumphed over absolutism and anarchy, established institutions have shown a remarkable resilience. By constantly adapting to new circumstances while upholding the rule of law, they have survived periods of unrest and crises to enable social change to take place peacefully.

Ignoring the somewhat selective history upon which such an interpretation is based, one can safely conclude that such certainties concerning the 'remarkable resilience' of 'established institutions' are no longer with us. And in their absence it is neither surprising that the spectre of 'violent political conflict' should occupy the imaginations of our rulers, nor that they should seek to hold socialism at least partly responsible for disturbing their reveries. The accusations are familiar. Socialists initiate and/or condone the use of violence for political ends, and in so doing demonstrate not only their scant regard for the legitimate arena of political debate and the rule of law, but also their ambivalence towards the value of reasoned discussion.

Socialist arguments

Socialists resort to such tactics because they have failed to win support for their arguments and beliefs as evidenced by their poor performance at general elections down the years. And moreover since socialists display at best an ambivalence towards violence in winning support for their cause, isn't it obvious that their victory will be maintained by large doses of repression, intimidation and terror, as witnessed before in the states of Eastern Europe and the Soviet Union?

Given the crudity with which many of these views are expressed it is tempting to dismiss them out of hand; but since they do enjoy a degree of popular support, and because they raise more serious questions than their rhetoric perhaps suggests, they need to be taken more seriously than that. Instead it is as well to start with the way in which the term 'political violence' has been employed. Major Clutterbuck considers that the period 1971–74 was: '. . . the most violent for over 60 years (since 1911) in terms of internal political violence: in strikes, demonstrations and terrorism'.[3] The late Reginald Maudling in a similar vein considered that: '. . . by political violence I mean everything from the wickedness of the IRA or bombers who murder to those protesters who sit down and block the traffic'[4], while Sir Robert Mark asserts somewhat triumphantly:

'Already workers have rejected the extreme policies of trade union leaders and an Anglo-Indian running a small business has courageously and successfully stood firm against politically motivated violence on the streets of Grunwick.'[5]

Finally, the intellectual chaos of Paul Johnson[6]:

Nor will the men of violence be content with the mere patronage of Labour. They are on the march. Violence feeds on its triumphs over the law. Labour's leaders may think that beastliness on a picket line is acceptable. But violence is an evil continuum which begins with the inflammatory verbal pursuit of class war, continues with Grunwick and the lawless use of union power, progresses to the knives, clubs and acid-bombs of Lewisham and Ladywood and then – as we may well fear – rapidly accelerates into full-blooded terrorism with firearms, explosives and an utter contempt for human life.

Now clearly a lot is being claimed for 'political violence' here, much of which falls outside a commonsense view that violence has something to do with the use of force to injure persons or damage property. It can apparently include talking about class, or participating in strikes and demonstrations which are lawful and more peaceful than most football matches, and it can also include unlawful acts such as blocking roads, where when charges are brought they are invariably for breaching the peace or obstructing the highway – neither of which involve even the accusation of violent behaviour. Indeed these approaches also produce a strange anomaly with regard to the IRA who, we are repeatedly told, are 'common criminals' yet here they are engaged in 'political violence'. What is very clear is that the above approaches are more concerned with condemning the politics and actions of those involved than with offering any serious and consistent consideration of what violence is, or the extent to which it is employed for political ends. For that reason, if for no other, they are capable of encompassing both lawful activity and patently non-violent actions such as blocking roads at the same time as they systematically exclude activities by the police and army, for whom a comprehensive job description would include amongst other things, intimidation, violence and killing people.

Of course the slide from civilian lawlessness to the behaviour of police and soldiers is not without its problems. It is certainly the case that in pursuing their duties the police force and the army are circumscribed by codes of behaviour which prescribe legitimate and illegitimate ways of going about their business, and there are occasions when charges are brought against individual police officers and soldiers for assault and manslaughter. But this should not obscure two important arguments. Firstly it is not only the extra-legal activities of the police and armed forces which involve the use of violence. Its employment is deeply inscribed in their lawful day-to-day activities, supported by tradition, training and a tendentious distinction between force and violence. Secondly, the use of this distinction between force and violence, enshrined in such mystificatory maxims as 'a timely show of force can prevent violence breaking out', suggests that we are not talking about violence at all but about who is legally entitled to be violent. The euphemism 'force' is employed to characterize the legitimate activities of the State, while the term 'violence', replete with all the moral condemnation associated with its use, is reserved for actions by other people or organizations deemed illegitimate. Now it is entirely understandable that the State should wish to dissociate itself from the accusation that it is involved in violence, but such a dissociation rests not on the claim that it does not employ violence – it clearly does, but on the claim that it is legitimately entitled to do so. The basis of this claim, namely that the State represents the interests of all the people as expressed through the electoral process, has been discussed and criticized elsewhere.[7] What we need to stress here is that a part of the socialist reply to the accusation that we engage in violence because we have no regard for the legitimate political process is the observation that a substantial body of socialist opinion disputes the State's claim to represent the interests of the people as a whole and anticipates that the transition to socialism will require the dismantling of the existing State machinery. The second part of the reply is to question the assertion of the necessary linkage of socialism and violence. The methods adopted by socialists to win support for their views in this country are invariably those of the political campaign, demonstration and meeting. Violence is not a central part of the political strategy of the vast majority of socialists in Britain today, and when the anticipation of violence does figure in their politics it is invariably defensive, a reaction to the unprovoked violence of others, a way of defending those sections of the community who are subject to increasing physical violence from individuals and organizations on the far Right in British politics – and even that only because of the failure, reluctance or refusal by the State to do anything about these attacks. As has recently been argued in *Race and Class*[8]:

No community should have to defend itself. That, in a democracy, is the function of the forces of law and order. But when those self-same forces have repeatedly and over a period of time shown, beyond any reasonable doubt that they are unable to protect that community, that inability becomes a refusal. If then such a denial of the right to be protected is upheld by judicial decision (or indecision), compounded by bad law and justified by the media (if only by default) such a community is reduced to one of two choices. It can either submit to indignity, harassment, brutalisation and even murder or it can defend itself.

And in conceding this much to those who would equate socialism with violence it should be remembered that the right to employ force/violence for the purposes of self-defence is an important feature of the common law tradition and is to be found in the 1967 Criminal Law Act, with the important proviso that such rights are generally held to apply only to individuals in situations where their person or property is immediately threatened and not to communities subject to persistent humiliation, intimidation and violence. In claiming self-defence as a justification for employing force/violence, socialists and black organizations are challenging not only the general claim by the State to represent the interests of the people as a whole, but also the appropriateness of a legal framework which confers little in the way of redress when the State is failing in its obligations.

It is a deeply depressing argument to have to advocate and no socialist would ever claim that it represents a sufficient response to either racism or racist attacks.[9] And that is why demands are also made for a more positive application of the Race Relations Act, the use of the Public Order Act to ban racist marches (a view endorsed by the Scarman Report), and for a serious consideration of the extent to which the police force is deeply imbibed with racist attitudes. To those who would condemn the advocacy of self-defence, the retort is obvious: on what grounds can one possibly stand aside and permit a section of the community already subject to widespread discrimination and abuse to be further persecuted by persistent attacks, harassment and murder? Moreover we have a right to question our critics about the particular narrowness and focus of their definition of violence and their hypersensitivity to only particular forms of human suffering. Why should we assume, as they do, that victims of violence (as conventionally understood) suffer to a greater extent than the victims of other forms of human suffering? What is not necessarily involved here is any rigorous attempt to quantify human suffering,[10] but simply the recognition that forms of suffering such as occur in situations of inequality or unemployment demand as much concern as is shown to the suffering caused by violent assault. It is after all worth pausing to ask why our sensibilities are frequently more responsive to a bloody nose than to a homeless family and why the definition of violence should not be extended to include forms of suffering and deprivation which are the result of force, albeit non-physical force, but are not characterized by the blood'n bruises imagery of conventional violence. Obvious examples might include inequality, starvation and the numerous forms of coercion and domination that exist in everyday life. One advantage of defining violence in this wider way is to remind us that the normal conditions of society are violent, and that much of what is taken for granted as natural or inevitable is nothing of the sort, but the result of specific economic and political forces which necessarily involve both coercion and suffering. This inevitably raises the question of responsibility: not simply for the direct and bloody violence of an individual to another, but for the violence done to the many by the inequalities and deprivation of a class society. To define violence too narrowly, that is, helps to obscure 'the violence of things' endemic to the market process of capitalism itself.

The point is polemical of course. There are genuine dangers of collapsing all forms of suffering into the one heading of violence. There is, for example, some difference between the form of coercion involved in the 'violence' of an eviction and the 'violence' associated with poverty and the non-payment of rent; or between an eviction carried out using hired thugs brandishing chair legs and a polite request to vacate property. But the importance of these arguments is that they seek to dispel any illusions that either violence or our responses to it are as straightforward a matter as many would have us believe, that they suggest that much of the human suffering and deprivation which is conveniently dismissed as inevitable is in fact a problem of capitalism, and that this kind of human suffering demands as much if not more concern than is persistently shown to the 'victims of violence'. If those who would criticize socialists for violence were as vocal on the suffering of the poor and the unemployed we would have greater cause to treat their concern for violence as genuine. But in their silence on this wider dimension of the problem, they reveal all too often that their real concern is not with the violence of socialism but with its radicalism, not with its supposed methods but with its goals that threaten the power and privileges that they would protect.

Having raised some general problems with the question of what violence is and our attitudes towards it, let me return to some of the more specific charges made against socialists. One noted earlier was that by engaging in or advocating violent activity socialists demonstrated a lack of interest in reasoned discussion. The charge is a much wider one suggesting that reason and violence are antithetical, that political violence is therefore irrational, and that the business of politics in Britain and indeed all 'civilized' countries is concerned with the exercise and application of reason. William Whitelaw, commenting on the riots of last summer, hoped: '... that it [the House of Commons] will not at any time get into the habit of imagining that there can be any reason or excuse for mindless violence in a free society'.[11] From a perspective such as this, any attempt to explain why the riots took place quickly comes to be seen as an attempt to legitimate them. Explanation is conflated with justification to establish an invidious moral position from which all attempts to explain are dismissed as both morally inadequate and politically unacceptable. Yet in fact there are good grounds for believing that the antithesis between reason and violence is a false one. The antithesis implies that there is no violence or threat of violence on the side of reason or the political order which it sustains. Yet it is surely difficult to argue that any society equipped with a police force, army and nuclear weapons is ruled by reason alone. The issue in any class society, including this one, is always that of the balance between rule by reason/consent and rule by force/coercion: and as a society strengthens its police force and its army that balance can be said to be tilted away from reason and not towards it. Moreover the presumed antithesis between reason and violence ignores the extent to which the precondition for the much-vaunted 'triumph of reason' was the systematic and widespread use of violence both at home and abroad. The social and economic conditions underpinning contemporary British democracy emerged as a result of complex historical processes in which the slave trade, the empire, the Highland clearances and much more played a central part. To put the point more generally, capitalism did not triumph in any major advanced country in the world without armed conflict or civil war. As Anthony Arblaster has argued[12]:

The point is not that the West today is held to be guilty of the sins of its forefathers . . . It is rather that the peace, order and civilisation which the West now enjoys are seen as the results of a history of bloodshed, conflict and ruthless exploitation of the non-Western world. If such fruits can only be won through violence, then those who enjoy them have no moral right to lecture others on the virtues of non-violence.

And it is this which makes one somewhat cynical about simplistic assertions that violence never achieves anything – in itself perhaps not, but it has invariably been an important characteristic of the transition from one form of society to another. It is unlikely that the transition to socialism will be any more peaceful, not because socialists have some perverse predilection to kill, throttle or maim, or because socialism possesses some inevitable relationship with violence, but because reason and history suggest that the structural shifts in the balance of power which socialism anticipates have always been characterized by a considerable degree of *resistance* which not surprisingly finds its ultimate form in armed conflict.

If, then, the neat antithesis between reason and violence raises some important questions on the side of reason it raises some equally important ones on the side of violence. There are invariably reasons why violence is employed both by the State and by those who challenge the authority of the State. It was suggested earlier that what is ultimately at issue here is the question of the State's legitimacy and that much of the way in which political violence is regarded and discussed is premised on the view that the State is legitimately entitled to be violent whilst opponents of the State are not. It is this which helps to explain the persistent duality of language in descriptions of the same action or event: force/violence, common criminal/revolutionary, terrorist/freedom fighter. It is this that provides some indication of why the struggle over the question of legitimacy is in part a struggle to define what is going on and who or what is responsible for it, and why that struggle necessarily precludes any agreement on either the terms being employed or the meanings attached to them. In other words, what on the face of it appears as wilful semantic confusion or plain muddled thinking apparently resolvable by a good dictionary is in fact part of the very struggle for legitimacy itself

For those socialists who dispute the State's claim to legitimacy, the question is not why do socialists employ violence – all the evidence suggests that in the main they do not – but rather why socialists eschew both breaking the law and the use of violence, and under what conditions might they not do so? The answer to that question has much to do with what the socialist project is all about and the conditions under which it is likely to be successful in advanced capitalist countries. The most obvious factor here is that socialism requires *mass* political support, and mass political support is not won by isolated campaigns of violence. Indeed such campaigns would be rightly condemned by socialists as simply making the task of winning that political support more difficult. There are exceptions of course. We have already considered the argument about self-defence and there are in addition certainly spontaneous outbursts on picket lines and demonstrations. But the scale of violence involving socialists is trivial compared with the persistent threat and use of violence by the State, and the vicious and brutal campaigns of racist organizations. Indeed such is the scale of attacks by racists that they have now been officially recognized by the government[13] and a leading Conservative spokesman on terrorism and counter-insurgency has argued that[14]:

The greatest internal threat facing the western democracies today is Right-wing and racist extremism. In Britain racial attacks ranging from swastika-daubing to brutal racist murders and firebombings, are reaching almost epidemic proportions

In certain situations, therefore, socialists would and do condone the use of violence. But this is to say very little, since in certain situations just about everyone would condone, however reluctantly, the use of violence. And it is precisely because of this that it is patently ridiculous to suggest that socialism in power will necessarily be characterized by intimidation, terror and repression, or to claim that the complex question of violence can be resolved by invoking an abstract and frequently hypocritical morality which condemns its use. Having said that, socialists need to be acutely aware of the dangers of employing violence. In and by itself violence can neither achieve nor sustain anything of which socialists can be proud, and in fact the problem faced by socialists in relation to violence is exactly the reverse of that implied by our critics: not that socialists introduce violence into a society hitherto free of it, but that socialism demands and requires a political support based not on coercion but on consent and yet has to win that support in a society characterized by disparate and complex forms of coercion, domination and violence.

Finally it was suggested above that historically the shifts in the balance of power which delineate the transition from one form of society to another have invariably been characterized by resistance from the class whose power, wealth and position is being challenged. In the case of capitalism this resistance has and will take many forms, from investment strikes and State repression to the engineering of coups and the propping-up of brutal regimes. It would be naive of socialists to suggest that in the face of this one can remain inactive, but it is clear that the catalyst in such situations has nothing to do with the nature of socialism and considerably more to do with the way in which the morally indefensible is indeed defended.

SOCIALISM AND HUMAN NATURE

As a Christian I am bound to shun utopias on this earth and to recognise that there is no change in Man's social arrangements which will make him perfectly good and perfectly happy
(Margaret Thatcher)

Our opponents are driven by their vision, a messianic vision of the perfectability of man. It may have been conceived with fine intentions, it may have been born of a passion, but it has become an engine of tyranny, impoverishment and unemployment
(Keith Joseph)

One of the most persistent and frequently raised objections to socialism is that the principles and values which it supports and struggles for are 'contrary to human nature'. Socialism is little more than a dangerous Utopian fantasy premised on a naively optimistic appraisal of the capacity of men and women to live and work in peace, cooperation and equality. There is something to be said for this view, though not much. There is more to be said about what arguments concerning human nature are actually about and why they figure so predominantly in political controversy.

Historically conceptions of human nature have played an important role in attempts to defend, explain, condemn and change the character and organization of society. Rousseau considered that 'man is naturally good', Machiavelli that 'men are wretched'. For Hobbes, greed, egotism and selfishness were the essential characteristics, a view satirized in Mandeville's treatment of early capitalism where 'every Part was full of Vice, Yet the whole Mass a Paradice',[15] while Marx considered that the search for some essential human nature was a waste of time, because that nature changed over time and that accordingly, scholarship could more fruitfully be spent accounting for these changes and establishing the conditions under which men and women could develop and realize their full potential. Marx aside, the role that conceptions of human nature played in these diverse accounts was to provide a basis for making certain recommendations as to how society could best be organized in accordance with an invariably static and arbitary view of human nature. What is absent from these and many subsequent appeals to human nature, appeals which range from excessive optimism to racist bigotry, is the important distinction between 'human nature in general' and 'human nature as historically modified in each epoch' (Marx).

Looking at contemporary conservative accounts of human nature we can identify two main features. The first of these is the argument that those values and attitudes celebrated by capitalism constitute the most worthy side of the human condition and the associated denial that these characteristics are in any way specific to capitalism, the assertion that is, that they are 'natural' and will therefore appear in any society. Combined with this is a series of grim warnings of the darker, weaker side of human nature from which society must be protected. The 'workshy' and the 'scrounger' are well-known contemporary exemplars of this sinful dimension. Increasingly these particular views are claiming support from the pseudo-science of sociobiology[16]:

We are what we are, greedy, rapacious, self-serving individuals, out to get what we can for ourselves and Devil take the hindmost. If this is how we are, if this somewhat mordant description of mankind does exactly describe us, as the sociobiologists claim that it does, it is as foolish to condemn it as it is to condemn the fact that our noses are exterior rather than interior organs . . . . Science now seems to have caught up with Adam Smith. To support an economic lame-duck is not merely bad economics, but apparently is also against our deep-seated nature.

226

In a second and more liberal variant of this argument, it is suggested that because of the wide range of observable human behaviour, and the absence of any good reasons why some alternative form of society would correspond better to human nature or indeed be more humane than the existing one, the method of trial and error is the most appropriate way of bringing about social change. What both of these arguments claim is that any radical transformation of society would be at variance with the dictates of human nature and could only be brought about by an excessive degree of coercion resulting in an unjustifiable amount of human suffering and misery.

In response to this socialists have argued a number of things. They have argued firstly that both human nature and what is considered good or bad about it are largely determined by the character of the society in which it appears, and that as a result there are no good grounds for believing that those highly esteemed attributes of competitiveness, acquisitiveness and egotism are inevitable characteristics of human nature. When a system of production is informed by the principles of competition, profit and accumulation it is hardly surprising that their virtues are extolled or that the consumption habits and social mores they sustain are paraded as immutable and beneficial to society as a whole. Far from seeing the much publicized 'bad' side of human nature as some essential part of being human, socialists would argue that it is often better understood as little more than a quite intelligible response to those experiences of exploitation, powerlessness, and that sense of failure and frustration which pervades contemporary society. Socialists have argued too that capitalism not only promotes and sustains certain values and particular forms of human behaviour, but also frustrates the development of others. As a result men and women possess a considerable amount of human potential which remains unrealized, and which will remain unrealized until the structures and forms of organization which frustrate its development have been removed. A third strand in the socialist response has been the recognition that there is clear evidence of the existence within capitalism of forms of cooperation and of a commitment to those values which socialism seeks to generalize and establish as guiding principles for a future society. Examples of these developments are readily available in factories, clubs, women's organizations, campaigns and personal friendships. It is axiomatic for socialists that in attempting to change society men and women also change themselves, and that this process is already under way, illustrating not only the depth of resources and capabilities that people do possess but also the very real barriers this process inevitably encounters in a capitalist society. Finally it is as well to guard against 'excessive socialist optimism' of the kind which considers that all the nefarious ills, prejudices and bigotry which stalk the world will be swept away by waves of virtuous, morally wholesome, socialists. Firstly it will not be true and nor does socialism require it to be true. Secondly it exposes one to considerable ridicule – try it and see. Thirdly one needs to be realistic about the very real obstacles socialism will encounter and to acknowledge that not all of them have their origins in the values and attitudes promoted by capitalism. Sexism is an obvious example. And finally, as can be seen by the remarks of Thatcher and Joseph above, the case against socialism frequently relies on an exaggeration of what socialism claims to be able to achieve and there is no need to encourage our critics.

Writing in 1944 on the question of socialism and human nature John Strachey suggested that an equally important question was whether capitalism was contrary to human nature[17]:

Is it contrary to human nature to give the highest pay to those who do no work at all? . . . is it contrary to human nature to keep several million people permanently idle while they, and many others, lack the very goods that they ought to be producing? Is it contrary to human nature deliberately to destroy food, clothes and many other forms of wealth, in order to render the production of wealth more profitable again? Is it contrary to human nature to send millions of men to slaughter each other in order to decide who shall possess the markets of the world? Is all this contrary to human nature? I think it is.

'WHY DON'T YOU GO TO RUSSIA?

'Why don't you go to Russia?', from pub to pavement the invitation is extended. And although it is doubtful whether those who extend such invitations are aware of the questions they raise, socialists need to be. By this I mean that they need to do more than simply refine their public repertoire of verbal retorts and acerbic insults. For that injunction to emigrate raises the vital question of socialist attitudes to the Soviet Union and the Eastern bloc, and the need to differentiate our criticism of developments in Russia since 1917 from the pervasive anti-Soviet rhetoric of the new cold-warriors. The injunction raises, too, the complex question of the legacy of the Soviet and East European experience for our ideas about what socialism is and the conditions under which it would be possible in both the Eastern and Western blocs. It forces us to confront the political consequences of the absence of any viable model of a socialist alternative, and by implication it puts onto our agenda the question of what such an alternative might look like, both with regard to its organizational and institutional form and to the principles and procedures which should inform their operation. Far from being unimportant, these questions are so central that they will be discussed at length in subsequent volumes in this series; and what I want to do now is to consider in very general terms why the questions are important, and to indicate in broad terms the nature of a socialist answer to them.

The spectre of the Soviet Union as a fearful warning of what might be, has occupied a central place in anti-socialist propaganda from the days of the October Revolution, and this is hardly surprising, given that it signified the first major challenge to the rule of capital in the world economy. Today the advocates of the build-up of nuclear arms justify their initiatives by invoking the 'Soviet threat' to the democratic traditions of the 'free world', while Denis Healey harangues the Labour left for employing 'Stalinist tactics'. In the face of this, socialists are right to expose the degree of distortion and caricature that informs much of official Western opinion on the Soviet Union. But there is also a need, long recognized by socialists, to expose the Soviet Union and the regimes of Eastern Europe for the bureaucratic, anti-democratic and frequently repressive regimes that they are, and to explain how and why these developments came about. Considerable controversy surrounds these questions, though most socialist accounts emphasize the impossibility of socialism in one country, the low level of development of the productive forces, the failure to resolve the tension between the laws of the market and the principles of planning to meet human need, the early consolidation and subsequent dominance of the party bureaucracy, and the failure to combine public ownership with popular and democratic control. Clearly a number of these problems can only be explained by referring to the specific historical conditions under which the Soviet Union and the Eastern bloc emerged and some of these conditions will be considered below, but it is also clear that the problems of bureaucracy, the conflict between planning and the market, the question of socialist internationalism and popular democratic control will emerge in any socialist initiative. Indeed many of these questions are highlighted in the struggle of the Solidarity movement in Poland today.[18] The point to emphasize is that by developing our understanding of the Soviet experience we are not only concerned with exposing some of the cruder interpretations of that regime emanating from Western leaders and political pundits, but also with examining some of the general problems that socialism has and will encounter anywhere.

It is important first to grasp the particularities of the Russian experience – the extent to which you *cannot* generalize from the Soviet case. That in its turn requires some familiarity with the detail of post-1917 Russian history. For in the wake of the October Revolution, the Bolsheviks were faced with massive social and economic dislocation, exacerbated by the commitment of the Provisional Government to persist with the war effort, the looming threat of counter-revolution which materialized in the Civil War, and the threat of foreign intervention and sanctions to smash the nascent Revolution. The political support enjoyed by the Bolsheviks was extremely uneven, for although they commanded, at least temporarily, considerable urban-based support from sections of a disintegrating army and the industrial working class, they lacked substantial support amongst the peasantry which comprised some 80 per cent of the population. Moreover the failure of the Revolution to act as a catalyst for further revolutionary successes elsewhere in Europe added to the immense obstacles that had to be overcome if the Revolution was to be defended and consolidated in accordance with that principle of egalitarianism that had been so vital a factor in undermining the power and position of privileged groups and the overthrow of the feudal Tsarist State. In the face of all this, the need to build an effective State administration virtually from scratch became the pressing imperative of the revolutionary leadership, an administration which was required not only to reorganize and redirect the economy, but one which of necessity had to mobilize and sustain the requisite political support to defend the Revolution against armed opposition. From within these extremely unfavourable parameters the State/party relationship emerged and consolidated itself, and the building and subsequent victory of the Red Army in the Civil war and the withering away of the immediate threat of direct foreign intervention ensured the physical if not the economic security of the country. But the cost of the Civil War was not only high in terms of the havoc it wreaked on the economy, but also in the blow it dealt to the soviets as forms of popular democracy, long recognized by Lenin as essential forms of popular power[19]:

. . . just as socialism cannot be victorious unless it introduces complete democracy, so the proletariat will be unable to prepare for victory over the bourgeoisie unless it wages a many-sided, consistent and revolutionary struggle for democracy.

The fragility of the soviets must be seen not only in the context of the strains placed upon them by the logistical and organizational imperatives of waging a conventional civil war, but also against that absence in Russia in 1917 of an environment which provided even the minimal historical conditions for the functioning of parliamentary forms of democracy (this was illustrated dramatically by the widespread indifference that marked the dispersal of the Constituent Assembly in 1918 following the decision to pull out of the First World War and the endorsement by the Bolsheviks of land seizure by the peasants). The demise of democracy therefore, and the Bolsheviks' refusal to tolerate organized opposition, was premised on the stark fact that 'no opposition party was prepared to remain within legal limits',[20] and in the face of this, the erosion of that embryonic form of popular power that the soviets undoubtedly consituted becomes not only comprehensible, but serves to highlight the point that democratization is not simply an optional extra for socialists but an essential feature of all socialist initiatives – and one, moreover, which appears to be much more difficult to sustain in societies which have not enjoyed a previous tradition of liberal democracy.

To dwell still further on the detail of recent Russian history for a moment, it is worth remembering that the period of War Communism that operated throughout the Civil War was superceded in 1921 by the New Economic Policy (NEP), in which market forces in agriculture as well as private initiatives in small-and medium-sized industrial concerns were revived as a concession to capitalist tendencies and peasant interests in the economy. But NEP was not without its problems: the interplay of State planning and market forces in the social conditions of the 1920s did threaten the gains of the Revolution and acted as a powerful barrier to industrialization. The peasant producers in particular were always in a position to frustrate national economic strategy, and especially State-directed industrialization, and in so doing provoked a series of crises in the 1920s which culminated in the latter part of that decade in the forcible collectivization of agriculture and the policy of rapid heavy industrialization which laid the foundations for the consolidation in the 1930s of an 'ultra-centralized command economy'[21] under Stalin's now triumphant banner of 'socialism in one country.'

The costs in terms of human suffering and the subsequent tyranny of Stalin are well known. There is no wish to minimize them here, but set against this there remains a need to acknowledge the very real achievements of the Soviet Union since 1917, as E. H. Carr has reminded us[22]:

> . . . the transformation of Russia from a country more than eighty per cent of whose population consisted of illiterate or semi-literate peasants into a country with a population more than sixty per cent urban, which is totally literate and is rapidly acquiring the elements of urban culture . . . And these things have been brought about by rejecting the main criteria of capitalist production – profits and the laws of the market – and substituting a comprehensive economic plan aimed at promoting the common welfare.

The general lesson to be drawn from all this is that Russian experience is a poor basis for conjecturing about the character of socialism in late twentieth-century Britain. For the reality of Soviet society today can only properly be understood by taking full account of the particular historical conditions that prevailed in Russia in 1917 and their profound implications for the subsequent development of the Soviet Union. Russia can be used as a model, of course, but hardly now for the West. The Russian achievement in economic terms goes some way to explaining why the Soviet system is attractive to so many Third World countries. It is a model for their industrial development. But since it also demonstrates the impossibility of achieving socialism in one country, so many of its lessons for us must be negative ones – warnings of things to avoid rather than blueprints on how to proceed. For the very fact that Russia began its transition to socialism at a time when Russian capitalism was *under*developed makes its experience after 1917 particularly inappropriate as a model and guide to the transition to socialism in *advanced* capitalist societies: and it is for this reason, more than any other, that the invoking of the Soviet experience as a warning of 'what will be' must be dismissed as little more than a crude exercise in political mystification.

Of course one cannot deny that the Soviet experience has had a profound impact on the political thinking of socialists and a resonance within the Communist Parties of both Eastern and Western Europe. There has long existed the possibility of a tension within all Communist Parties between the pressures and demands stemming from national politics and those international pressures emanating from the Soviet Union as part and parcel of Soviet foreign policy. The avenues open to other Communist Parties for initiatives at variance with the wishes of Moscow have varied greatly down the years, and have increased dramatically lately, but are obviously at their most restricted in Eastern Europe. But even here, as recent developments in Poland indicate, there is a growing body of opposition to Russian domination and to one-party control. And here it is necessary to differentiate carefully between the 'dissident' movements that feature so prominently in the antisocialist invective of the Western Press, and the very real socialist initiatives that have and are being made by workers, intellectuals and peasants in parts of Eastern Europe. The struggle for a democratic socialism is on again in Eastern Europe, and deserves the active support of socialists worldwide. And in Western Europe, too, Khrushchev's denunciation of Stalin and the Soviet invasion of Hungary in 1956 ensured the continuation of a long, complex and uneven process within Western Communist Parties of distancing themselves from the Soviet Union and devising and mobilizing support for a political initiative adequate to challenge the realities of State power in advanced capitalist countries. This is not the place to assess either the adequacy of these strategies or the level of support that they command throughout Europe. It is enough to make the point that the most persistent and clear-thinking critics of the Soviet Union have invariably been socialists themselves. For if Western Communist Parties have few illusions about the socialist nature of the Soviet Union, then those outside Communist Parties have none. Some have characterized it as 'State Capitalist', whilst others refer to it as a 'degenerate workers state', but all have agreed on the need for its total transformation if the claims it makes for itself as socialist are to be realized in practice.

Finally, any assessment of the significance and legacy of the Russian Revolution must be tempered by what Trotsky referred to as the need to measure the process of vast transformations by an adequate scale. With regard to the Russian Revolution the legacies for socialists in advanced capitalist countries are deeply contradictory. On the one hand the October Revolution served to emphasize the central question of State power in any socialist initiative and this is a positive gain. But at the same time the combined spectre of 'actually existing socialism'[23] and the excessive sluggishness of Western social democracy remain in the eyes of many people the two alternatives of what socialism is all about. And in the face of such grim alternatives it is perhaps not surprising that considerable cynicism surrounds even the mentioning of something called the 'socialist project'. The Russian experience has not only provided lessons, both positive and negative, to guide socialists in the West. It has also made their task immeasurably more difficult by helping to discredit the very idea of socialism itself. Our job is to try to undo that legacy, by facing again the vital and extremely difficult task of specifying the organizational and institutional form that socialism might take and the principles and procedures which should inform their operation. That specification will, of course, have to be a provisional one. But even in its provisional form it needs to be made, and made quickly, if socialism is ever to break from its association in the popular mind with the horrendous consequences of the Bolshevik failure in Russia after 1917.

NOTES

I should like to thank David Coates for his helpful comments on an earlier draft of this chapter and Carolyn Taylor for clarifying a number of points of law.

1. Sir Robert Mark, former Commissioner of the Metropolitan Police, *The Listener*, 4 Aug. 1977 (my emphasis)
2. 'Extremism and the Left', *Politics Today*, No. 13, Conservative Central Office 1981, 122
3. R. L. Clutterbuck, *Britain in Agony*, Penguin 1980, p. 19
4. Quoted in *The Guardian*, 18 May 1972
5. Sir Robert Mark, *In the Office of Constable*, Fontana 1979, p. 317
6. P. Cormack (ed), *Right Turn*, Lee Cooper 1978, pp. 85–6
7. See Ch 4
8. *Race and Class* **XXIII** (Autumn 1981–Winter 1982) 236
9. See Ch 9
10. See Ted Honderich *Violence For Equality*, Penguin 1980, for a discussion of this question
11. *Hansard* 6 July 1981, Col. 23
12. *The Socialist Register*, Merlin 1975, 248
13. See Home Office Report on Racial Attacks (Home Office, November 1981). Copies available from: Home Office Library, Room 1007, 50 Queen Anne's Gate, London SW1H 9AT
14. Prof. Wilkinson quoted in *The Guardian* 3 Nov. 1981; see also P. Wilkinson, *The New Fascists*, Grant McIntyre 1981
15. Bernard de Mandeville, *The Fable of the Bees*, Penguin, 1970, p. 67
16. Quoted in Martin Barker, *The New Racism*, Junction Books 1981, p. 146
17. J.Strachey, *Why You Should Be A Socialist*, Gollancz 1944, p. 76
18. See Neal Ascherson, *The Polish August*, Penguin 1981, and Andrej Wajda's film *Man of Iron*
19. V. Lenin, *Collected Works*, Vol. 21, Lawrence and Wishart, p. 408

20. *New Left Review*, No. 111, Sept.–Oct. 1978, 26.
21. A. Nove, *An Economic History of the USSR*, Penguin 1972,p. 374
22. E. H. Carr, *The Bolshevik Revolution 1917–23*, Vol. 1, Penguin, p. 190
23. The phrase is from Rudolf Bahro's *The Alternative in Eastern Europe*, New Left Books 1978

'. . . an answer less often suffices to rid the world of a question
Than a deed.'
Bertolt Brecht
'The Gordian Knot', *Poems 1913–1956*, Eyre Methuen 1981, p. 120

INDEX